THE WORLD
IN SO
MANY WORDS

THE WORLD
IN SO
MANY WORDS

A Country-by-Country Tour of Words That

Have Shaped Our Language

Allan Metcalf

HOUGHTON MIFFLIN COMPANY   Boston   New York

Picture Credits: **penguin** © 1999 PhotoDisc, Inc. **geyser** © 1999 PhotoDisc, Inc. **dynamite** © 1999 PhotoDisc, Inc. **dodo** Tech-Graphics **robot** Corbis-Bettmann **Zouave** Corbis **okra** Laurel Cook Lhowe **basenji** © Houghton Mifflin Company/Evelyn Shafer **marimba** © 1999 PhotoDisc, Inc. **aye-aye** Animals Animals/G.I. Bernard **teff** Corbis/Paul Almasy **shish kebab** © 1999 PhotoDisc, Inc. **baluchithere** Tech-Graphics **polo** © 1999 PhotoDisc, Inc. **ginger** © 1999 PhotoDisc, Inc. **catamaran** Corbis/Neil Rabinowitz **tae kwon do** © 1999 PhotoDisc, Inc. **bonsai** © School Division, Houghton Mifflin Company **kangaroo** © 1999 PhotoDisc, Inc. **bikini** © 1999 PhotoDisc, Inc. **tattoo** © 1999 PhotoDisc, Inc. **poncho** Corbis/Owen Franken **hurricane** © 1999 PhotoDisc, Inc. **dory** Corbis/The Purcell Team **moccasin** © 1999 PhotoDisc, Inc. **wapiti** © 1999 PhotoDisc, Inc. **hogan** Corbis/Buddy Mays **dunk** © 1999 PhotoDisc, Inc. **mukluk** Laurel Cook Lhowe **kayak** © 1999 PhotoDisc, Inc.

Library of Congress Cataloging-in-Publication Data

Metcalf, Allan A.
    The world in so many words: a country-by-country tour of words that have shaped our language / Allan Metcalf.
       p.   cm.
    Includes bibliographical references and indexes.
    ISBN 0-395-95920-9 (cloth)
    1. English language—Foreign words and phrases. 2. Language and languages—Influence on English. 3. English language—Foreign elements. 4. English language—Etymology. I. Title.
PE1582.A3M48 1999
422'.4—dc21   99-29849
                                                       CIP

Book design by Margaret Ong Tsao

Manufactured in the United States of America

DOH 10 9 8 7 6 5 4 3 2 1

For Thomas Allan Metcalf

This is your world!

CONTENTS

Introduction   ix
   Note on Sources   xv
   Acknowledgments   xvii

Europe   1

Africa   61

Asia   109

Oceania   167

The Americas   199

Indexes   279
   Word Index   281
   Language Index   293
   Country Index   297

INTRODUCTION

*I*f you speak English, you know at least a bit of a hundred languages. Or more.

It's true. You're a savant in French, a genius in Latin, a philosopher in Greek. If you made it through kindergarten, you've mastered a bit of German. If you have a yen to be a *tycoon*, whether or not you become one, you're speaking Chinese and Japanese. If you *trek* to *paradise*, you're going through Afrikaans and Persian.

You are what you eat. Taste *goulash* and you're Hungarian, *shish kebab* and you're Armenian, *chocolate* and you speak the Nahuatl language of the Aztecs. Use *okra* to make *gumbo* and you're speaking Ibo and Tshiluba of Nigeria and the Congo, respectively. Wash it down with a *cola* and it's the Temne language of Sierra Leone.

You are what you wear. In a *dashiki*, you're speaking the Yoruba language of Nigeria. In a *cashmere* sweater, it's the Kashmiri language of India and Pakistan. In a *parka*, you're using the Nenets language of Siberia. Take it off to reveal a *bikini*, and it's Marshallese, spoken in the South Pacific.

You are what you do. *Pamper* someone, *rip* another, and you're speaking Dutch and Flemish. Encounter a *horde* of *Yeti*, and you're speaking both Polish and Tibetan. Eat a *mango* and you're mouthing Malayalam. Play the *marimba* and you're in the Kimbundu language of Angola.

Dance the *hora* in Rumanian, the *tango* in the Ibibio language of Africa (helped by Argentine Spanish). Observe *shibboleths* in Hebrew and *taboos* in Tongan. Play *polo* in the Balti language of Pakistan. Or just *yabber* away in the Wuywurung aboriginal language of Australia.

In short, when you speak English, you're speaking a world of languages. This book is a tour of that world.

English is so worldly that it could be called a language of immigrants. Of the half a million words that have accumulated in the vocabulary of present-day English, only a small minority are native to the language as far back as we can trace it, that is, to the Anglo-Saxon invasions of England some 1500 years ago. The rest have immigrated in subsequent years. The immigrants have come in such numbers that they seem as much at home as words of native stock.

In the previous paragraph, for example, the very word *native* is an immigrant: from Latin, via French. So are *language*, *million*, *present*, *minority*, *trace*, *invasions*, *subsequent*, and *numbers*. Directly from Latin, without the mediation of French, are *immigrant*, *accumulate*, and *vocabulary*. Yet those words do not look *bizarre*; they are our *pals*; they speak our *lingo* (to use words from Basque, Romani, and Provençal, respectively). Our language could be said to have run *amok* (Malay) with the *jumbo* (Mandingo) possibilities, as any language *guru* (Hindi) or *maven* (Yiddish) could tell you.

Some of the immigrants to our language have been brought by human immigrants to English-speaking countries. French speakers immigrated first, conquering England in 1066 and bringing with them what eventually amounted to over one-quarter of our vocabulary. Later, immigrants to England and especially the United States have continued to carry their words with them, everything from the *dunk* of Pennsylvania German to the *bhangra* dance of India and Pakistan. Africans, brought to the Americas against their will, also brought with them foods, music, and magic like *benne*, *marimba*, and *voodoo*.

Other immigrant words have been brought home by traders and tourists. There is exotic clothing like the Samoan *lavalava* and the Khmer *sampot*, plants and animals like Bengali *jute* and Montagnais *husky*, foods like Indonesian *tempeh* and Amharic *teff*, objects like the Dharuk *boomerang* and the Finnish *sauna*, diseases like Fore *kuru* and Ga *kwashiorkor*, skills like the Japanese *bonsai* and Tahitian *tattoo*.

When we have *slogans* with *spunk*, we have imported from Scottish Gaelic. We have words *galore*, and *phony*, from Irish. We indulge in Arabic when we drink *alcohol*, Tlingit when we drink *hooch*, Chinese when we drink *tea*, Hindi when we put on *pajamas* to sleep on a *cot* in our *bungalow*. American Indians gave us everything from *succotash* (Narragansett) to *kachina* (Hopi) and *Sasquatch* (Halkomelem), as well as at least three kinds of salmon: *sockeye* (Northern Straits), *kokanee* (Shuswap), and *haddo* (Nisqualli). Canadian speakers of English also contributed to the language, *eh?* It's enough to make an etymologist go *berserk* (Old Norse).

And if *etymologist* is Greek to you, that's understandable. It's a Greek word, coming to us via Latin and French. It combines the word for "true" with the word for "study," and we use it to mean the study of the true origins of words. As in this book. We are careful to distinguish it from *entomologist*, a Greek word for somebody who studies bugs.

Looking at the etymologies of English words, we find more than two hundred languages that have contributed words to ours. In this book we will make a whirlwind world tour, continent by continent, visiting words from these languages in their native habitats. The tour will tell us not only about other languages, customs, and cultures, but about how we have welcomed words and traditions from other languages and what we have done with them to construct our own increasingly multicultural world of English.

The rest of the world may be influenced by American cultural imperialism, or "Coca-Colonization," as Harvard scholar Henry Louis Gates Jr. has called it. But American culture may be so exportable because the English language has been so generous in importing from around the world, "all things bright and beautiful, all creatures great and small." How different from the French, for example, who gave our language so much, yet who have a stern Academy to resist imports that might detract from the purity of their own language. They have France to consider; we have the world.

To make it possible to visit the whole world of English, our tour will stop at only one word for each language—with the exception of French and Latin, which get two apiece because they are so important. In fact, if we gave each language proportional representation, French, Latin, and Old English with other Germanic languages would each command about twenty-five percent of the book. An additional five percent would go to Greek. No other language has even a one percent share of the present-day English vocabulary. But in this book, to show the diversity of English, every language will have equal representation.

Even though there are so many immigrant words, it is still a distinction for a language to have contributed to the English vocabulary. According to the Summer Institute of Linguistics in Dallas, which maintains a complete list, there are about 6,700 languages in the world today: 225 in Europe, 2,000 in Africa, 2,200 in Asia, 1,300 in the Pacific, and 1,000 in the Americas. Of all these, scarcely two hundred are represented in English, if we leave out proper names for places, people, and currencies.

That is because getting into the English vocabulary isn't easy. Though new words and meanings knock at the door every day, few are admitted. A word can't bully its way in; it has to have special value to get its linguistic green card. Successful foreign words may name a plant, animal, or food that has no counterpart in the borrowing language, like *banyan* (Gujarati), *muntjac* (Sundanese), or *muffuletta* (Sicilian). Or the word may name an exotic cultural trait worthy of comment and sometimes emulation, like *siesta* (Spanish) and *potlatch* (Nootka). Often words change their meaning as they become naturalized and adapted to English-speaking circumstances, as in the cases of *gung ho* (Chinese) and *Kwanzaa* (Swahili).

Other immigrant words do not name new things or concepts but give us alternative ways of discussing things we already knew. The result is greater subtlety of expression. So, for example, among the numerous immigrants from French, we have *infant* differentiating itself from English *child*, *mansion* from *house*, *saintly* from *holy*, *charity* from *love*, *entire* from *whole*. Nor is it just French imports that have this effect; thanks to other languages, for example, we can choose between a *parka* (Nenets) and a *poncho* (Mapudungun).

And while words enrich the receiving language, they have the advantage over some other kinds of imports in taking nothing from the giver and doing no damage to the receiver or the environment. We can accept *cannibal* (Carib) without allowing cannibalism, and we can bring in the name of the deadly disease *kuru* (Fore) without the disease itself. No plants or animals were harmed in the making of the English language.

Because the words we visit have become English words, they will require no translation. Some, like *cola*, *bikini*, and *rip*, are so familiar that they need no introduction, just recognition of their immigrant status. Others, however, like *indaba* and *galah*, are obscure enough to require an explanation. Well over a hundred languages have contributed familiar words, and another hundred have given us words that are less well known or known only locally: the *dhandh* of Pakistan, the *bunyip* that amuses children in Australia, and the interjection *lah* in Singapore and Malaysia.

As we visit different languages, we will talk about their relatives. Some languages are isolated, but most of them come in families, that is, groups of related languages that have a common ancestor. English belongs to a family called Indo-European because the ancient homelands of the members of this family stretch from India on the east to Europe on the west. Nowadays Indo-European languages extend throughout most of the world, predominating not only in India and Europe but in the Americas and Australia, as well as in parts of Africa and Asia. Almost one-third of the words on our tour are from Indo-European languages. Four of the five languages of the United Nations are Indo-European: English, Spanish, French, and Russian. But there are many other language families with no ancestral connection to Indo-European, and they too are well represented in this book.

Some cautions are in order before we set out on our tour. We have chosen the best native guides and linguistic experts, but even the experts are not always in agreement about the origins of words, and often there is not enough evidence to know for sure where a word came from. It may be possible to say that a word is of West African origin, for example, but if that word is found in several West African languages it may not be possible to identify a particular language as the sole source.

Nor are dates of immigration always definitive. When a date "as early as" is mentioned, that is just the date of the word's first known use in an English document. In many cases the word was spoken or written in English before that time. This book reflects up-to-date research, but some dates of immigration into English will no doubt be pushed back as scholars make new discoveries.

Finally, there is unavoidable confusion about the names of languages. We have no problem in naming English or French, Swahili or Maori; but there are many cases of languages having several names, even among native speakers. Is it the Tungus or Evenki language which gave us the word *shaman*? They aren't two different languages, just two different names for a language which is also known as Chapogir, Avanki, Avankil, Solon, and

Khamnigan. We will generally follow the policy of the Summer Institute of Linguistics, when possible choosing the name preferred by those who speak the language.

So if our *mojo* (Fula) is working, we should manage to get a good look at the diversity of the English language with our world tour. Put on your *huaraches* (Tarascan), *moccasins* (Virginia Algonquian), *shoepacs* (Unami), or *mukluks* (Yupik); get in your *kayak* (Inuit), *catamaran* (Tamil), or *dory* (Miskito), and let's take advantage of our *freedom* (Old English) to visit the world.

Note on Sources

If you want to know about the languages of the world, the best book—in fact, just about the only comprehensive book—is *An Introduction to the Languages of the World* by Anatole V. Lyovin (Oxford University Press, 1997). It mentions some 1,500 languages by name; tells about their families, locations, and special qualities (like the "brother-in-law language" of Guugu Yimidhirr in Australia), and has detailed sketches of eleven languages, ranging from Finnish to Hawaiian. Parts of it are technical, but anyone can appreciate the diversity of the world's languages from this book.

If you want a complete list of the 6,700 languages of the world, together with information about language names, language families, locations, number of speakers, writing systems, even Bible translations—you'll find them in *Ethnologue: Languages of the World*, Thirteenth Edition, edited by Barbara F. Grimes (Summer Institute of Linguistics, 1996). It's also conveniently available on the Internet.

If you want to know about the sources of the English vocabulary and the proportions of words from different languages, you'll find detailed and thoughtful discussion in a book by Thomas Finkenstaedt and Dieter Wolff, *Ordered Profusion: Studies in Dictionaries and the English Lexicon* (Carl Winter, 1973).

If you want etymologies of individual words, there are quite a few books to choose from. A good starting point is a desk dictionary that presents accurate and precise information on the origins of the general vocabulary of English. *The American Heritage Dictionary*, Third Edition, from Houghton Mifflin, and *Merriam-Webster's Collegiate Dictionary*, Tenth Edition, have been invaluable in the preparation of this book, especially because they both are available on CD-ROM.

For greater detail, there is, above all, the monumental *Oxford English Dictionary* from Oxford University Press. It explains the etymologies and gives quotations illustrating the histories of half a million words of English. Its 1989 second edition is also available on CD-ROM and is augmented by an *Additions Series* of three volumes.

Other more specialized dictionaries are equally thorough. There are two important works still in progress, the *Dictionary of American Regional English*, edited by Frederic G. Cassidy and Joan Houston Hall (3 volumes, A–O; Belknap Press of Harvard University Press, 1985–1996) and the *Random House Historical Dictionary of American Slang*, edited by J. E. Lighter (2 volumes, A–O; Random House, 1994–1997). Also essential are *A Dictionary of American English on Historical Principles*, edited by William A. Craigie and James R. Hulbert (4 volumes, University of Chicago Press, 1938–44) and *A Dictionary of Americanisms on Historical Principles*, edited by Mitford M. Mathews (2 volumes, University of Chicago Press, 1951).

Further valuable etymological information is found in *A Comprehensive Etymological Dictionary of the English Language*, by Ernest Klein (Elsevier, 1971); *The Oxford Dictionary of English Etymology*, edited by C. T. Onions (Oxford, 1966), and the *Barnhart Dictionary of Etymology*, edited by Robert K. Barnhart and Sol Steinmetz (Wilson, 1988).

So much for words and languages. Most of the other information in the book comes not from print but from the world of the World Wide Web. There it is possible to get up-to-the-minute information from the Finnish Sauna

Society, Supima Cotton Association (for *pima*), the Welsh Mountain Zoo (for *penguin*), and the Wyo-Braska Museum (for *baluchithere*). On the Web you can discover where to order *lekvar* or a *muffuletta* sandwich, how to put on a *lavalava*, and why *tiki* is back in style in California. You can hear "Waltzing Matilda" and read the full text of its original version (for *billabong*). Because Web sites come and go, there is no point in listing their addresses here, but searching the Web for almost any of the words in this book will bring a rich harvest. One print source has also been essential for many American languages: *Encyclopedia of North American Indians*, edited by Frederick E. Hoxie (Houghton Mifflin, 1996).

Acknowledgments

This book was made possible by the encouragement and support of Joseph Pickett, Executive Editor at Houghton Mifflin, and made clearer and more accurate by his acute editing. At Houghton Mifflin I also benefited from David Pritchard's expert commentary on the native languages and cultures of the Americas, Carol Rigsby's acute copy editing, and Margaret Anne Miles's expertise with illustrations.

In the making of this book I have also had valuable help from these people, among others: Richard W. Bailey, Suzanne Cook, Meghan Chenoweth, Gerald Cohen, James Davis, Natalie Maynor, David Metcalf, Robert and Mary Beth Metcalf, Victoria Neufeldt, Sara Park, Barry Popik, Luanne von Schneidemesser, Mary Wambach, Charles and Amy Witzke, and Walt Wolfram. Members of the American Dialect Society have wittingly and unwittingly provided stimulating ideas and important information. The staff of the MacMurray College library has been unfailingly helpful, in particular Mary Ellen Blackston and Ronald Daniels. In Julian Hall at MacMurray College I have again enjoyed the hospitality and encouragement of William DeSilva and Nadine Szczepanski.

This book is a companion and counterpart to *America in So Many Words* (Houghton Mifflin, 1997), which tells the year-by-year story of words made in America. That book has been the inspiration for this. I am grateful to my collaborator on that book, David K. Barnhart, for his help on this one, whenever asked.

And I must acknowledge my debt to my wife, Donna Metcalf, who perhaps will see more of me now that this is done.

Jacksonville, Illinois
January 1999

EUROPE

*O*ur tour of the world's languages that have contributed to English begins at home, with the home continent of English. Here we find immigrant words so much at home that we don't recognize them as foreign: *rip, reason,* and *justice,* for example. But even Europe has exotic entries, from *berserk* to *bizarre.* Of all the continents that have contributed to our language, Europe's gifts are the most basic and the most varied. After all, as far as English is concerned, Europe had a thousand-year head start on the rest of the world.

Nowadays the European languages are quite diverse. They have been going their separate ways for many millennia. But it should be noted, before we set out, that despite this present diversity, most of the languages of Europe can be traced back to a single common ancestor spoken about ten thousand years ago. Thus the languages we visit in Europe are, for the most part, not utterly alien, even when we get as far away linguistically as the Celtic languages and as far away geographically as the Slavic ones. All these, like English, belong to the Indo-European language family, so called because the homelands of its members extend from Europe to northern India. Indo-European diverged into more than half a dozen major branches, ranging from Indo-Iranian on the east to Balto-Slavic, Hellenic, Italic, Celtic, and our Germanic on the west. These in turn became the separate languages we know today.

Even in Europe, however, some languages aren't members of the family. Hungarian and Finnish belong to a separate language family of their own, apparently unrelated to Indo-European, and Basque is a puzzling isolate, like nothing else.

All these languages will be on view in the European tour. It begins where the English language itself began fifteen hundred years ago, on an island off Europe's northwest coast. Members of a few Germanic tribes who had been raiding the island of Britain liked it well enough to settle there. As their numbers increased, they developed an insular way of speaking different enough from the ways of the mainland to make it a language in its own right. The Angles, one of the invading tribes, called this language "Angle-ish." Thus began the language we call *English*.

Like other invaders before and since, the speakers of Angle-ish took the lands and goods of the previous inhabitants but not much of their languages. As we begin our tour of other languages, we do not find ancient Welsh, Scots, or Irish words in ancient English. Our imports from these other languages of the British Isles are much more recent. Otherwise we would not expect to find a *penguin* in Wales, *glamour* in Scotland, and in Ireland *galore*.

To the north and east of these islands, we find ourselves in familiar linguistic territory. From Iceland to Scandinavia dwell the close relatives of English, the North Germanic languages, giving us everything from *geysers* to *Lego*. Even more closely related are the West Germanic languages just across the Channel from England, with immigrants to English ranging from *hunky-dory* to *rip*.

And then there is France. French is not as closely related to English as the Germanic languages; a descendant of Latin, it belongs to the Italic branch of Indo-European. Nevertheless, the impact of French on English is greater than that of all the Germanic languages put together. For three centuries, starting with the Norman invasion in 1066, the rulers of England spoke French. During those centuries, as the people of England struggled to understand their French masters, their language absorbed great quantities of French, so much that more than one-quarter of today's English vocabulary is from French. The exchange was by no means reciprocal; the conquered people learned the language of the conquerors but not vice versa. Even today the French defend the "purity" of their language against invasions from English. But in the Middle Ages, English was defenseless against French, and once that invasion had succeeded, English was open to the other languages of the world. Thus the Norman invasion had the unanticipated effect of making English a world language.

After suitable acknowledgement of our indebtedness to French, we make our way through Spain, Portugal, and Italy, visiting the other Romance languages that have also been influential in English. That influence culminates in Latin itself, the source of another quarter of the English vocabulary.

Latin, of course, was much influenced by the prestige of Greek philosophy and the Greek language, and so in turn was English. Next we travel to parts of Europe more remote from England and from influence on English, encountering *vampire* and *bora* and *robot*, not to mention *horde* and *Cossack*, but also enjoying the taste of *goulash*, *lekvar*, and *kugeli*, as well as the comfort of *sauna* and *divan*.

Here are forty-five words in English from the languages of Europe. Let the journey begin!

∼ ENGLAND

freedom *from English*

English had its beginnings about fifteen hundred years ago, when the "Angle-ish" spoken by Angles and Saxons separated from other Germanic languages as the Angles and Saxons themselves, crossing the water to settle in what they would call "Angle-land," separated from other Germanic tribes. Since that time, no word has been of more significance to English speakers than *freedom*. This word was not carried to England as part of the Angles' and Saxons' Germanic language heritage, nor was it imported from another language. Instead, it seems to have been a homemade invention, put together from two existing Germanic words to form a distinctive concept.

The elements of *freedom* are *free* and *doom*, to use the modern spellings. *Free* originally meant "beloved" and is related to the word *friend*. By the time English came into being, *free* had evolved to take on its modern meaning, with the idea that one who is beloved is a friend, free from bondage. The development of *doom* is more complicated. Nowadays we think of *doom* as a judgment—and a harsh one at that—or as an unhappy fate. A thousand years ago, in the time of the early English language, *doom* had a different emphasis. It did indeed mean judgment, but it meant a considered judgment, related to the present-day *deem*.

Put *free* together with *doom* and you have the condition of being judged to be free. It involves being free and thinking about it, being free and accepting the responsibility for making the judgments that being free entails.

Appropriately, one of the earliest appearances of English *freedom*, in about the year 888, is in the best-known translation of a philosophical work ever to appear in English. The translation was made by King Alfred himself, the only English ruler ever to be called "the Great." Fate or free will? Necessity or freedom? That was the question Alfred answered in favor of the latter in his translation of the *Consolation of Philosophy* by the Roman Boethius. For the Latin *libertas*, our present-day *liberty*, Alfred uses the newly created *freedom*. To be governed by righteousness, he writes, is to be "on tham hehstan freodome," that is, in the highest freedom. He writes of the "fulne friodom" or "full freedom" attained by those who do not seek earthly gains. Through such language Alfred made a Platonic work into a decidedly more Christian one. Alfred needed all the Platonic and Christian consolation he could find in the grim days of Viking invasions and the near anarchy of what we call the "Dark Ages" after the collapse of the Roman empire.

Freedom made itself thoroughly at home in English at an early date. In addition to Alfred's Boethius, about fifty other extant Old English texts use it, including English translations of St. Augustine's soliloquies, Pope Gregory the Great's book on pastoral care, and the Venerable Bede's famous history of the English church and people.

There are a thousand or so words like *freedom* that appear to be truly English, that is, that do not seem to have existed in the ancestors of our language but were newly made after English developed from Proto-Indo-European and Germanic and that appear in the written records of the earliest period of English, about a thousand years ago.

The rest of English-speaking history might be said to be the development of the meaning of *freedom*. Much later, in the fourteenth century, we admitted the French *liberty* to our language in equal partnership, but *freedom* has remained fundamental. It has certainly been the watchword of the American experience. "Those who deny freedom to others," declared Abraham Lincoln, "deserve it not for themselves." In the darkest days of World War II, President Franklin Roosevelt spoke with hope of "a world founded upon four essential human freedoms": freedoms of speech and worship, freedoms from want and fear. And Martin Luther King Jr. concluded his most famous speech with the refrain, "Let freedom ring."

✑ ENGLAND

brit *from Cornish*

No, it's not *Brit*, the nickname for a person from Great
Britain. This lowercase *brit* refers to the tiny sea creatures
that are dinner for a whale. Herman Melville describes brit
in Chapter 58 of *Moby-Dick* (1851):

> Steering north-eastward from the Crozetts, we fell in
> with vast meadows of brit, the minute, yellow substance,
> upon which the Right Whale largely feeds. For leagues and
> leagues it undulated round us, so that we seemed to be
> sailing through boundless fields of ripe and golden wheat.
>
> On the second day, numbers of Right Whales were
> seen, who, secure from the attack of a Sperm Whaler like
> the Pequod, with open jaws sluggishly swam through the
> brit, which, adhering to the fringing fibres of that
> wondrous Venetian blind in their mouths, was in that
> manner separated from the water that escaped at the lip.
>
> As morning mowers, who side by side slowly and
> seethingly advance their scythes through the long wet grass
> of marshy meads; even so these monsters swam, making a
> strange, grassy, cutting sound; and leaving behind them
> endless swaths of blue upon the yellow sea.

In less poetic language, brit are very small fish or crustaceans in very large schools or pools, collectively making
meals for the giant known as the Right Whale (because it
was the "right whale" to hunt, unless like Ahab you were
looking for a sperm whale).

Brit apparently comes from *brythel*, the name for
mackerel in the Cornish language, formerly spoken in the
southwest of England. As a name for the small fry of fish,
brit appears in English as early as 1602. Like nearby Welsh,
Cornish belongs to the Celtic branch of Indo-European.
Other somewhat obscure words that have immigrated
from Cornish to English are *wrasse* (a kind of fish, 1672),
porbeagle (a kind of shark, 1758), *gossan* (decomposed
rock, 1776), and *vug* (a rock cavity, 1818). Cornish itself

became extinct in the late eighteenth century, but conservation measures seem to be reviving it along with the whales. There are now said to be 150 fluent speakers of Cornish who have learned it from books and classes.

∼England

pal *from Romani*

"Where have you been all this day, pal?" "Why, pal, what would you have me to do?" That conversation was recorded in Herefordshire, England, in a deposition in 1682. At least from that time, we have had pals in English.

Nowadays *pal* is a term of endearment, but it had a disreputable aura in earlier times. In the eighteenth century, an author explained, "when highwaymen rob in pairs, they say such a one was his or my pal."

The word comes from the Romani language spoken by the people who call themselves Romani or Rom, and who are called by others Gypsies, a name they don't like. There are about a million and a half speakers of Romani throughout the world. The Romani of western Europe are one of three great populations that began a nomadic exodus from India about a thousand years ago. There are also the Lomarven or Lom of Central Europe and the Domari or Dom of the Middle East and Eastern Europe. All speak versions of Romani, an Indo-European language of the Indo-Aryan branch related to the Hindi language of India.

In Romani, pal means "brother." Because the Romani have kept their language to themselves in the midst of other peoples, few other words from Romani have made their way into English. We do, however, have from Romani the blackjack known as a *cosh* (1869), the term *cove* (1567) to mean "fellow" or "man," and possibly the knife called a *shiv* (1674).

∿ WALES

penguin *from Welsh*

There are no penguins in Wales. You will search for them in vain along the region's rocky shores. They are not to be found even at the Anglesey Sea Zoo on the Welsh Isle of

Anglesey, nor among the two dozen species of birds at the Welsh Mountain Zoo near Colwyn Bay. To find a penguin in its native habitat, you have to go to the other end of the earth. But the name we give the bird in English is Welsh.

Stranger still, in Welsh, *pen* means "head" and *gwyn* means "white," so *penguin* means "white head." But on a penguin, the head is mostly black. How did it come to this?

The solution to the mystery goes back to the late sixteenth century, when nautical adventurers from the British Isles were beginning to venture across the oceans. Among the first places they visited was Newfoundland. There they found an island crowded with gray and white birds as big as geese but unable to fly—and thus easy to catch for food. The sailors would "driue them on a planke into our ship as many as shall lade her," wrote an observer in 1578.

There must have been Welshmen among the sixteenth-century British sailors, because they called both the island and the bird *pen gwyn*. Why they called it "white head" we can only guess. The bird had large white spots next to its eyes, though it did not have a white head. Perhaps the island itself looked like a white head.

In any case, when English explorers ventured as far south as the Strait of Magellan later in the century, they found birds that reminded them of the ones they had encountered in Newfoundland. These southern birds also were flightless, with dark backs and white fronts, and they waddled upright on web feet. They were therefore called *penguins*, even though they were zoologically quite distinct from the penguins of Newfoundland.

The northern bird, which we now call the great auk, was such an easy catch that by the mid-nineteenth century it was extinct. The southern bird, living in remote places, escaped that fate. And so when we speak of penguins today, we mean only the birds of the south.

Welsh, like Scottish, Irish, and Breton, is from the Celtic branch of Indo-European. It was spoken in the British Isles long before anyone spoke English there, but as is typical of the language of a conquered people, very little of the Welsh language ever entered English. We do, however, have Welsh names like *Arthur* and *Merlin*, landscape features like *combe* (valley, as early as 770) and *crag* (1300), a stringed instrument known as the *crowd* (1310), a dog called a *corgi* (1926), the *eisteddfod* festival (1822), a dessert called *flummery* (1623), and a drink made from fermented honey called *metheglin* (medicinal liquor, 1533). There are about half a million speakers of Welsh in Wales nowadays, most of them also fluent in English.

~SCOTLAND

glamour *from Scots*

Where else would you find *glamour* but on a windswept Scottish heath? Though you might look elsewhere for glamour today, the Scottish dialect of English is where all other English speakers got the word. Of course the Scots had a more serious meaning for it.

Originally it meant nothing more or less than grammar, the study of the proper form of words and sentences. This was back in the Middle Ages, when only a few clerics and clerks (both words have the same origin) knew how to write. To others, *grammar* meant something mysterious and magical, as it still does to many who wrestle with the language today. Eventually *grammar* came to have a secondary meaning of "magic."

In Scots, the word had an *l* instead of the first *r*. We find writers from Scotland using this magical *glamour* in English as early as 1720. Later in the eighteenth century, the poet Robert Burns writes of

> Ye gipsy-gang that deal in glamor,
> And you deep read in hell's black grammar,
> Warlocks and witches.

And the novelist Sir Walter Scott discussed the magical *glamour* in his *Letters on Demonology and Witchcraft* (1830).

In the twentieth century, it was apparently American usage that transferred the glamour of magic to the glamour of fashion, personality, and life style. To make the word even more glamorous, Americans retained the British *our* ending instead of changing it to *or* as we usually do (in words like *color* and *flavor*).

Scots is the distinctive Scottish version of the English language. It has been spoken in the lowlands of Scotland for over a thousand years, almost as long as English English has been spoken in the south. Scots English is now spoken by almost all of Scotland's population of five million. The rest of the English-speaking world has learned from Scots words like *feckless* (1585), *jockey* (1670), *flunky* (1782), *rampage* (1808), and *wow!* (1513).

Until recently, the principal language in the highlands of Scotland was Scots Gaelic, a Celtic language and close relative of Irish and Welsh. About 90,000 people still speak Scots Gaelic. The several dozen imports into English from that language include such well-known words as *loch* (1375), *clan* (1425), *glen* (1489), *plaid* (1512), *slogan* (1513), *spunk* (1582), and *trousers* (1613).

～IRELAND

galore *from Irish*

There is Irish galore in the English language, thanks to the persistence of the Irish language in Ireland despite centuries of English rule. Among the finest of the Irish immigrants to our vocabulary is *galore*, which appears in English writing as early as 1675. It comes from the Irish phrase *go leór, go* translating as "to" and *leór* as "sufficiency"; so the phrase translates roughly as "sufficient" or "enough." That was enough for English speakers to make much more of it; we have an abundance when we have something *galore.* We keep the exotic flavor of *galore* by using it only after the noun it modifies, contrary to our practice with most other adjectives.

The Irish word was helped in popularity by the novelist Sir Walter Scott, who knew it from Scottish usage too, since Scots Gaelic and Irish Gaelic are closely related. And we have uses galore for the word today. Who doesn't remember the actress Honor Blackman in the 1964 movie *Goldfinger?* When James Bond (Sean Connery) first meets her, she says, "I'm Pussy Galore"; to which Bond replies, "I must be dreaming." Or consider the Tennessee State Poem "O Tennessee, My Tennessee" by Adm. William Lawrence, who wrote it while a prisoner of war in Vietnam:

> I Thrill at Thought of Mountains Grand;
> Rolling Green Hills and Fertile Farm Land;
> Earth Rich with Stone, Mineral and Ore;
> Forests Dense and Wild Flowers Galore.

Like Scots Gaelic and Welsh, Irish is from the Celtic branch of Indo-European. Long disfavored by the ruling English, Irish is now an official language of the independent Irish Republic and is taught in Irish schools, but it is spoken natively by only about 120,000 of the population of three and a half million.

Irish has given us such notable English words as *hubbub* (1555), *smithereens* (1829), *slob* (1861), (hockey) *puck* (1891), *hooligan* (1898), and *phony* (1900), as well as Irish-flavored words like *shamrock* (1577), *leprechaun* (1604), *brogue* (1705), *shebeen* (an illegal drinking place, 1787), *colleen* (1828), *brogan* (1835), *donnybrook* (1852), and *kelly green* (1935). Irish and Scottish have combined to give to the English language *bard* (1450), *bog* (1505), *whiskey* (1715), and *banshee* (1771).

～IRELAND

moniker *from Shelta*

If you have a moniker, it's thanks to a small group of travelers in Ireland known, logically enough, as Travelers. They are like the people called Romani elsewhere in Europe and North America (and commonly known as Gypsies), keeping to themselves, living in vans, moving from place to place, and living on odd jobs and trades such as barn painting and selling linoleum. But the Irish Travelers are Irish.

Like the Romani, Irish Travelers have their own secret language or cant. Theirs is called Gammon or Shelta. Its origins are uncertain and disputed, but to some degree it derives from the Irish language, which belongs to the Celtic branch of the Indo-European language family. From Irish *ainm* developed Shelta *munik*, meaning "name," and somehow speakers of English managed to decipher that word and adopt it as *moniker*. It had spread to London as an English slang word for "name" by 1851.

In Ireland's present-day population of three and a half million, there are about 20,000 Travelers. A recent estimate is that 6,000 of them speak Shelta. That language, along with the Irish Travelers who speak it, has spread to the rest of the British Isles, where it is spoken by an additional 30,000, and to the United States, where there are an estimated 50,000 speakers of Shelta.

Here is the first line of the Lord's Prayer translated into a modern version of Shelta: "Our gathra, who cradgies in the manyak-norch, we turry kerrath about your moniker."

∾FAROE ISLANDS

skua *from Faroese*

Richard Bach wouldn't have had a best-seller back in the 1970s if he had titled his inspirational book *Jonathan Livingston Skua*. Although closely related to the seagulls Bach wrote about, skuas don't seem inclined to introspection. They're too busy devouring baby penguins or dive-bombing tourists.

If you like penguins, you won't be fond of skuas. There are seven species of skua, ranging the length of the Atlantic Ocean. Only the Antarctic skuas devour penguins, but that's because there aren't any penguins up north. The northern skuas have to be content with fish and krill. Sometimes they let other birds do their hunting, then chase them away. Sometimes for good measure they eat the other birds' eggs.

Skuas are the crows of the ocean. Crow-sized, they have crooked claws for grasping their prey and hooked bills for gouging it. They are adapted to the ocean with completely webbed feet and with brown and white streaked coloring that makes them less visible in the waves.

We get our name for them from Faroese, spoken on the Faroe Islands in the North Atlantic 280 miles southeast of Iceland, a thirty-seven-hour ferry ride from Denmark. If the islands aren't in the midst of one of their frequent fogs or storms, they offer a good view of skuas because they have no trees to get in the way. The eighteen main islands have a rather independent population of Norwegian descent, mostly self-governing nowadays under the protection of Denmark.

Their Faroese language, like Danish, Norwegian, and Icelandic, is from the North Germanic branch of our Indo-European language family. It is spoken by the entire population of the islands, about 45,000 by recent count. No other words of Faroese have soared into English.

⌒ICELAND

geyser *from Icelandic*

In Iceland, in the year 1294, a strong earthquake shook the valley of Haukadal in the place called Stóri-Geysir. Some time after the quake was over and the earth had quieted down, Icelanders in the vicinity heard another rumbling sound, this time coming from a crack in the earth opened by the quake. Water that had poured into the crack and collected on hot rocks below the surface was beginning to boil. It built up pressure until it erupted in a column of steam and hot water.

That was not the first geyser in history, but it was the first to be called a *geysir*, taking its name from the name of the place. It erupted not just once but again and again, becoming a tourist attraction before there were tourists in Iceland. In the eighteenth century, when there were tourists, the Geysir was an "old faithful," letting off steam and water every

half hour. But it slowed down in the nineteenth century, eventually erupting only two or three times a week. Another earthquake in 1896 speeded it up, but it quit entirely in 1915, flooded with too much water.

Before the demise of the Geysir, however, the name *geysir* or *geyser* had spread to other such hot spring fountains in Iceland. It is mentioned in English in that generic sense as early as 1780. In the next century the word was thus ready for use by the English-speaking American discoverers of the great geysers of Yellowstone, which became our first national park in 1872. Yellowstone has more than two hundred active geysers, more than in the rest of the world combined. They include Grand, the world's largest geyser, which erupts every eight to twelve hours, and Old Faithful, the most famous, with intervals anywhere between half an hour and two hours, depending on the length of the previous eruption.

Icelandic is a North Germanic language in our Indo-European language family, closely related to Danish, Norwegian, and Swedish. It is the national language of the 250,000 residents of Iceland. From Icelandic English has also acquired *geyserite*, the name of a mineral (1814); *narwhal*, the name of a tusked sea mammal (1646); and *eider*, both the duck (1743) and its down (1774).

⌒NORWAY

berserk *from Old Norse*

In the early Middle Ages, the Vikings of Norway, Sweden, and Denmark were famous for going berserk—not because they were simply crazy, but because they were as crazy as a bear when they overran and terrorized England and northern Europe. In Old Norse, the Viking language, *berserk* meant "bear shirt." Instead of wearing body armor, berserkers would put on bearskins, which would transform them mentally, if not physically, into bears. By some accounts, they would also prep themselves by eating psychedelic mushrooms. They would then enter battle in a fearless rage, and if they won they would pillage afterwards with the same fury. The earliest king of Norway, Harald Fairhair (850–933), had berserkers as his household guard.

Not until nearly a thousand years later, when the berserkers were a safely distant memory, did their name appear in English. One of the first modern writers to describe them was Sir Walter Scott in his 1822 novel *The Pirate*. "Aye—aye," says an old woman, "the Berserkars were champions who lived before the blessed days of St. Olave [died 1030], and who used to run like madmen on swords, and spears, and harpoons, and muskets, and snap them all into pieces, as a finner [a whale] would go through a herring-net, and then, when the fury went off, they were as weak and unstable as water."

Since Scott's revival of the word, even though the original berserkers are long gone, there has often been occasion to speak of someone "going berserk." In 1940, for example, the *Chicago Tribune* wrote of "the recent addition of the word 'berserk,' as a synonym for crackpot behavior, to the slang of the young and untutored." In the 1990s, things got so wild that to the expressions *go berserk* and *run amok* we added a third, *go postal*.

Old Norse is the ancestor of modern Norwegian and Icelandic. Thanks to the uninvited presence of Vikings in England, hundreds of Old Norse words entered the English vocabulary much earlier than *berserk*. The very pronouns *they* and *their* are from Old Norse, as are basic verbs like *cast, crawl, hit, stagger*, and *take*; adjectives like *loose, low, odd, ugly*, and *weak*; and numerous nouns like *anger, bag, dirt, egg, gift, skill, skirt, skin, sky, thrift*, and *window*. All these Norse words became English during the Middle Ages, some as early as the 800s and none later than the fourteenth century.

∼SWEDEN

dynamite *from Swedish*

 Funny, it doesn't sound Swedish. That's because its ancestry is classical Greek. But *dynamite* was born in Sweden, in the mind of Alfred Nobel, later of Nobel Prize fame. Nobel invented a way to convert a hazardous liquid explosive, nitroglycerine, into a stable solid. He just poured the nitroglycerine into a nonexplosive filler—at first diatomaceous earth, made from the shells of microscopic sea creatures called diatoms, then something as simple as sawdust. Pressed into cylinders, this new material was easy to carry. More important, it had the advantage of not exploding before its time.

To name his new material, Nobel did not limit himself to everyday words of his native Swedish. He turned, as scientists still do, to Greek, the most respected language of the ancient world. He added *-it*, a Swedish suffix like English *-ite*, to *dynam-*, the root of the Greek word for "force," which also appears in words like *dynamo* and *dynamic.*

Nobel's explosive contribution to world technology and vocabulary made him rich. A pacifist, he worried about the effects of dynamite and in his will established what became the best-known prizes in the world, for science and for peace. He also armed our language with what is still a powerful word. *Dynamite* occupies nearly a full page in the *Random House Historical Dictionary of American Slang*, with examples like this from Saul Bellow's 1944 novel *Dangling Man*: "He didn't have to tell me. I could tell from the beginning she was dynamite."

Swedish is spoken by almost nine million people in Sweden and a few hundred thousand in neighboring Finland. It has contributed about a hundred words to present-day English, most of them more Swedish-sounding, including *spry* (1746), *scuffle* (1590), *nickel* (1755), *smorgasbord* (1893), *orienteering* (1948), *moped* (1955), and *ombudsman* (1959).

~DENMARK

Lego *from Danish*

Thanks to those little interlocking building blocks, the whole world plays with the Danish language. They are playing with Lego, a name constructed out of the Danish expression *leg godt,* meaning "play well."

The company's historians tell us exactly when it happened. In 1932 Ole Kirk Christiansen began manufacturing ironing boards, stepladders, and wooden toys in the town of Billund, Denmark. Two years later, when his company had grown to have half a dozen employees, he gave it the name *Lego.* It was noticed later that *lego* means "I study" or "I read" in Latin, but play remained the official interpretation of the company name.

For nearly two decades after that, Lego remained a Danish company, with no effect on English-speaking children or their language. Even in Denmark, Lego was not registered as a trademark until 1954. But in 1956 the company began opening sales offices in other countries; in 1958 the stable stud-and-tube style of brick was introduced; and within a decade children the world over knew the name. From then till now, according to the company, about 190 billion Lego bricks (they call them "elements") have been produced, as well as 11 billion of the Duplo double-size bricks. That's enough for everyone in the world to play well.

Danish is a North Germanic language of the Indo-European family and the national language of the more than five million inhabitants of Denmark. Along with Norwegian and Swedish, Danish is a likely source for such English words as *skulk* (1225), *scoff* (1300), *ballast* (1530), *dangle* (1590), *skoal* (1600), *troll* (1616), *walrus* (1728), *iceberg* (1820), and *aquavit* (1890). Other Danish contributions to English have been from Danes whose names have become scientific designations: *Jacobson's organ* (in the head, 1885), *Gram's stain* (for bacteria, 1903), and the *Bohr effect* (from carbon dioxide in the blood, 1939).

∼GERMANY

kindergarten *from German*

In the nineteenth century, it sometimes seemed that everything we needed to know came from Germany: Christmas trees, serious philosophy and science, the art of brewing beer, and kindergarten. The latter was the invention of a serious, philosophical teacher of teachers, Friedrich Wilhelm August Froebel, born in 1782.

Froebel himself was largely self-educated and therefore escaped the grim, rigorous drills that passed for education in his day. He was thus free to dream of a different ideal, and he dedicated his life to providing children with an education that developed their spirits as well as their bodies by making use of a child's natural playfulness and creativity. He was already noted as an educator when in 1837 he started the first preschool embodying his principles of guided play. Three years later, on May 1, 1840, he invented the name for it. Looking for a word to describe a sunny experience that would cultivate children like plants and let them bloom like flowers, he called it a children's garden, that is, a Kinder-Garten.

With that name embodying its cheerful philosophy, the kindergarten idea soon became world famous. That was a good thing, because his own government, fearing that kindergartens would not impart proper lessons in obedience, banned them for a while in the 1850s. Refugee teachers established kindergartens in England, where the word was adopted without translation as early as 1852. The first kindergarten in the United States was established in 1856.

Among the countless Americans since then who have learned everything they need to know in kindergarten, one of the most prominent was the architect Frank Lloyd Wright. His sense of design was profoundly influenced by the simple forms embodied in kindergarten blocks.

German is a close relative and neighbor of English. Both are West Germanic languages in the Indo-European family.

It is spoken by seventy five million people in Germany and about a hundred million worldwide. Over the past millennium it has contributed hundreds of words to our language. In the twentieth century, for a terrible decade or so, the German of the Nazi era gave us grim words like *fuhrer* (1934), *gestapo* (1934), *flak* (1938), and *blitzkrieg* (1939). But most of our words from German are more benign, ranging from *clown* (1563) to *muffin* (1703), *ouch!* (1838, Philadelphia), and the now all-American *hamburger* (1884). The psychological insights of German thinkers also gave us the useful words *schadenfreude* (1895), the pleasure we feel in the misfortunes of others, and *kitsch* (1925), would-be art that serves only to emphasize bad taste, like garden gnomes or portraits of Elvis on black velvet.

⌁NETHERLANDS

hunky-dory *from Frisian*

A Japanese performer in New York City seems to have invented the word *hunky-dory*. But we trace its beginning to Friesland on the north coasts of the Netherlands and Germany.

According to John Russell Bartlett's 1877 *Dictionary of Americanisms*, *hunky-dory* was the invention of a performer called Japanese Tommy, who was popular in the 1860s. He is said to have based it on the name of a street in Tokyo, or perhaps Yokohama, called *Honcho-dori*. (In Japanese, *Honcho-dori* means something like "Main Street," and many cities have one.) But Tommy wouldn't have thought of it if there hadn't already been the adjective *hunk* in English meaning "safe" or "in a good position." This particular *hunk* derived from a Dutch word meaning the goal or "home" in a game. And that in turn evidently came from Frisian. In West Frisian *honck* means "house" or "safe place"; in East Frisian *hunk* means "nook" or "retreat" or "home" in a game. Before becoming obsolete, that *hunk* spawned *hunky*, and whether it was really Japanese Tommy's doing or just children's play, somebody added *dory* to make *hunky-dory*, first noted in print in 1866.

West Frisian is spoken by 700,000 people in the Netherlands. North Frisian and East Frisian, related but different languages, are spoken by about 10,000 people each in Schleswig-Holstein, Germany, near the Danish border. Like English, Dutch, and German, the Frisian languages belong to the West Germanic branch of our Indo-European language family.

In fact, Frisian is the closest foreign language to English. Sixty percent of its basic vocabulary is similar to ours. You can almost understand a Frisian sentence posted on the World Wide Web: *Lowlands-L is in automatisearre diskusjelist, dy't ferspraat wurdt fia e-mail*, that is, "Lowlands-L is an automated discussion list that is spread via e-mail." Many English words have Frisian cousins, but the *hunk* of *hunky-dory* is the only Frisian word that is definitely an ancestor of an English one. The most famous Frisian in recent times, by the way, was Mata Hari, dancer, spy, and femme fatale.

∽NETHERLANDS

pamper *from Dutch*

From the point of view of English, Dutch is a 1 percent language. That is, about 1 percent of the general English vocabulary has been imported from Dutch. This is nothing like Latin and French, with about 25 percent each, but only those languages plus Greek with 5 percent and Old Norse with nearly 2 percent have pampered our language more than Dutch. And unlike most other languages, Dutch has given us many verbs. It seems appropriate, then, to let our Dutch representative be the verb *pamper*.

When it first appeared in English, as long ago as 1380, it had a narrower meaning, "to overfeed or stuff with rich food." At a time when food was not always abundant or even adequate in supply, overeating was the ultimate pampering. By the 1500s, it meant any kind of overindulgence, not just eating, and it had developed the kinder, gentler modern sense of complete but not necessarily too much indulgence. We now happily accept the instruction of advertisers or counselors to pamper ourselves.

Dutch is a close relative of English, a member of the West Germanic branch of the Indo-European language family. It is spoken by the nearly sixteen million inhabitants of the Netherlands. A very similar language, Flemish, is spoken next door in Belgium by half of its population of ten million, and another very similar language, Low German, is spoken next door on the other side, in Germany, by a few million more.

A sampling of verbs that we owe to Dutch includes *scour* (1297), *slip* (1300), *gulp* (1380), *grumble* (1586), *rant* (1602), *rumple* (1603), *slurp* (1648), *smuggle* (1687), *hustle* (1751), and *snoop* (1832). Adjectives include *plump* (1569), *slim* (1657), and *gruesome* (1816). And the many nouns from Dutch include *block* (1305), *bundle* (1382), *tub* (1386), *deck* (1509), *bully* (1538), *suds* (1581), *landscape* (1598), *boss* (1679), *cookie* (1703), and *snack* (1402 as a snap or bite, 1757 as a quick meal).

∽BELGIUM

rip *from Flemish*

Without the assistance of Flemish, the English language would be impoverished. We would not be able to rip a seam, rip open an envelope, rip apart the opposition. Romance novelists wouldn't be able to rip bodices. And nobody could rip off someone else's property.

Rip is a word so much at home in English that it needs no introduction. English obtained it in the late Middle Ages, around 1477. We didn't have to go far to get it; *rip* was in the vocabulary not only of Flemish but of Frisian,

Dutch, and Low German. All four are Germanic languages located just across the Channel from England. They are closely related to each other and to English.

Flemish is, in fact, a variety of the Dutch language. It is spoken in Flanders, a region that includes parts of northern France and the northern half of Belgium. We count it as a separate language from Dutch because it is in a different country; it has been said that a language is a dialect with an army and a navy of its own. Nowadays standard Flemish and standard Dutch are the same, but in earlier times Flemish was a distinct dialect.

The historical importance of Flanders in trade with England has brought several dozen Flemish words into the English language. These include *cambric* (1530), *dock* (in court, 1586), *funk* (1743), and in this century *waterzooi* (a thick creamy stew, 1949).

～FRANCE

reason, fashion *from French*

What language has better reason than French to compliment itself on gracing our language with fashion? During the three hundred years in the Middle Ages when the royalty, nobility, and courts of England conducted their affairs in French, the English language imported from French a vast number of *royal* (1374), *noble* (1225), and *courtly* (1450) words. Our provincial language thereby became international and adorned with *chivalry* (1300) and *honor* (1290). More than a *quarter* (1375) of the present-day English vocabulary comes to us *courtesy* (1225) of the French. What can we offer but our *gracious* (1303) *approval* (1690) in words adopted from the French?

With good reason, we can say that we owe our appreciation of *reason* (1225) to the French. Consider the French philosopher René Descartes, who in the seventeenth century wrote *Discourse on the Method of Conducting One's Reason*

Well and reasoned into existence himself, God, and the world, starting with nothing more than a sense of doubt.

As for *fashion* (1300), French has been in fashion with the English language ever since the models of fashion were the French nobles who followed in the wake of William the Conqueror to occupy every exalted place in England. Even today, France remains a center for fashion and fashion models. Though France and England went through centuries of bitter rivalry from the late Middle Ages to the time of Napoleon, the sovereignty and elegance of French vocabulary in English have remained uncontested.

True, we have other less agreeable vocabulary to thank French for: *felony* (1290) and *misdemeanor* (1487), *arson* (1680), *assault* (1297), *burglary* (1533), *fraud* (1330), *libel* (1297), *perjury* (1387), and *slander* (1300), for example, as well as *crime* (1382) itself. French has given us *vice* (1297), *grief* (1225), *decadence* (1549), *defeat* (1374), *error* (1300), *treason* (1225), and *torture* (1540). But to balance that, we have *achievement* (1475) and *praise* (1430), *comfort* and *joy* (both 1225), *leisure* (1303) and *pleasure* (1390), *amusement* (1603) and *sport* (1440).

French is a Romance language, one of the descendants of Latin in the Indo-European language family. Today it is spoken as a first language by nearly sixty million people in France and perhaps twenty-five million elsewhere around the world, and as a second by many more. In number of speakers, it is the thirteenth most populous language in the world; in influence, it is perhaps unequalled by any other except English, to which it has given so much.

⌒ FRANCE

druid *from Gaulish*

If you had religion back in ancient Celtic Gaul, the land we now call France, you probably had an oak grove for a church, mistletoe for a holy plant, and animal or even human sacrifice for a ritual. During a religious service you might listen to sacred stories. You would believe in the immortality of the soul and a place to go to after death—better or worse, depending on how you lived your present life. You wouldn't restrict your worship to one god but would respect dozens, if not hundreds. And to guide you in all this you would have a druid for a priest. If you didn't do what the druid said, you'd face a fate worse than death: exclusion from the rituals and shunning by the community.

Being a druid was a full-time occupation. Druids needed to know the names and attributes of the gods, the sacred tales about them, the intricate lunar calendar, and the rituals. Julius Caesar, the Roman conqueror of Gaul, wrote that druids also acted as judges in all cases involving tribes and individuals. The Gauls, he said, sent their apprentice druids to Britain for as long as twenty years to learn their profession. According to Caesar, druids memorized the verses about their gods rather than allowing them to be put in writing.

And that is a difficulty for modern historians. What we know about the druids comes not from the Gauls themselves but from Greek and Roman writers who were fascinated with, and scornful of, the religion of the big blond barbarians.

We do know that the name *druid* is a Celtic one, most likely from the Gaulish branch of the Celtic language. The Greeks and Romans learned *druid* from the Gauls, and English took it from Latin much later, in a 1563 translation of Caesar.

Although Celtic, to which Gaulish belongs, and Italic, to which Latin belongs, are separate branches of our Indo-European language family, the Continental Celtic languages were fairly close to Latin. Caesar is said to have written his dispatches in Greek instead of Latin so that the Gauls would not be able to decipher them. In Caesar's day, two millennia ago, all Gaul spoke Gaulish, but today nobody does. All that remains of the language is a few inscriptions.

∼ FRANCE

bijou *from Breton*

It's a little gem, this pretty gift from the Breton language to English. That's the present-day meaning of *bijou*, which was nicely delivered to our language by the French as early as 1668. An English document of that date refers to "Perfumed gloves, fans, and all sorts of delicate bijoux for each lady to take att her pleasure."

Reflecting our awareness of its foreign charm, we have kept the French pronunciation of *bijou* (with a zh sound for the middle consonant) and the strikingly French *x* to mark the plural. To the French, centuries before the English, it was also a charming import. It came from Breton, a Celtic language spoken in the region of northern France appropriately called Brittany.

In Breton, the word *biz* means "finger." The related word *bizou* means "ring for the finger." By the 1500s the French had learned the word and generalized it to mean any kind of small jewel or gem, as it does in our language today.

English speakers have generalized the word still further. Anything that can be a little gem can have the exotic sparkle of *bijou*, whether a book, a painting, a farm, or a house. In *Ulysses* (1922), recently said to be the greatest novel of the twentieth century, James Joyce wrote of "the most prominent pleasure resorts, Margate with mixed bathing and firstrate hydros and spas, Eastbourne, Scarborough, Margate and so on, beautiful Bournemouth, the Channel islands and similar bijou spots." For a time in the mid-twentieth century, *Bijou* was a favorite name for an elegant movie theater.

Breton is a member of the Celtic branch of the Indo-European language family, along with Welsh, Scottish, and Irish. Northwestern Europe was once dominated by Celts; the name *Britain* as well as *Brittany* attests to the former importance of Celtic languages. Nowadays there are still about 700,000 speakers of Breton, mostly in France.

Aside from place names, only a few words of Breton have made their way into English; the conquering French and English speakers did not have to learn the language of the peoples they subjugated. In the nineteenth century, however, interest in antiquity brought two more Breton gems into English: *menhir* (1840) and *dolmen* (1859), both referring to mysterious stone formations raised by humans in prehistoric times. A menhir is a lone tall upright stone, also called a *standing stone* in Britain; a dolmen is a man-made cavern, a structure of two or more upright stones with a capstone on the top.

∼FRANCE

lingo *from Provençal*

If there ever was a lingo that sweetened and charmed our English language, it was Provençal, the Romance language spoken in the southeast of France. We may well have the light-hearted word *lingo* itself from Provençal. In English, it was noted in a 1660 court case at New Haven colony: "To which the plaintiff answered, that he was not acquainted with Dutch lingo." William Congreve's play *The Way of the World* (1700) also uses the word: "Well, well, I shall understand your lingo one of these days, cousin; in the meanwhile I must answer in plain English." In 1702, Cotton Mather's *Magnalia Christi Americana*, referring to American Indians, mentions the "verbs of which their linguo is composed."

Authorities are not agreed on where this *lingo* of ours comes from. It might be an abbreviation of *lingua franca*, the Italian name for a language used to communicate among people of different languages. Or it might come from *lingoa*, the Portuguese word for language. But Provençal has the very word *lingo* itself, also meaning language.

Whatever the uncertainty about the origin of *lingo*, there is no doubt that Provençal has enriched English. It has done so through its gift of words to French, which has brought them to the attention of English speakers. Thus Provençal has satisfied our appetites with *fig* (1225), *nutmeg* (1366), *salad* (1390), *truffle* (1591), and *escargot* (1892). It has charmed us with *amour* (1300), *ballad* (1492), *perfume* (1533), *sonnet* (1557), *cavalier* (1589), *aubade* (1678), *viola* (1724), *troubadour* (1741), and *charade* (1776). Provençal has built us *cabins* (1400), *camps* (1528), *bastilles* (1741), and *boutiques* (1767). It has outfitted us with *canes* (1398), *velour* (1706), *camisoles* (1795), and *berets* (1827). And it has enabled us to see *dolphins* (1387), walk on a *terrace* (1515), and wrap ourselves in *cocoons* (1699).

Provençal is a Romance language of our Indo-European family. Geographically and linguistically it is located between French and Italian, and like them it is a descendant of the Latin spoken by the ancient Romans. Today in Provence there are about a quarter of a million fluent speakers of Provençal.

⌒SPAIN

siesta *from Spanish*

At the sixth hour of the day, after the midday meal, speakers of Spanish have a sensible occupation: the siesta. For an hour or two or three, shops close and people close their eyes, awaiting the abating of the heat of the day. In the later afternoon and evening, life awakens with new vigor.

English speakers have discussed the siesta since the seventeenth century. A letter dated 1655 comments on the "Siesta (as the Spaniard calls it) or afternoon sleep." English-speaking travelers to Spanish-speaking countries have continued to comment on, and often happily partake in, the siesta. Back home, however, we have kept our stores open at siesta time.

As Texans know, the siesta made possible their independence in 1836. After Mexican general Santa Anna defeated the defiant Texans at the Alamo, he pursued the rest of the rebels, who had retreated to Galveston Island. On April 21, on the coastal plain at San Jacinto near Galveston, Santa Anna and his troops took their customary afternoon siesta. That was the time the unsleeping Texans, led by Sam Houston, chose to attack. In eighteen minutes the battle was over, the Mexican army was routed, Santa Anna himself became a prisoner, and Texas won its independence.

Spanish is one of the Romance languages, a descendant of Latin, in the Indo-European language family. Worldwide, about 300 million people speak Spanish as a first language, 28 million in Spain and most of the rest in Central and South America. Numerous Spanish words have immigrated into English, from both the old world and the new. The words in this book from Indian languages of Central and South America have mostly been brought to us by speakers of Spanish.

Among the many other Spanish words in English we have space to mention just a few: *tuna* (1555), *breeze* (1565), *alligator* (1568), *mosquito* (1583), *bravado* (1599), *embargo* (1602), *sherry* (1608), *desperado* (1610), *cockroach* (1624), *cargo* (1657), *vanilla* (1662), *avocado* (1697), *cigar* (1735), *ranch* (1808), *patio* (1828), *stampede* (1834), *silo* (1835), *bonanza* (1844), and *tango* (1913).

~Spain

placer *from Catalan*

California had just become part of the United States when gold was discovered there in 1848, but the state's Hispanic heritage was pervasive. The names of California places were mostly Spanish. Canyons, arroyos, and sierras were Spanish then, as they are now, and Spanish-derived words like *ranch*, *plaza*, and *adobe* (originally from Coptic) have remained familiar too, reflecting the Spanish-speaking Californians' way of life.

Gold mining, however, brought in new and mostly non-Hispanic terminology as it brought in the forty-niners, new and mostly non-Hispanic adventurers from the eastern parts of the United States. Their mining vocabulary included terms like *bar*, *diggings*, *gulch*, *pay dirt*, *tailings*, *rocker*, and *wing dam*, to use examples from an 1859 glossary of "Californianisms" published in a San Francisco newspaper. But even in the getting of gold, some Spanish influence could be noted, in the terms *arastra* (a mill for crushing quartz), *color* (visible gold), and *placer*. The last was the name for gold-bearing beds of sand and gravel, a special attraction of California's gold country. The 1859 glossary defined *placer* as "a place where gold is found in dirt near the surface of the ground."

What do these Spanish words have to do with Catalan, an Indo-European Romance language spoken in northern Spain by more than six million people? The explanation is that *placer*, like several dozen other words, seems to have been imported from Catalan into Spanish before being passed on to English. In Catalan, *placer* means a shoal or underwater sandbar. By the time the word got to English, as early as 1842, it could also mean a sandy place along a streambed but above water.

Catalan is also the likely source of these words brought by Spanish into English: *frijoles* (1577), *brocade* (1588), *barracks* (1686), *capsize* (1788), *mirador* (a window or tower with a view, 1797), and *fajita* (1984).

∿SPAIN

bizarre *from Basque*

Can a beard be bizarre? Of course. Can a bizarre beard be Basque? How bizarre! There is no question that the Basque language, spoken on the border between Spain and

France, from which so many English words have come, has a word *bizarra* that means beard. There is no question, furthermore, that *bizarro* means "handsome" or "brave" in Spanish and Portuguese.

Furthermore, coming at it from the present day, there is no question that we got our *bizarre* directly from the French, in about 1648. And there is no question that the French were the ones who took *bizarre* meaning "brave" or "warlike" and twisted it to our present-day meaning of "strange, weird, grotesque."

But what happened in between? Did a Spaniard, observing a fierce bearded Basque, hear the word *bizarra* and by misunderstanding give it a new meaning? Did the French then borrow this "brave" *bizarre* from the Spanish? So could it be that *bizarre* comes from the Basque word for beard?

The experts aren't sure, but then the experts aren't sure of a lot of things about the Basque language. It has a bizarre history. It seems completely unrelated to other European languages, or indeed to any other languages at all, although efforts have been made to link it with languages of the Caucasus, the Americas, and Pakistan.

Basque is spoken by more than 600,000 people in the northeast of Spain, where it is recognized as an official regional language, and by 90,000 across the border in France, as well as some 8,000 in the United States.

Via Spanish, Basque has also given the English-speaking world what is said to be the world's fastest game. In Basque, *jai* means "festival" and *alai* means "happy." The game of *jai alai*, which involves flinging a hard rubber ball against a wall at high speed, is thus a "happy festival." It is a popular spectator sport in Florida and Latin America.

Yet another likely Basque word in English is *chaparral* (1842), the term for dense brush in the American Southwest. We know this word comes to us directly from Spanish, but Spanish may well have obtained it from Basque.

⟲PORTUGAL

dodo *from Portuguese*

It was a stupid bird, and that is what the Portuguese called it when one of their world-ranging expeditions found it on the

remote Indian Ocean island of Mauritius. In Portuguese, *dodo* means stupid or silly. An Englishman visiting Mauritius in 1628 reported the name in a letter, writing of "a strange fowle, which I had at the Iland mauritius, called by the portingalls a DoDo." The clumsy, squat birds were good eating and could not fly, so they could not escape capture by hungry sailors. Three or four dodos were said to be enough to feed a hundred men. It is not surprising that before the seventeenth century was over dodos were extinct.

But their reputation was not. With the image of the dodo in mind, speakers of English have used *dodo* ever since as a four-letter word to express exasperation with a stupid person or stupid behavior. Reflection on the fate of the bird gave us, as early as 1904, a proverbial phrase, *dead as a dodo*, to go along with the much earlier *dead as a doornail* or *dead as a herring*.

Because the Portuguese were first among Europeans to voyage to remote parts of the earth, through their *palaver* (1735) and *savvy* (1785) they obtained well over a hundred exotic words that later made their way into English. These include *molasses* (1582), *pagoda* (1588), *flamingo* (1565), *emu* (1656), the *coco* of *coconut* (1613), *caste* (1613), and back home, *port* (1691), a kind of wine made in the Portuguese city of Oporto.

Portuguese is an Indo-European language of the Romance family, descended from Latin and a close relative of Spanish. The two languages are so close that it is sometimes hard to tell which one is the source of an English word. Words that could just as well have come from either Spanish or Portuguese include *junta* (1622) and *albatross* (1672). Nearly all of the 10 million inhabitants of Portugal speak Portuguese, of course. Brazil adds 165 million, and there are a few million more in the rest of the world.

～SWITZERLAND

avalanche *from Romansch*

Alpine adventurers are always assiduously advised: act alert about avalanches! Better begin by buying beacons, but beware: Crashes can cause catastrophically confining circumstances. Dangerous drops don't effectively enable escapes. Finally—well, it's easier to break loose of the confines of the alphabet than to get out from under an avalanche.

If you're not killed outright, you have about half an hour to be rescued alive. According to avalanche authorities, nearly everyone who is dug out within fifteen minutes survives; after thirty-five minutes, fewer than half of those buried by snow get out alive. An avalanche rescue beacon, which requires practice and training to use, reduces average rescue time from two hours to thirty-five minutes, but that still does not bode well for survival. In Europe between 1985 and 1991, more than 700 people died because of avalanches; in the United States between 1950 and 1993, 420 died. A majority of the American victims inadvertently started the avalanches that killed them.

How do you avoid the danger? Consider slope lines, fractures, tender spots, and stress concentrations, say Jill Fredston and Doug Fesler in their book *Snow Sense*. Hammer on the snow. Stay alert and objective. "Remember that the avalanche dragons do not care if you are tired, hungry, grumpy, or late for work. . . . When evaluating avalanche hazard, you need to think like an avalanche."

An avalanche is an alpine experience, so it is not surprising that we look to the Alps for the origin of the word. It is also clear that the word comes from a Romance language, one of the descendants of Latin in the Italic branch of our Indo-European language family. That is because *avalanche* evidently derives from something like *à val*, meaning "(falling) toward the valley" in the Romance language French.

A likely candidate for the original of the word is *avalantz* in the Romansch language, spoken in the southeast corner of Alpine Switzerland. Though Romansch has fewer than 50,000 speakers in a country of more than seven million, it has been protected and supported by the government since 1938, when it was designated Switzerland's fourth official language. (The others are German, French, and Italian.) In English, an author mentioned Alpine *avalanches* as long ago as 1771. No other words of Romansch have made their way across the Alps to English.

∾ ITALY

graffiti *from Italian*

In ancient Rome, when you had a written message for the public, you scratched it on a wall. What else could you do? You didn't have a fax machine, a photocopier, or the World Wide Web. You couldn't even take out an ad in a newspaper.

The walls of Pompeii, preserved for two thousand years under volcanic ash, are marked with numerous examples of this Roman custom. Here are some translated graffiti:

—Successus was here.
—Gaius Julius Primigenius was here. Why are you late?
—Lovers, like bees, lead a honey-sweet life.

—I don't want to sell my husband.

—Burglar, watch out!

—Someone at whose table I do not dine, Lucius Istacidius, is a barbarian to me.

—The fruit sellers ask you to elect Marcus Holconius Priscus as aedile.

—I am amazed, o wall, that you have not collapsed and fallen, since you must bear the tedious stupidities of so many scrawlers.

The custom of wall writing has occurred worldwide and continues to the present, though advances in the technology of paint have made it more of an opportunity both for art and for defacement on a grand scale. But it was the example of Pompeii that gave the world, and the English language, an Italian word for it: *graffiti*. The word was used in English as early as 1851 with regard to runic inscriptions in Orkney, and in 1873 with regard to Greek poets: "Even the Graffiti of Pompeii have scarcely more power to reconstruct the past." In Italian, *graffiti* is the plural of *graffito* meaning "a scratch," so purists in English distinguish "one graffito" from "many graffiti."

Many hundreds of words besides *graffiti* have migrated from Italian to English. Most numerous are the musical terms, everything from *opera* (1644) to *piano* (1803). But there is also the language of business, including *manager* (1588), *tariff* (1591), and *bankrupt* (1533), and such other words as *miniature* (1586), *bandit* (1593), *umbrella* (1609), *ghetto* (1611), *portfolio* (1722), *dilettante* (1723), and *studio* (1819), not to mention foods like *broccoli* (1699), *pasta* (1874), and *caffe latte* (1927).

Italian is a Romance language, that is, a descendant of Latin, belonging to the Italic branch of our Indo-European language family. Nearly seventy million people speak Italian nowadays, including fifty-seven million in Italy, a million and a half in Argentina, and about a million each in France and in the United States.

~ITALY (SICILY)

muffuletta *from Sicilian*

You won't find *muffuletta* in the *Oxford English Dictionary*, and it's hard to find it anywhere in the English-speaking world outside of New Orleans. But it's worth a visit, if you ever need an excuse to visit the Big Easy.

The world has Salvatore Lupo to thank for thinking of this sandwich that is a complete gourmet meal. Early in the twentieth century he was proprietor of Central Grocery, which is still located at 923 Decatur Street in New Orleans, open daily to 5:30 P.M. and still said to make the best muffuletta. Back in Lupo's day, Italian workers would stop at the grocery to get the ingredients for a four-course meal: meat, cheese, salad, and bread. It was in 1906, we are told, that Lupo combined all four into a single item called the *muffuletta sandwich* because it was made with the bread known as *muffuletta*.

At first glance, this muffuletta sandwich, nicknamed *muff*, looks something like the sandwich known variously as a *submarine, grinder, hero, hoagie,* or (in New Orleans) *poor boy*. But there are two crucial differences. The muff is made on muffuletta bread, a round seeded Sicilian loaf, and it includes an Italian salad or relish. The latter is so important that it appears in cookbooks like *The New Joy of Cooking* and was featured in two issues of *Bon Appétit* in 1996. Key ingredients in the relish are chopped olives and other vegetables and seasonings, along with olive oil. Add the relish to ham, salami, and provolone cheese in a loaf of freshly baked muffuletta bread, and you have a genuine Central Grocery muff.

Other stores and restaurants in New Orleans make delectable muffs too, and the word is spreading. *Bon Appétit* gave a muffuletta recipe from a hotel restaurant in Rochester, New York, and there's now a Muffuletta Cafe upstream from New Orleans at the other end of the Mississippi River in St. Paul, Minnesota. You can also order muffs from Central Grocery for delivery anywhere in the country by next-day air express.

Sicilian is a distinct version of the Italian language, spoken on the island of Sicily to the south of the Italian mainland. Like Italian, Sicilian is a descendant of ancient Latin and a member of the Italic or Romance branch of our Indo-European language family. It is the language of the nearly five million inhabitants of Sicily. Two notorious Sicilian words that have also immigrated to English are *Mafia* (1875) and *omertà* (1909), the Mafia's code of silence.

∾ITALY

justice, universe *from Latin*

All roads lead to Rome, and so do the majority of English words. There is no way this book can do justice to Latin, which directly or indirectly has provided well over half of the vocabulary of present-day English. So we will content ourselves here with doing *justice* and a word big enough to encompass everything else, *universe.*

Both *justice* and *universe* have taken the most often traveled road from Latin to English, the one that leads through French. But the form and meaning of both words remained essentially unchanged, so that our English understanding of justice and of the universe has clear roots in ancient Rome.

In English, courtesy of the French, we find *justice* as early as 1137 in a chronicle of unjust King Stephen. He was "a mild man, and soft, and good—and did no justice." The same chronicle has higher praise in the year 1140 for the man who became Stephen's successor, Earl Henry of Anjou: "Then was the earl received at Winchester, and at London, with great worship; and all did him homage, and swore to keep the peace. . . . And the earl went over sea; and all people loved him; for he did good justice, and made peace."

In about 1375, Geoffrey Chaucer brought the universe into English. His great poem *Troilus and Criseyde* uses the phrase *in universe*, meaning "universal": "Ye folk have set a law in universe." But it was the Elizabethan era, two centuries later, that began to discuss the universe as we know it today. Another poet, Edmund Spenser, in his 1596 *Hymn of Heavenly Beauty* exclaims, "Look on the frame of this wide universe, and therein read the endless kinds of creatures."

It was the English Renaissance of the sixteenth and seventeenth centuries that saw the greatest direct influx of Latin words to English, with minimal assistance from French. Scholars exulted in enriching our language with Latin imports, and many of them became commonplace words. These include nouns like *genius* (1513), *appendix* (1542), *circus* (1546), *vacuum* (1550), and *idea* (1563); verbs like *exit* (1538), *meditate* (1560), and *erupt* (1657); adjectives like *compatible* (1490), *enormous* (1531), and *insane* (1550). So many Latin words became English that there is nothing foreign-looking about them, and to the present day they continue to immigrate without attracting special notice. Examples of more recent Latin additions include *hallucination* (1629), *museum* (1672), *ultimate* (1681), *propaganda* (1718), and *bonus* (1773).

While adding Latin we have often kept our older English words, as in "last will and testament," where *will* is a word from our Germanic ancestors and *testament* (1330) is an import from Latin.

Latin is the head of the Italic branch of our Indo-European language family. Two thousand years ago it was the common language of the Roman Empire, as we would know even without documents from those times, because descendants of Latin are spoken in former provinces of the empire, ranging from Spain on the west to Romania on the east.

∼GREECE

philosophy *from Greek*

To the ancient Greeks we owe our love of wisdom. Or at least the word *philosophy*, which is the same thing, *phil* meaning "love" and *sophy* meaning "wisdom." Combined, the two elements mean both a love of wisdom and a desire for it. In English, *philosophy* first appears in writing as early as 1340, when it is explained for the benefit of readers unfamiliar with the word as "love of wysdome." *Wisdom* is a word native to English, but we had no term for the love of learning or the desire to gain wisdom. Like the rest of the Western world, we learned that from the Greeks.

Greek is one of the great contributors to English, and *philosophy* a great example of the Greek contribution. Like many other Greek words, it came to us not directly from the Greek but first through Latin and then through French, the two languages that have contributed even more than Greek to the English we know today.

The two parts of *philosophy* recombine themselves in numerous other words. *Phil-* is found, for example, in *philanthropy*, the love of humankind; *philharmonic*, loving music; *philodendron*, a plant that loves to hang around trees (*dendron* being tree); and *Philadelphia*, or the love of brother or sister. We are so comfortable with Greek that we can use it to make stunt words such as *philopatrodomania*, or the mania that comes from loving one's homeland, that is, homesickness. *Phil* with an added *e* also appears at the end of dozens of words from Greek like *bibliophile*, a lover of books; *ailurophile*, a lover of cats; *oenophile*, a lover of wine; *Anglophile*, a lover of things English, and *Francophile*, a lover of things French; and *pedophile*, one with a (perverted) love of children.

The *soph* part of *philosophy* also finds itself in English words, notably *sophisticated*, full of a certain kind of wisdom; and *sophomore*, combining the words for "wise" and "foolish" to represent the state of mind of a second-year college student.

It is thanks to the Greeks that we have *schools* and *scholars* in the first place; both of those English words are from the Greek. Even today, scholarly fields of study are named in Greek, using the suffix *logy* from *logos* meaning "word" or "discourse." The three hundred *logy*s in present-day English include *archaeology*, discourse about old things; *biology*, discourse about life; *oology*, discourse about eggs; *neurology*, discourse about the nervous system; *geology*, discourse about the earth; *psychology*, discourse about the mind; *theology*, discourse about God; *eschatology*, discourse about the last days of the world; *graphology*, discourse about writing; *cosmetology*, discourse about cosmetics; *terminology*, discourse about terms; and *criminology*, *demonology*, *ufology*, and *sexology*, which need no introduction. And then, we have *philology*, the love of words, of discourse, of learning, the name formerly given to scholarship in language and literature.

English has many other words of Greek origin as well, everything from *catalog* (1460) to *zeal* (1382). All told, about 5 percent of the general English vocabulary comes from Greek. Even today, science and technology use elements of Greek and Latin to construct new English words. One hybrid example, is *television*, which uses *tele* (meaning "distant") from Greek and *vision* from Latin.

Like English, Greek is an Indo-European language. It is the sole member of the Hellenic branch. Modern Greek is spoken by about eleven million inhabitants of modern Greece. But it is the classical language, the ancestor of modern Greek, that is the basis for our philosophical borrowings.

⁓Yugoslavia, Croatia, Bosnia-Herzegovina

vampire *from Serbo-Croatian*

Thanks to Bram Stoker and his ilk, we know all about vampires. We know that they once were people but now are dead; that they can't stand sunlight and spend their days in their coffins; that they have no reflections in mirrors because they have no souls; that they cannot enter a house without being invited but once invited can enter again and again; that for convenience they can change into vampire bats; that they drink the blood of others with the result that these others become vampires after death; and that, being dead already, they're very hard to kill, the effective methods being beheading, cremation, or a stake through the heart.

But what about the name *vampire*? Where did that come from? That's harder to determine. We know that words like *vampire* were thick as bats in the Slavic languages of eastern Europe in the Middle Ages. Russian, Polish, Czech, Bulgarian, and Serbo-Croatian all had *vampir*, while Bulgarian also had *vapir* or *vepir*. There is also a variant beginning with *u*, as in Polish *upiór*, Russian *upyr'*, Ukrainian *uper* or *upyr*. It is possible that this *u*-word came from Turkish *uber*, meaning "witch," and also possible that that *u*-word was the ancestor of *vampire*. And perhaps not. For our purposes, Serbo-Croatian is as good a candidate for the word's source as any other. Its word is *vampir*, the same form that made its way through such intermediate languages as Hungarian, German, and French to arrive in England by 1734. An English document of that date declares that "These Vampyres are supposed to be the Bodies of deceased Persons, animated by evil Spirits, which come out of the Graves, in the Night-time, suck the Blood of many of the Living, and thereby destroy them." That about sums it up.

Serbo-Croatian is a Slavic Indo-European language spoken both by Serbs and by Croats in Yugoslavia, Croatia, and Bosnia-Herzegovina, more than 20,000,000 people altogether. But since the people are not all together, and since the two cultures have recently become enemies, or at least gone their separate ways, they prefer to consider themselves speakers of two separate languages, Serbian and Croatian. The chief difference between the two is that

Serbian is usually written in a Cyrillic (or Russian) alphabet, Croatian in a Roman one. From this language, or these languages, English has also imbibed *slivovitz* (1885) or plum brandy and has learned to wear a *cravat* (1656) or necktie, a word that traces back from French to German to the Serbo-Croatian word meaning a Croat. Neckties were worn by Croatian mercenaries in France.

～BULGARIA

bora *from Bulgarian*

This is not Bora-Bora, the gentle tropical island in the South Pacific. Far from it. The *bora* is a biting wind on the opposite side of the world, and it seems to blow nothing but ill to those who have to endure it.

Consider the Russian port of Novorossiysk or "New Russia" in the northeast corner of the Black Sea. Founded some 150 years ago, it has the only deep-water bay on Russia's Black Sea coastline. In Novorossiysk, the bora rules. It howls through the mountain passes from the north so fiercely that it makes an airport impossible; you have to go forty kilometers west to Anapa to catch an airplane. Even for shipping, the bora is so strong that it closes the harbor about seventy days of each year. In April 1997, bora winds of sixty knots created ten-foot waves right at the pier and sank many ships.

Other nations on the Black Sea feel the bora too, including Bulgaria. And it is there that the bora seems to have found its name. Some have speculated that the word is a borrowing from Latin, which calls the north wind *boreas*. But it seems just as likely that *bora* is an immigrant to our language from Bulgarian, a Slavic language closely related to Serbo-Croatian in the Indo-European language family. Bulgarian is spoken by about seven million people or all but 15 percent of the population of Bulgaria.

Another English word that is certainly from Bulgarian

is *gamza* (1959), the name of a grape grown in northern Bulgaria and the wine made from it. Suhindol Winery's Gamza 1994 is described by Delf Group Wines as "a deep brilliant ruby-red in color, with tawny nuances, and . . . a richly scented nose; full-bodied, round, and fruity on the palate. An exceptionally well balanced wine with good acidity, tannin, and wood in the finish. Oak aging is quite obvious in the finish and nose."

∾BULGARIA

heathen *from Gothic*

The woman was an outsider. She was a Greek, born in Syrian Phoenicia, definitely not one of the Jews to whom Jesus had been ministering. Chapter 7 of the Book of Mark tells us that Jesus met her when he went up the Mediterranean coast to the vicinity of Tyre and Sidon. There this woman asked Jesus to drive out a demon in her daughter. He hesitated to heal anyone other than his own people, saying rather harshly, "Let the children first be fed, for it is not right to take the children's bread and throw it to the dogs." But the foreign woman had a ready answer: "Even the dogs under the table eat the children's crumbs." That was enough. "For this saying you may go your way; the demon has left your daughter," said Jesus, and it was so.

Three centuries later, when Bishop Wulfilas of the Visigoths was translating this story into his native tongue, he described the woman's otherness by saying she was *haithno*, our *heathen*. This may just have been to say she was figuratively living on the *heath*, out in the countryside away from the community. But apparently thanks to Wulfilas's choice of words, the religious meaning of *heathen* as "outside the faith" spread to the other Germanic languages, including English, as they changed their allegiance from heathen to Christian. The word appears in English sermons written as long ago as the year 971.

In our Germanic branch of the Indo-European language, the oldest documents by far are written in Gothic, the language of the Goths who were so helpful in bringing the Roman Empire to a close. Most of the Gothic we know is in Wulfilas's fourth-century translation of some parts of the Bible, preserved in an elegant sixth-century version with gold and silver letters on purple parchment, the Codex Argenteus now at the University of Uppsala in Sweden. Wulfilas probably did his writing in the land we now know as Bulgaria; Goths at other times went as far north as Ukraine and Poland, as far west as Italy and Spain. There were some Gothic speakers in the Crimea on the Black Sea as late as the eighteenth century, but the language is extinct now. Aside from this one example of *heathen*, East Germanic Gothic and the West Germanic English had little to say to each other.

∾Romania

hora *from Romanian*

Put your right arm in, put your right arm out. . . . No, that's the wrong dance. Let's try again: Stand in a large circle. Put your hands on the shoulders of your neighbors, and let them do the same to you. Then move to the left, stepping with your left foot, stepping over with your right, stepping again with your left, swinging your right foot in front of your left, then stepping back on it in place; and so on. Got it? That's the hora. We have spoken of it in English since 1878.

Danced slow and solemnly or fast and furiously, the hora is the national dance of Israel and has been so since that nation's founding in 1948. But it was not invented there. It came from Romania, where it is also the national dance and has been so at least since Romania was the Roman province of Dacia nearly two thousand years ago. When Romanians want to celebrate a historical moment, they dance and sing the "Union Hora," written in 1855 by poet Vasile Alecsandri. In 1998, when Romania defeated England in the World Cup soccer tournament, fans gathered in the streets of the capital, Bucharest, shouting "Romania! Romania!" and forming large circles to dance the hora.

As the name of the language suggests, Romanian is a Romance language, a descendant of Latin in the Indo-European language family. It is spoken by most of the more than twenty-two million people of Romania. Because it is so remote from English-speaking countries, Romanian has contributed far fewer words to English than its siblings French, Spanish, Portuguese, and Italian, not to mention Latin itself. But from Romanian we do have two kinds of food, *halvah* (1846) and *pastrami* (1936), both via Yiddish.

⌇HUNGARY

goulash *from Hungarian*

Cowboys invented it. Hungarian cowboys, that is. More than a thousand years ago, they created their own version of Meals, Ready to-Eat by stewing and sun-drying cubed beef. They would pack this dried meat in bags and carry it with them. When they wanted a meal, they would cook the meat in a little water to make goulash, or a little more water to make goulash soup.

In Hungarian, *gulyá* means "herd of cattle," "herdsman" or "cowboy," and *hús* means "meat." Put *gulyá* and *hús* together and you have "meat cowboy style."

The word and the dish came into English as *goulash* in the nineteenth century, mentioned as early as 1866. In the twentieth century, at least according to a Gallup poll taken in 1969, *goulash* was among the five most popular meat dishes in America. Like its spelling, however, American goulash was not exactly the same as its Hungarian original.

A true Hungarian goulash, it is said, begins with onions browned in lard or bacon fat in a kettle or cast iron pan. To these you add water, beef cut into small cubes, and a generous amount of sweet paprika, Hungary's national spice. This simmers over low heat for an hour. Additional ingredients are possible, including potatoes, tomatoes and green peppers, salt, bay leaves, marjoram, garlic, caraway seeds, even cloves. Health-conscious cooks have substituted unsaturated vegetable oil for the lard, and there is a vegan meatless recipe featuring potatoes and rutabagas.

The one ingredient common to all these recipes is *paprika* (1896), another word which came into English in the nineteenth century courtesy of the Hungarian language and cuisine. *Paprika* ultimately comes from the same Latin word that gives us English *pepper*, but paprika is a distinctive mild spice ground from a red pepper cultivated in Hungary and ultimately borrowed from the Turks. Like goulash, paprika sometimes suffers a little in translation; one goulash recipe cautions that it is "most important to use real Hungarian paprika for ultimate flavor."

Unlike most languages of Europe, Hungarian does not belong to the Indo-European family but rather to a family known as Uralic; its one well-known relative is Finnish. More than ten million people, 98 percent of the population of Hungary, speak the language, along with two million more in Romania and about half a million each in Slovakia, Yugoslavia, and the United States. Aside from food, the Hungarian language has given us a dozen or so words, including the names of three dogs: the *komondor* (1931) and *puli* (1936), both sheep dogs, and the *vizsla* (1945), a hunting dog.

∼SLOVAKIA

lekvar *from Slovak*

In the latter part of the twentieth century, *lekvar* spread from the Slovak language into English, at least into pockets of North American English. Fresh from eastern Europe and first noted by lexicographers in 1958, lekvar is a prune jam used especially with pastries. You can make it by cooking prunes until they are soft, then mashing them with sugar. Or you can buy lekvar ready-made. If your neighborhood grocer doesn't have it, you can order Kettle Fresh Prune Lekvar from Bunge Foods of Atlanta. It comes in forty-four-gallon containers.

Lekvar makes a delicious filling for cookies, but it seems especially destined for pirohis. Here is how you prepare pirohis, according to the Lekvar Page on the World Wide Web:

> Recipe for Lekvar Pirohi: 3 cups flour, 6 eggs, 1 tsp salt, warm water if necessary. Mix into a firm dough and roll out thinner than for a pie crust. Cut into 3 x 3 squares and fill. Fold over to make a triangle and pinch edges securely. Drop into boiling water and cook for about 10 minutes. Drain. Saute onions in butter, and pour over pirohis.

Lekvar is from Slovak, the national language of Slovakia. The full history of the word, according to the *American Heritage Dictionary*, has Slovak giving *lekvar* to Hungarian and thereby to English. Before Slovak, it was Czech; before Czech, it was German; before German, it was French; and before French, it was Latin.

Pirohi (or *pirogi*, or *piroghi*, or similar spellings) is from Russian or Polish, languages related to Slovak in the Slavic branch of our Indo-European language family. But *lekvar* seems to be the only Slovak word that has immigrated to English.

About five million people in Slovakia speak Slovak, and nearly half a million more in the United States. Closest to Slovak is Czech, the language of the other half of the former Czechoslovakia that split into two countries in 1993. Anyone who speaks Czech can understand Slovak, and vice versa.

∾CZECH REPUBLIC

robot *from Czech*

The Frankenstein monster of nineteenth-century science, brought to life in Mary Shelley's novel of that name, was an English creation in a Swiss setting. The monster of twentieth-century science, the *robot*, was a Czech creation in an English setting.

Like Frankenstein's humanoid, the *robot* was created not in a scientist's laboratory but in the literary imagination. It was the work of Czech brothers Josef and Karel Čapek. Josef invented the *robot* for a short story of 1917; Karel made the word famous in his world-famous 1921 play *R.U.R.* Although the play was in Czech, the word *robot* was used in English in the name of the company that manufactures robots and that gives the play its title, *Rossums Universal Robots*. Čapek chose English, the most international of languages, to emphasize the worldwide effects of modern science and technology.

Robot comes from the Czech (and Russian) word for forced labor. But Čapek's robots, who did all the work in his imagined world, weren't forced labor. They were imitation humans, designed to want to work while humans sat back and enjoyed life. Lacking the fulfillment of work, the humans in the play become sterile and then victims of a worldwide robot rebellion. Ironically, the victorious robots take on human characteristics. They learn to love and procreate, and life goes on.

In 1923, with the play translated into English, robots were the talk of the English-speaking world. These first robots, creatures of the literary imagination, were fearsome because they were nearly human. In *R.U.R*, a visitor to the factory can't tell robots from humans.

By the end of the century, there were real robots, but they seemed less of a threat to humanity. Our more confident view of robots may have been shaped in part by a science fiction writer, Isaac Asimov, who in his 1942 story "Runaround" proposed three laws for robots:

> 1. A robot may not harm a human, or allow a human to come to harm through inaction.
> 2. A robot must obey a human's orders unless they conflict with the first law.
> 3. A robot must protect itself unless this conflicts with the first or second law.

And as science caught up with science fiction, and industry created industrial robots, they indeed turned out to be more benign.

The Czech language from which *robot* came is spoken by most of the ten million inhabitants of the recently created Czech republic. It belongs to the Slavic branch of our Indo-European family, closely related to Polish and Slovak. Just a few other words have been borrowed from Czech into English, including *haček* (1953), the *v*-shaped mark over the *C* in Čapek that indicates the *ch* pronunciation; *kolache* (1918), a square, sweet, fruit-filled pastry (1919); and *pistol* (1570), which shot through German and French before hitting English. Newly notorious in English is the explosive *Semtex* (1985), named after the Czech village of Semtin where it is made.

∼POLAND

horde *from Polish*

In 1241, a fearsome army invaded Poland. They were the Mongols or Tatars, fresh from incorporating Russia into the largest empire the world has ever seen and efficiently moving westward to make it larger. Their main objective was Hungary, but to divide and mislead the European forces they sent a diversionary army of 20,000 north to

Poland. There the efficient and disciplined Tatars defeated Polish and German armies and captured the cities of Sandomir and Krakow. A final victory for the Tatars, over the army of Duke Henry II of Silesia, came on April 9, 1241, near the city of Legnica. Duke Henry himself was killed, but the Tatars were finished with Poland, and their army turned south to Hungary to battle there. To this day, April 9 is celebrated in Poland not as a defeat but as a day when the Tatars were stopped.

In Hungary, the Mongols accomplished great military victories too. Just as they were about to push further west, however, they got word of the death of their Great Khan, Ogadei, the son of founder Genghis Khan. It was necessary for all the leaders to return to Mongolia to choose a successor. They left central Europe and, as it happened, never came back.

The Tatars had brought a terror to Europe that would be remembered for many hundreds of years. They also brought a name for an awesome military force that would be remembered in the languages of Europe: the horde.

This word had its beginning in the Turkic *orda* or *ordu* meaning "residence of the Khan." The Ukrainians, subjugated by Mongol armies, learned the word as *orda*. One dialect of Ukrainian added a *g* at the front of the word, and Polish changed the *g* to *h*. Polish, then, is the source of the word as we know it today. It was from this Polish version, via medieval French and German, that *horde* came into English, as long ago as 1555.

By then, the Tatars were history. The Mongol empire had divided into competing factions before the thirteenth century was over, and in 1502 its last stronghold in Russia ceased to exist. But hordes live on in our language. We speak of hordes of shoppers at a sale, hordes of autograph seekers surrounding a celebrity, or on a summer evening in the north woods, hordes of mosquitos.

Polish belongs to the Slavic branch of the Indo-European language family. It is closely related to Russian and Czech, among others. There are nearly forty million speakers of Polish in Poland and another two million in the United States.

Among the other Polish gifts to English are the foods *baba* (a cake, 1827), *bigos* (a stew), and *kielbasa* (sausage, 1939); *rendzina*, a kind of soil (1922); *uhlan*, a kind of cavalry modeled on the Tatars (1753); and a dance, the *mazurka* (1818). Two famous dances have English names that mean "Polish" but come from other languages: *polka* is Czech and *polonaise* is French.

∼LITHUANIA

kugeli *from Lithuanian*

Lithuanian has a special appeal for historians of language because it seems to be the most old-fashioned of the present-day Indo-European languages. That is, words and their inflections in Lithuanian seem less changed from ancient Proto-Indo-European than in any other. Even an ordinary desk dictionary may therefore have hundreds of references to Lithuanian in its etymologies: *absorb* akin to Lithuanian *surbti* "to sip," for example, or *zone* akin to Lithuanian *juosti* "to gird." But "akin" means only that it is a relative, not an ancestor; English got *absorb* from French, which got it from Latin; English got *zone* from Latin, which got it from Greek. In both cases, Lithuanian was just a cousin.

We have to look hard for a word that was imported into English from Lithuanian. But there is one savory example: a creamy potato pudding known as *kugeli*. It made its English debut relatively recently, attested in a 1965 cookbook.

The main ingredient of kugeli is russet potatoes, peeled and grated very fine. To five pounds of potatoes you add one onion, likewise grated very fine; half a pound of cooked bacon, diced very fine; a can of evaporated milk, heated; five beaten eggs, salt, pepper, and a cup of bread crumbs. You bake the mixture in a large greased and floured casserole dish at 375 degrees for about seventy-five minutes, then serve hot with sour cream.

Lithuanian belongs to the Baltic branch of Indo-European. It is the national language of Lithuania, spoken by about three million people there and by another million elsewhere in the world, including 300,000 in the United States.

~FINLAND

sauna *from Finnish*

When Finnish immigrants settled on homesteads in the United States during the nineteenth century, the first structure they built was not a house but a sauna. For many centuries that had been the custom in Finland, too, because the sauna was a place to get warm, relaxed, and clean. Even in the midst of an arctic winter, you could take off your clothes and open your pores in a sauna. It was a haven even for cooking, childbirth, and care of the sick.

The old-fashioned sauna was something of a rugged place compared with the electric-heated saunas of today. Until this century, a sauna would be dug into a hill or built of logs, with a stone stove whose smoke was made to circulate throughout the room before finally escaping through a ceiling vent or the open door. The fire would be doused and water poured on the hot rocks to raise the humidity. Soot was everywhere, sweet-smelling and supposedly hygienic. Sweat and the *vihta* or *vasta*, a birch whisk, did the cleansing, along with jumping in the lake or rolling in the snow after sitting in temperatures approaching two hundred degrees Fahrenheit. Soap was not introduced until the nineteenth century.

As the Finns still take pains to explain, a sauna should be a sacred and relaxing place, not an exciting one. No sex, please. (Men and women generally go to separate saunas.)

No television or newspapers. Don't even raise your voice. In a sauna, according a Finnish saying, you must behave as in church.

Nowadays there are slightly over five million Finns in Finland, and slightly over one and a half million saunas. In the United States there are many thousands of saunas, and even sauna clubs. More than 25,000 residential saunas were sold in 1985. And if you can't get to a sauna, you can enjoy a virtual Finnish sauna on the Internet, complete with lessons in sauna etiquette.

The Finnish language is different from the Scandinavian and Slavic languages of its neighbors. It does not belong to the Indo-European language family but to the Uralic, and is related only to Hungarian among the European languages. Aside from *sauna*, very few Finnish words have become part of English. One is *kantele* (1903), a kind of zither; another is a genus of tropical plants, *tillandsia* (1759), named after the Finnish botanist Elias Tillands.

∿RUSSIA

tundra *from Sami*

Trees don't grow on the tundra of the arctic regions. But then, what tree would want to? The earth is frozen solid except in the brief summertime, when it thaws only a foot or two down from the surface. The surface, of course, is wet, since water can't sink into the soil. So when it's not frozen, it's swampy. That short summer season is a busy breeding time for billions of insects, who in turn attract millions of birds. The vegetation sustains caribou and reindeer, voles and lemmings, and those in turn sustain wolves, foxes, and birds of prey.

No wonder Stalin, starting in the 1930s, chose the tundra of Russia and Siberia as a suitably inhospitable environment to house "enemies of the people" in his prison camps, the gulags. And yet there are people who like life in the cool, wide-open tundra: the Sami, who have lived there since prehistoric times. (They are better known as Lapps, but they don't like that designation.)

The Sami were the first to inhabit the tundra of what is present-day northern Norway, Sweden, Finland, and Russia. When southerners first heard of them, thousands of years ago, the Sami made their living by hunting reindeer. About five hundred years ago they began herding reindeer instead of hunting them. Despite the growing political and social pressures of European civilization, about 10 percent of the 80,000 ethnic Sami still herd reindeer today, using snowmobiles and modern telecommunications.

We know that *tundra* is from one of the languages spoken by the Sami. Which of the Sami languages is not certain, but since *tundra* came to us through Russian, it would likely be from Kildin Sami, Skolt Sami, or Ter Sami, the three Sami languages of Russia's Kola Peninsula on the Barents Sea next to Finland. Sami belongs to the Finno-Ugric branch of the Uralic language family.

The Sami languages are most widely heard in Norway, where there are about 17,000 speakers, and in Sweden, where there are nearly 10,000. Finland has about 4,000 and Russia just 2,000. Aside from *tundra*, no other Sami word is of general circulation in English.

∼RUSSIA

czar *from Russian*

Many countries have had kings and emperors, monarchs and tyrants, dictators and autocrats. But only Russia has had a real czar.

The character of a czar was established by the first Russian ruler to bear that title, Ivan IV. When he was seventeen, in 1547, he was crowned czar of all Russia. By the time of his death thirty-seven years later, he had earned the nickname Ivan the Terrible. He governed absolutely, and he ruthlessly eliminated anyone who stood in his way, including not only the nobility but also his son and heir, Ivan, whom he killed in a rage. He had seven wives, not at once but in succession. When he tired of one, she would be murdered or sent off to a nunnery. But he was also intelligent, learned, and a talented writer. It was during his reign that printing was introduced to Russia.

Thus Ivan, and his successors, gave a twist to a 1600-year-old name for a ruler. It had begun in ancient Rome with the family name of Julius Caesar. Julius's adopted son Octavius, later Augustus Caesar, became the first Roman emperor. After him, Roman emperors took Caesar as a title. The word made its way into Russian as *tsar*. Our spelling *czar* comes from a Latin commentary on Ivan's coronation published in 1549; *czar* appears in English writing as early as 1555. In the wake of *czar* came *ukase*, the Russian word for an imperial decree and thus for any authoritarian edict. We began using it in English as early as 1729.

In present-day English, *tsar* is the usual spelling for Ivan and his successors who ruled Russia. We tend to use *czar* more figuratively, for someone who exerts great authority, especially someone appointed to deal with a particular activity. There can be a drug czar to prevent drug use and a gang czar to stop gangs. A government can have an economic czar or a county health czar. There have been Olympics czars and a baseball czar, a company marketing czar and an auto parts czar, as well as Internet czars in companies and the White House.

Russian is spoken by over 150 million people in Russia and the other countries of the former Soviet Union. It is in the Slavic branch of the Indo-European family. From Russian more than a hundred words have immigrated to English, including *mammoth* (1706), *balalaika* (1788), and *samovar* (1830). The *Potemkin village* (1937) is a Russian invention, named after Catherine the Great's minister

Grigori Potemkin, who arranged for fake villages to be constructed for Catherine to visit as she toured the country. In the twentieth century Russian has given us political words ranging from *pogrom* (1903) and *intelligentsia* (1907) to *gulag* (1974) and *glasnost* (1986). As the first in space, Russian speakers taught us *sputnik* (1957), *cosmonaut* (1959), and most recently *Mir*, the name of a sometimes malfunctioning space station but also the Russian word for peace.

〜UKRAINE

Cossack *from Ukrainian*

Across the open, fertile plains of Ukraine six hundred years ago came the raiding Tatars, descendants of the Golden Horde of the Mongols. They were disrespectful in the extreme to the local populations. With Tatars constantly interfering, Ukrainians found it hard to get a life, let alone make a living. So they invented self-defense forces, the Cossacks, fierce enough to stop the Tatar hordes. They took their name from the South Turkic word *qazaq* meaning "adventurer" or "free person."

The Cossacks got their strength from local autonomy and leadership. They were not troops belonging to some distant government but members of democratic self-governing communities, each community electing its leader, known as an ataman, and the whole assembly of Cossacks electing a leader known as the hetman. Cossack communities welcomed diverse members, including Poles, Russians, and runaway serfs.

In later centuries, having defeated the Tatars, Cossacks fought the encroaching Polish and Russian governments. But by the end of the eighteenth century the Russians had overcome Cossack resistance and converted them into an elite military class within the Russian army. Cossack communities managed to survive Russian imperialism and communism, and Cossack forces have continued to be an elite within the Russian army.

Ukrainian, an Eastern Slavic and Indo-European language, is closely related to Russian. The two languages and their respective countries share much history and vocabulary. They are close enough that it is often difficult to tell whether an English word of Slavic origin comes from Russian, Ukrainian, or another related language. *Cossack*, for example, which has been in English since 1589, comes to us also from Polish and Russian, though the original Cossacks were in Ukraine. From Ukrainian we also have *dumka* (music that alternates between sad and happy, 1895) and *gley* (a kind of clay soil, 1927) as well as *hetman* (1710). In the independent republic of Ukraine, Ukrainian is spoken by more than forty million people.

∿UKRAINE

shashlik *from Crimean Turkish*

The Crimea is a peninsula extending from the south shore of Ukraine into the Black Sea. In English it was made famous by a war with Russia in the 1850s that stimulated Alfred Tennyson to write "The Charge of the Light Brigade" and stimulated Florence Nightingale to revolutionize the treatment of wounded soldiers. But though the Crimea remained in Russian hands after that war, it had been Turkish for the three preceding centuries, and much of the population had spoken a version of Turkish known as Crimean Turkish.

It would take too long to tell of the Russian and then Soviet dispersal of this population, especially to Uzbekistan, and the return of large numbers of them after the collapse of the Soviet Union. But in their tribulations and travels, speakers of Crimean Turkish seem to have taken time to present the Turks, the Russians, and the rest of the world with a particular kind of food and their name for it: *shashlik*. It reached English relatively recently, attested in the 1925 book *Paris on Parade*, published in Indianapolis.

Lamb or sturgeon is especially recommended as the main ingredient of shashlik. You cut the meat or fish into cubes, marinate it overnight perhaps in oil, lemon juice, salt, pepper, bay leaf, dill, garlic, and celery, and then cook the cubes with vegetables on skewers over a fire.

This sounds like *shish kebab*, our term from Armenian and Turkish. And in fact, thanks to the mixing of populations and recipes, *shashlik* and *shish kebab* have become synonymous in English. One is often defined as the other. But in Russian it is just *shashlik*, and in Russian contexts we can find *shashlik* evoking a Crimean scene, as in Bruce McClelland's translation of Osip Mandelstam's poem about Theodosia, a Crimean resort where he lived in 1919:

> The person tends to be old,
> But the lamb, young,
> And under the sinewy moon,
> With rosy wine vapor
> The smoke of shashlik begins to drift.

Today Crimean Turkish is spoken by perhaps 200,000 people in the Crimea and elsewhere in Ukraine, and by nearly 200,000 in Uzbekistan, as well as a few in Turkey. It is distinct enough from the national language of Turkey to be considered a separate language, but the two are closely related members of the Altaic language family. Nothing else of Crimean Turkish is part of the general English vocabulary.

AFRICA

*L*eaving Europe, we leave behind the languages English grew up with, the close neighbors like Old Norse and French that had such a profound effect on our vocabulary. The rest of the world has provided a bountiful share of immigrant words for English, but these are not as plentiful or as commonplace as some of the European arrivals. No longer will we find so many adopted words that seem home-grown like *rip* and *pamper*, slang like *moniker, lingo,* and *pal,* fundamentals of thought like *reason* and *philosophy*. But in other parts of the world there is the appeal of the exotic as well as the surprisingly familiar.

We cross the Mediterranean to Africa, whose gifts to the English language are relatively new. Aside from Egypt and the Mediterranean coast, Africa was unknown territory for English speakers until well into the so-called Age of Discovery. Appropriately enough, one of the first words we will encounter south of the Sahara is a name for remoteness: *Timbuktu*. Nevertheless, Africa, the cradle of civilization, has affected our language from cradle to grave. It has given us plants and animals, customs, costumes, musical instruments, diseases and medicine.

The first substantial African imports to English came from western Africa. In the seventeenth and eighteenth centuries, the dismal business of the slave trade brought Africans, their cultures, and some of their agriculture to the English-speaking West Indies and North America. As a result, English knows the religious and magical practices involving *voodoo, obeah, juju, mojo,* and *zombie;* we drink *cola* and cultivate *okra* to make *gumbo;* we are acquainted with hard-shelled *cooters* and biting *chiggers*. In more recent times, West Africans have taught us to breed the barkless *basenji,* wear the colorful *dashiki,* and dance the *tango* (with assistance in the last from Argentina).

Southern and eastern Africa were even later in contributing to English, but since South Africa, Zimbabwe, Tanzania, Uganda, and northern Somalia were all under British rule for at least a while during the nineteenth and twentieth centuries, it is not surprising that the languages of these countries also have left their mark on our language. We have gained the names of animals from the *gnu* to the *suni* and the *tsetse fly*, musical instruments including the *mbila* and the *mbira*, customs like the *indaba* of South Africa and the African-inspired *Kwanzaa* of recent North American invention.

From Africa we have also learned about deadly diseases: *kwashiorkor*, the disease of starvation, from western Africa, and *chikungunya* and *o'nyong-nyong*, both mosquito-borne viruses, in eastern Africa. And there is both poison and medicine in the *ouabain* of Somalia. Returning to North Africa, we find an ancient *oasis* and a more modern *adobe* in the deserts of Egypt.

Like Europe, Africa is dominated by one language family. But it is a different one, not Indo-European but the Niger-Congo family that stretches from Gambia in the west to Tanzania in the east and everywhere south. Of the thirty-eight languages we will visit in Africa, twenty-nine are Niger-Congo languages. In the northern parts of Africa are seven members of the Afro-Asiatic family, which includes languages of Algeria, Egypt, Ethiopia, and Somalia. We will encounter more Afro-Asiatic languages in our Asian tour, notably Hebrew and Arabic. There is also one transplanted Indo-European language, Afrikaans, and one Austronesian language, Malagasy of Madagascar.

There is no doubt that a number of English words have their origins in West African languages, but in many cases it is hard to tell which one. This part of Africa has dozens of widely spoken languages and hundreds more that are of local importance, and often several neighboring languages share the same word. Thus it is often the case that any of several languages could be the source of an English word. Among such words are *cola*, *voodoo*, *obeah*, *tango*, and *mojo*.

ᔛ**ALGERIA**

Zouave *from Kabyle*

It rhymes with "suave," and that's what the American Zouaves of the nineteenth century thought they were, suave beyond compare. They were soldiers named, drilled,

and dressed after the Zouaves of the French Army, fierce and colorful fighters who served in Algeria and Morocco. In peacetime, the American Zouaves were a brilliant spectacle in their North African-inspired attire. According to one account, the Zouave uniform consisted of "A short, collarless jacket; a sleeveless vest (gilet); voluminous trousers (serouel); 12-foot long woolen sash (ceinture); white canvas leggings (guetres); leather greaves (jambieres); and of course the tasseled fez (chechia) and turban (cheche)." No camouflage for these warriors!

At first, the American version of the Zouaves seemed just for show, suited to shine at a Fourth of July parade. But when the Civil War came, the Zouaves' exploits for the Union were as brave as their uniforms. They were said to act "as though warfare were merely a game and their lives simply the table stakes." General George B. McClellan, using an appropriately French phrase, called the Zouave the "beau-ideal" of a soldier.

The original Zouaves were so called because they came from the Zouaoua tribe in the hills of Algeria. In 1830 some of the Zouaoua volunteered for the French colonial army, enough to form two battalions of auxiliaries. They kept their distinctive uniforms and their reputation for heroism even as the Zouave units became more and more composed of Frenchmen. In 1852, Emperor Louis Napoleon made the Zouaves entirely French by relocating them in Paris. Until World War I they were the elite French troops.

The Zouaoua speak Kabyle, a Berber language of the Afro-Asiatic language family. There are two million speakers of Kabyle in Algeria today and another half million in France. One other Berber word known in English is *aoudad* (1861), a wild sheep originally found in North Africa. Nowadays you can get a hunting license for auodad in Texas.

ᘛMALI

Timbuktu *from Timbuktu Tamasheq*

Unlike Shangri-La, Xanadu, and Atlantis, the fabled city of Timbuktu really exists. It remains remote from the rest of the world, but its former fame is remote now too. There is not much to attract a present-day traveler to the sleepy town of barely 20,000 located way up the Niger River, at the edge of the Sahara Desert, in the West African republic of Mali. Hundreds of years ago, however, that oasis was an important crossroads for caravans from the desert and merchants from all over West Africa. Timbuktu was known for its wealth and for its learning; it was the starting point for Muslims in western Africa making the pilgrimage to Mecca, and it was a mecca of Muslim scholarship.

The fame of Timbuktu first spread far and wide when it became part of the Mali Empire in the fourteenth century. Sultan Mansa Musa, the Mali ruler, attracted the outside world's notice in 1324 with his opulent pilgrimage from Timbuktu to Mecca and back. He had tens of thousands of attendants and fifteen thousand camels carrying food, salt, perfume, and gold. After that, the wealth of Timbuktu seemed truly fabulous.

In Europe and the Middle East, the city's remoteness enhanced its charm. In the English language, as the city's prosperity became only a distant memory, the name Timbuktu came to stand for any remote place, a usage we find as long ago as 1863.

We owe the name to the Tuareg people who founded the town in about 1100. They spoke a language known as Timbuktu Tamasheq, still used by about a quarter of a million people in Mali. It is from the Berber branch of the Afro-Asiatic language family. No other words from Timbuktu Tamasheq are found in English; it's too remote.

∾Gambia and Mali

jumbo *from Mandingo*

One of the biggest words in the English language is an import from Africa. Before it attained its current meaning, it was imported in the phrase *mumbo jumbo*, introduced to English by one Francis Moore in a 1738 account of his African travels: "At Night, I was visited by a Mumbo Jumbo, an Idol, which is among the Mundingoes a kind of cunning Mystery. . . . This is a Thing invented by the Men to keep their Wives in awe." And in 1799, another Englishman, Mungo Park, in his *Travels in the Interior Districts of Africa Performed Under The Direction and Patronage of the African Association*, wrote about "A sort of masquerade habit . . . which I was told . . . belonged to Mumbo Jumbo. This is a strange bugbear . . . much employed by the Pagan natives in keeping their women in subjection."

Later travelers to West Africa have been unable to find any trace of this supposed custom. Meanwhile, however, *jumbo* was beginning to make itself hugely useful in the English language. By the early nineteenth century, *jumbo* was noted in a slang dictionary as referring to "a clumsy or unwieldy fellow." But it had a jumbo increase in popularity and meaning when P.T. Barnum bought Jumbo, an enormous elephant, from the London zoo in 1882 and exhibited this elephant as the star of his circus. Soon other animals and things were also called *jumbo*. In 1883 the generators in Thomas Edison's first electric power station were so large they were called "Jumbo." At the other end of the scale, there were "jumbo" crickets that year too. We have since seen such jumbos as peaches (1897), peanuts (1916), malted milk (1940), martinis (1958), burgers (1959), and jets (1964). If a soft drink isn't jumbo nowadays, it's hardly worth buying.

Mandingo is actually a group of closely related languages in West Africa belonging to the Mande branch of the Niger-Congo language family. The seventeen Mandingo languages are spoken by more than two million people in Mali, Gambia, Senegal, Guinea, Burkina Faso, and adjoining countries. Mandingo includes the Malinke and Bambara languages, which we will visit individually, but Moore's account does not allow us to be more specific for *jumbo*. The Mandingo group has not had a jumbo influence on the English language, but we can thank it for half a dozen additional words, including a couple of good things to eat: *banana* (1597) and possibly *yam* (1657).

⌁MALI

cooter *from Malinke*

"If you've got facilities to house a big aquatic turtle, cooters can't be beat," writes Mary on the Internet Turtle & Tortoise Forum. "They're pretty and friendly and can become quite the puppy dog characters, following people around the pond area."

If you don't know a cooter from a turtle, that's because a cooter is a turtle. But it's a turtle of a particular kind, or rather of several particular kinds. Mary was writing about "*Pseudemys floridana floridana*—one big turtle. Florida cooter females can reach 16 inches." In the *Pseudemys* genus of redbelly turtles and cooters, there are also, among others *P. suwanniensis*, the Suwannee River Cooter; *P. concinna metteri*, the Missouri River

Cooter; *P. texana*, the Texas River Cooter; *P. gorzugi*, the Western River Cooter; *P. concinna*, the Eastern River Cooter; and *P. concinna hieroglyphica*, the Hieroglyphic River Cooter. (There is no Hieroglyphic River; the turtle is called Hieroglyphic because of the markings on its shell.)

In the United States, cooters and their names are found mostly in the southern and eastern states. Cooters seem especially well known in South Carolina, and it is from that state in 1832 that we have the earliest evidence of *cooter* used in English. In recent times, *cooter* has also been used as the name of a dance, the Cooter Stomp, a country solo that begins "touch, hold, touch, hold, touch, touch, stomp, stomp" at the Club Danse Québec. And *cooter* has a vulgar slang use as a name for a central part of the female anatomy. That may relate to the obsolete verb *coot*, dating back to 1667 and referring to the long slow mating practice of turtles.

It is very likely that *cooter* is from an African language, brought over by slaves. And it could well have come from more than one language at the same time, since several languages have similar words for turtle. Among the likely candidates are Malinke and Bambara. Both are Mandingo languages of the Mande branch of the Niger-Congo language family, and in both, *kuta* means turtle. Since the next word is Bambara, we will let this one be Malinke, which is spoken by three-quarters of a million of the ten million people of Mali, and by an additional quarter of a million in Senegal. Another English word definitely from Malinke is *boubou* (1961), a large flowing dress worn by both women and men.

∽MALI

juke *from Bambara*

Before there was a jukebox, there was a juke. And before there was a juke, there was a wicked word in the Bambara language of present-day Mali in West Africa: something like *dzugu,* meaning "wicked." There is also a *dzug,* meaning "live wickedly," in the neighboring Wolof language, so that too may have contributed to the English *juke.* Whatever the exact origin, it was brought across the Atlantic centuries ago by slaves.

In the American South, in due course, it became the name of a place where the descendants of slaves could have wicked fun. Novelist and anthropologist Zora Neale Hurston explained it in *Jonah's Gourd Vine* in 1934: "*Jook,* the pleasure houses near industrial work. A combination of bawdy, gaming, and dance hall. Incidentally the cradle of the 'blues.'" Jukes were generally located in the countryside rather than the city, sometimes near the camps of turpentine workers.

In the late 1930s, coin-operated phonographs in jukes were jokingly called *juke organs* and then *juke boxes.* And while jukes seem extinct, juke boxes remain fixtures in bars and other places of entertainment.

Bambara is a Mandingo language of the Mande branch of the Niger-Congo language family. It is the national language of Mali, where it is spoken by nearly three million people. Another English word from Bambara is *shea* (1799), the name of a tree with oily seeds used to make *shea butter.*

∿SENEGAL

chigger *from Wolof*

There are chiggers and then there are chiggers. One kind causes itching and the other causes pain, but they both get under your skin.

The English language applies the name *chigger* to two quite distinct species of insect that share the common quality of being very small and burrowing into the skin. Widespread throughout the United States is a tiny red mite, *Trombicula irritans,* that sits on plants waiting for humans or other animals to show it some skin. It's only about one-fiftieth of an inch across, and it takes four to eight hours for its feeding to create an itch, so by the time you notice it the mite may be already gone. There's nothing to do but wash the bite and try to avoid scratching it.

A more painful kind of chigger is a flea, *Tunga penetrans*, which is at home in the tropics. In the United States, it is found mainly in the Southeast. The female looks for bare human feet and hops on between the toes or under the toenails. She cuts open the skin, burrows most of the way in, feeds, and lays eggs. Three or four days later the eggs hatch and new fleas are born. These chiggers go through a complete life cycle in about seventeen days, so a minor nuisance can soon become a major invasion. The engorged chigger makes her habitat very painful for its owner, and her activity can lead to secondary infections like tetanus and gangrene. But she can be killed with ethyl chloride spray.

The name *chigger*, which has been used in English since 1756 (deriving from *chigoe*, 1691), has two possible languages of origin, both spoken in tropical areas where the chigger of the second kind thrives. One possible source is Kalihna or Galibi, a Cariban language of Guyana and Suriname in South America. The other source, at least equally likely, is Wolof, a language of the Niger-Congo family spoken by more than two and a half million people in Senegal on the far western coast of Africa. Africans brought to America would have brought the name. Wolof has also given the names of two monkeys to English, *potto* (1705) and *galago* (1848), and is a possible language of origin for *banana* (1597).

◆SIERRA LEONE

cola *from Temne*

The most intensely marketed beverage in the world comes not from Atlanta but from Africa. Or at least its family name does.

It's a real nut. The cola nut, that is, the white, pink, or purple seed of a tree found in the rain forests of western Africa. The tree grows twenty-five to fifty feet tall and produces crops of fleshy "nuts" once or twice a year for fifty years or more. You harvest the nuts before they are ripe, splitting the seed pod and removing the nuts, three to six in each pod. Toss the nuts in a pile and allow them to ferment for five days before storing them. You can enjoy the nuts without further treatment just by chewing them, or you can send them off to be made into a patented drink.

In Africa, and originally when imported to America, cola was known for its medicinal properties. Its caffeine, kolanin, and theobromin make it a treatment for headaches, motion sickness, diarrhea, mental fatigue, and depression. In the nineteenth century (we've had the word since 1795) it was also said to cure pneumonia and typhoid fever. Cola nuts have more caffeine than coffee beans, but most cola drinks have less than coffee.

The name *cola* is widespread in the languages of West Africa. It might be from the Malinke language of Senegal and Gambia, but it could just as well be from the language we designate here, Temne, a Niger-Congo language of the Atlantic-Congo and Temne-Banta branches. Temne is spoken by more than a million people, about 30 percent of the population of Sierra Leone. No other words from Temne seem to have made their way into English.

∿SIERRA LEONE AND LIBERIA

benne *from Mende*

In most of the English-speaking world, sesame is *sesame*. (In the seventeenth century we got that word from Latin, which got it from Greek, which got it from one of the ancient Semitic languages of the Middle East.) But in South Carolina, influenced by the Mende language of Africa, sesame is also known as *benne*. Interviewed for the *Dictionary of American*

Regional English in the 1960s, residents of South Carolina spoke of several kinds of candy made with benne seed, including benne brittle and benne wafers.

Benne was brought into English by slaves from Africa who were speakers of Mende, a Niger-Congo language now spoken by one and a half million people in Sierra Leone and Liberia. We find the word in a 1769 letter from Georgia, just south of South Carolina, to the American Philosophical Society: "I send you a small keg of Bene or bene Seed, which you will please to present to your Society for their inspection." One other Mende word more recently arrived in English is *nomoli* (1910), the name for small soapstone carvings of men and animals found in caves and fields in Sierra Leone. No one knows who made these figures or for what purpose.

The Mende language had a starring role in the 1997 movie *Amistad,* a largely true story about the trials in America of slaves from Sierra Leone who captured the ship in which they were being transported. The historical version is slightly different from the movie. To learn the Africans' language, Professor Josiah Gibbs of Yale College visited them in jail and held up his fingers, counting aloud. When he said "one," one of the Africans responded with "hita" in the Bandi dialect of Mende. Gibbs learned the Mende numbers and walked the docks of New Haven, Connecticut, counting aloud: *hita, fele, sawa, nani, dolu, woita, ngofera, ngohakpa, tau, pu.* (In the main dialect of Mende the numbers are *yilá, felé, sawá, nááni, lóólu, wóíta, wófela, wáyákpá, táálú, pu.*) By this means he found translators who knew Mende and English.

kwashiorkor *from Ga*

In the United States, our chief nutritional problem is eating too much. Not all of the rest of the world is so fortunate. Other places have to contend with too little food, if not outright starvation, and it can make you sick. One such sickness, a protein deficiency that especially affects children, is called *kwashiorkor*.

Lacking sufficient protein, the sufferer from kwashiorkor becomes both lethargic and irritable before proceeding to more severe symptoms, including loss of hair, thinning of muscles, loss of color in the skin, and a protruding abdomen, a picture of children all too familiar in times of famine. If kwashiorkor persists, it prevents a child's physical and mental development and leads to early death. Kwashiorkor often affects an older child weaned from breast milk to an inadequate diet after another child is born.

To prevent kwashiorkor, it's not enough to have adequate amounts of protein; you must get all twenty of the amino acids that make up human proteins. You can get them all from meat or dairy products, but plants provide only some of them. If meats aren't available, or if you're a strict vegetarian, your body requires several varieties of vegetable protein. Through trial and error, different cultures the world over have learned the appropriate combinations. American Indians, for example, learned that corn and black or pinto beans will do, but not corn alone or beans alone, no matter how much you eat. Asians found that a diet of rice needed to be supplemented with soybeans or lentils. Europeans discovered that with wheat or barley you need peas or lentils. So the cure, or better yet the prevention, for kwashiorkor is adequate nutrition.

Kwashiorkor was well known in Ghana as a disease affecting weaned older children (the word means "deposed child") when it was first described in English, using its Ga name, in a medical journal in 1935. More than a million people in Ghana speak Ga, a language of the Volta-Congo branch of the Niger-Congo language family. Our language has no other words from Ga.

∾GHANA

harmattan *from Twi*

It is an ill wind that blows nobody good, and around the world it has many names. There is the world-famous *monsoon* of Asia, a word ultimately derived from the Portuguese. On the pampas or plains of Argentina, there is the cold westerly *pampero*. The United States has, among others, the *Chinook* of the Pacific Northwest, the *Santa Ana* of southern California, and the *blue norther* of Texas. In the Alps the *foehn* (a German word) blows warm. Southern France has its cold northerly *mistral*, derived from the French word for mastery. In Italy the *bora* brings cold air from the north and the *libeccio* (both Italian words) brings warm air from the southwest, while the *sirocco* (from Arabic) brings hot air from the southeast. The *levanter* is an easterly wind of the Mediterranean, from French *lever*, to rise, referring to the rising sun in the east.

Africa has its winds too. The deserts of North Africa have such troublesome winds that they have given three Arabic words for them to English: *simoom* or *simoon, ghibli,* and the Egyptian wind called *khamsin*. Further to the south and west, in Ghana where Twi is spoken, is the dusty wind from the north and east called *harmattan*. As early as 1671 English adventurers spoke of it, one of the few words of Twi that have entered the English vocabulary.

Does English need so many words for winds? Evidently so, because winds are closely associated with the places where they blow and the type of pleasure or pain they bring. The *harmattan* of West Africa is a dry wind that blows from the land to the sea during the winter months. In 1845 the naturalist Charles Darwin saw the harmattan "raise clouds of dust high into the atmosphere."

Twi, a member of the Niger-Congo language family, is spoken by about one and a third million people in southern Nigeria. Twi and Fante make up a language group known as Akan used by seven million people, nearly half the population of Ghana. Aside from *harmattan*, one other English word that may have come from Twi is *akee* or *ackee* (1794), the name for a tropical tree whose seed cover is poisonous until mature but is eaten as a delicacy when ripe, at least in Jamaica where it has been transplanted.

GHANA

voodoo *from Ewe*

If you bring together the religious practices of dozens of West African cultures, mix vigorously, and season with Catholic Christianity, you will have something like voodoo. That is what happened in Haiti as slaves from Africa were brought to the island to work plantations there, starting in the 1500s. They were baptized as Catholics, but instead of praying to the saints they worshiped their familiar tribal gods, called loa. Their rituals, led by voodoo priests or priestesses, involved offerings to the loa and sometimes possession of the worshipers by the loa. Since the loa were very powerful, some followers of voodoo used rituals to enlist their aid in black magic.

Again and again the Haitian authorities, first Spanish and after 1697 French, tried to suppress all African religions, rightly seeing the potential for defiance and rebellion, but such efforts only strengthened the determination of the slaves to continue their practices in secret. In 1791 it was voodoo priests who instigated and guided the rebellion that eventually led to Haiti's independence in 1804.

Despite opposition from the Catholic Church, voodoo has continued to thrive in Haiti and places to which Haitians have gone, including Louisiana. It is there that we have early attestations in English. A Carolina newspaper reported in 1820 that in New Orleans a house was being "used as a kind of temple for certain occult practices and the idolatrous worship of an African deity, called Vandoo."

The form we know in English today, *voodoo*, appeared in the writing of New Orleans author George Washington Cable in 1880.

Voodoo mixes many African cultures. According to one source, it incorporates elements from "Fon, the Nago, the Ibos, Dahomeans, Congos, Senegalese, Haussars, Caplaous, Mondungues, Mandinge, Angolese, Libyans, Ethiopians, and the Malgaches." The name *voodoo* also has a number of possible sources, including Fon *vodun* and Ewe *vudu.* Since the Ewe form is closest to modern English, we will use it here.

Ewe is spoken by more than one and a half million people in Ghana, about 15 percent of the population, and it is an official literary language there. Nearly a million people in Togo also speak Ewe. It is a member of the Volta-Congo branch of the Niger-Congo language family.

One other contribution to English from Ewe is the obscure and obsolete name *John Canoe.* In pre–Civil War North Carolina, that name designated the leader of a group of slaves who went from house to house at Christmas time singing and asking for gifts. According to research by Frederic Cassidy, the name came from an Ewe word sounding like John Canoe and meaning "sorcerer-man."

⌒NIGERIA

obeah *from Efik*

It's magic: magic and folk medicine to get you through the aches and pains of life, from love to straying spouses to childbirth. It's big in the Caribbean, especially in Jamaica, where it was introduced by slaves hundreds of years ago. They used all the magical practices they knew from their African homelands to resist the powerful magic of the white people who had enslaved them. And they called it obeah.

Centuries before comic-book superheroes began catching bullets in their bare hands, obeah is said to have enabled rebellious slave heroes and heroines to perform that feat in Jamaica. In the 1730s Queen Nanny, an obeah woman, taught warriors to catch bullets in their left hand and fire them back. She showed her own disdain for the magic of European firearms with a greater magic, catching bullets safely between her buttocks.

By 1760 we have early evidence for *obeah* in English. That year the Jamaican assembly enacted a bill "to remedy the evils arising from irregular assemblies of slaves . . . and for preventing the practice of obeah." It was in vain; even after the introduction of Christianity to the slaves of Jamaica later in the eighteenth century, obeah maintained its presence, as it still does today, long after the abolition of slavery. The religious practice known as Revivalism incorporates both Christianity and obeah, and there are still obeah men and women in Jamaica and elsewhere in the Caribbean. The main character of Jamaica Kincaid's 1985 novel *Annie John*, for example, grows up in Antigua in a family that practices both Christian and obeah rituals.

There are obeah thinkers, too. "Obeah discloses the African insight into the cosmos as constituted in spiritual energy," declares writer Burton Sankeralli in the *Trinidad Express*. "Obeah represents an ontological challenge to the modern, secular, individualist, antihuman world view."

There is no question that both obeah and its name come from West Africa. A number of African languages have words that could be the source of *obeah*: Twi, Ibo, and Efik. As good a candidate as any is Efik, whose word *ubio* means "a bad omen" or "any harmful object."

Efik is a national language in Nigeria, though it is spoken by only 360,000 people as their first language and another two million as their second. It belongs to the Volta-Congo branch of the Niger-Congo language family and is closely related to Ibibio. The general vocabulary of English has no other words from Efik.

⌒NIGERIA

juju *from Hausa*

One of Nigeria's chief exports to the English-speaking world is oil. Another is juju. It's a little bit of voodoo and a lot of music.

Juju of the more sinister sort was mentioned in 1997 by Reuben Abati, member of the editorial board of the Guardian Newspapers of Lagos, Nigeria. He told of a Nigerian in the United States who "had built a strong network for credit card fraud. He repatriated funds regularly to Nigerian banks. After his arrest, his associates were afraid to testify against him. The fellow was said to have strong 'juju.' Even the presiding judge was advised to be careful lest the accused gave him an incurable ailment by 'remote control.' "

But the juju that is more prominent among Nigerian exports today is music. Modern juju music, as Andrew Frankel of Graviton African Music Productions explains, is "a lively mixture of traditional Yoruba social dance drumming, songs, and praise poetry, Latin American rhythms, and Christian church hymns, performed on guitar, percussion, and talking drums." Talking drums? Yes, because many African languages convey meaning not only with vowels and consonants but with different tones of voice, so you can have something of a conversation using drums of different tones. I. K. Dairo was the first of Nigeria's juju musicians to attract international attention. Another performer has been known as King Sunny Ade since he was crowned King of Juju Music in a grand ceremony in 1967.

Although the music is based in the Yoruba culture, the word *juju* apparently has its source in the Hausa language. Hausa is one of the principal languages of Nigeria, spoken by nearly twenty million people there, one-fifth of the population. It is also the language of an additional three million people in Niger. Hausa is a Chadic language in the Afro-Asiatic language family. *Juju* was noted in English as long ago as 1894 in a book about West Africa. One other word of Hausa which has recently immigrated to English is the name of a long, straight trombone, the *kakaki*.

∿NIGERIA

okra *from Ibo*

Although to Americans it seems native to the southeastern United States, *okra* is an import from Africa. Both the word

and the plant come from Ibo territory in Nigeria, at the inside corner of the continent where West Africa turns south. This okra plant grows five to ten feet tall or more. When we talk of cooking okra, we mean its narrow, pointed, gooey seed pods, best picked at two to four inches before they reach full maturity.

A basic Nigerian recipe goes like this: Chop okra into small pieces, cover with water in a pot, and cook for fifteen minutes. It makes a side dish to go with amala (boiled elubo flour) or obe ata (pepper soup).

But you can do far more with okra. Thanks to its thickness yet near-tastelessness, okra can show up in almost any recipe. Okra can be boiled, fried, stewed, pickled, or stir-fried with dried fruit in Syrian style. You can serve a dish from India called Okra Kaalun (Okra in Spicy Yogurt). There's a Texas recipe called Confetti involving okra with chopped onion, tomatoes, and fresh corn, sauteed and cooked in a skillet. In a pinch, dried okra seeds make a tolerable coffee substitute. The ultimate okra dish, though, is gumbo, which deserves an entry all to itself (and gets it a little later in our African tour).

Okra was brought to the Americas from Africa long ago, and ever since it has prompted a love-hate relationship. It is described in English in a 1707 account of

Jamaica. An 1834 traveler to the West Indies wrote, "The only native vegetable, which I like much, is the ochra, which tastes like asparagus."

Ibo is one of the principal national languages of Nigeria, spoken by seventeen million people, about one-sixth of the population. It is a Benue-Congo language of the Niger-Congo language family. Ibo has also given English the name of an enormous deep-water fish, the *opah* (1750), a.k.a. moonfish. You don't have to go to Africa for opah; the brightly colored fish, weighing one hundred pounds or more, can be caught in the waters of Hawaii too. And in 1995, a five-foot-long opah, with bright red fins and gold and silver scales, washed up in the Orkney Islands north of Scotland.

∿NIGERIA

dashiki *from Yoruba*

In Nigeria, it was worn for comfort in the hot climate. In America, it was worn to send a message.

That was the situation when the dashiki, and the Yoruba name for it, were imported into the English language in America in the late 1960s. The dashiki rebelled against men's fashions of the day: brightly colored instead of drab, loose instead of tight, worn outside the pants instead of tucked in. It could be worn defiantly on occasions that normally would call for a coat and tie.

The dashiki was introduced as a way to protest society's disrespect for African Americans. It was a symbol of affirmation, standing for "black is beautiful," a return to African roots, and insistence on full rights in American society. Marion Berry, later to become mayor of Washington, D.C., was then one of the rebels leading the "Free DC Movement" to gain voting rights for the mostly black residents of Washington. Sam Smith, editor of *The Progressive Review,* recalled that in those days the press would describe him as "dashiki-clad Negro militant Marion Barry." The 1960s were the hippie era, too, and whites in the counterculture sometimes adopted the dashiki for its rebellious symbolism as well as its anti-mainstream fashion statement.

The militancy of the 1960s has faded, but the dashiki has not. It still serves as a symbol of Africanness within American culture, as in the celebration of Kwanzaa. It is also sometimes an ingredient of high fashion or just a colorful, comfortable shirt for all occasions.

Yoruba, from the Atlantic-Congo and Benue-Congo branches of the Niger-Congo language family, is the official language of southwestern Nigeria, spoken by nearly twenty million people there. One other word English has acquired from Yoruba is *iroko* (1890), a tree whose wood is resistant to insects and is often used as a substitute for teak.

⌇NIGERIA

tango *from Ibibio*

Who does not know the tango? Well, not everybody knows the steps, but most speakers of English are aware of the often slow, sometimes mournful Argentine ballroom dance whose pauses are as important as its movements. Where did it come from? Historians agree that the tango began in Argentina late in the nineteenth century as a somewhat boisterous style of music and a shockingly intimate dance for couples to go with that music. Millions of Europeans immigrated to Argentina early in the twentieth century, and some of those Europeans brought the low-class tango back to France, where it became the rage in the early teens of the century. That made it respectable and admired by the better classes in Argentina and around the world. The tango is mentioned in English as early as 1913, when a London newspaper calls it "a most graceful and beautiful dance."

But what was the origin of this dance and the word for it? Nobody knows, though there are many guesses. The influences on it seem diverse; in the tango you can find hints of both the waltz and African dances. Some see the tango developing from two dances of mixed African-Latin American-European origin, the slow Habanera and the faster Milonga. The Spanish name *tango*, which emerged along with the dance late in the nineteenth century, could well come from an African source. And one possible African source is the Ibibio language of Nigeria, where, as the *American Heritage Dictionary* informs us, the word *tamgu* means "to dance." A substantial number of African slaves had been imported to Argentina, as elsewhere in the Americas, and elements of African culture remained strong among their descendants.

We do know about the Ibibio language. It belongs to the Volta-Congo branch of the Niger-Congo language family and is closely related to Efik. Today Ibibio is spoken by more than three million Nigerians, a little more than 3 percent of the total population. No other words of Ibibio have become part of the general English vocabulary.

⌒CAMEROON

mojo *from Fula*

If your mojo is working, you lead a charmed life. That's because mojo, in its original sense, is a charm, kept in a cloth bag. Depending on which conjure doctor you go to, the charm can be roots, rats, snakes, lizards, pumpkin seeds, dirt, clay, or steel wool. Those were ingredients mentioned in North Carolina in 1962. Back in the late 1930s, in Memphis, Tennessee, to make a mojo one expert said you would sew a red flannel bag with these ingredients: High John de Conker (a plant known also as Solomon's seal), black lodestone, Adam and Eve root, and violet incense powders. A 1946 account from New Orleans said that the mojo was "the leg bone of a black cat that's been killed in a graveyard at midnight."

If your mojo is working, you have sex appeal. But if someone else touches or even sees your mojo, it can lose its power. That's the explanation of the lyrics in the 1928 blues song: "My rider's got a mojo and she won't let me see. . . . She's got to fool her daddy, she's got to keep that mojo hid; but papa's got something for to find that mojo with." Written evidence for the word goes back to 1926 in the song title, "My Daddy's Got the Mojo, But I Got The Say-So." Nowadays the word is widely used, often with no reference to a magical cloth bag but simply meaning power, influence, or advantage.

The word is African American. Its origin is uncertain, but it seems probable that *mojo* ultimately came from Africa. If it did, a good candidate for the source is *moco'o*, meaning a conjure doctor or person who works magic. That word is from the Fula or Fulfulde language, a member of the Fulani branch of the Niger-Congo language family. Fula is spoken as a native language by two-thirds of a million people in Cameroon, and by four million more in Cameroon as a second language. One other English word that may possibly come from Fula (if not from Mandingo) is *yam* (1657).

⁓GABON

bongo *from Kélé*

You play with this bongo a little differently than with the familiar bongo drums. In fact, it's hard to play with this bongo at all, since it weighs a good six hundred pounds. And it's hard to see, at least in its native habitat. Boldly striped white on red, the bongo blends almost invisibly into the dappled sunshine of the equatorial forests of Africa. It is an antelope, husky and hump-backed. Aided by horns that curve backward, the bongo is strong enough to plow through the dense forest with clearance as low as two and a half feet, or to jump six feet from a standing start. It finds forage and safety in bushes, brambles, and vines. It is a vegetarian, munching new plant growth and saplings as well as bamboo leaves and rotten logs.

Outside its homeland, there are about two hundred bongos in zoos around the world, and many have been bred in captivity. But it remains relatively rare and elusive. Until the 1940s, only the zoos in New York City and Rome had bongos in captivity; even by 1970 only a dozen had been exhibited. As early as 1861, however, its name *bongo* appeared in English, in a book on equatorial Africa. The *bongo* drum that makes music, a term from American Spanish, is a totally different word and a relative latecomer; it did not immigrate into English until 1920.

In Africa, bongo antelopes live in forests from Sierra Leone on the west coast to Kenya on the east, though they are not easy to find even there. The name *bongo* is from one or more of the Bantu languages spoken in that area. Kélé, a Niger-Congo language spoken by about 100,000 people in Gabon on the west coast, is a likely candidate. Nothing else from Kélé has made its way into English.

⌇CONGO, DEMOCRATIC REPUBLIC OF THE CONGO, AND ANGOLA

zombie *from Kongo*

Don't try this at home! but here's a recipe. First put on some gloves and catch a bouga toad. Carefully collect some of its gland secretions, said to be a hundred times more powerful than the heart medicine digitalis and hallucinogenic. Then (perhaps keeping your gloves on) catch some puffer fish for their tetrodotoxin, said to be one of the strongest poisons in the world. Add tarantulas, millipedes, seeds and leaves of poisonous plants, and skins from poisonous tree frogs. Mix the poisons together, and for extra effect add ground-up human bones. Then sidle up to an unsuspecting victim and surreptitiously apply a little of the brew to that person's skin.

There! The victim will keel over and appear dead. Go ahead, have a nice funeral. Then give the victim a potion known as "zombie's cucumber," and your prey will wake up and seem to have risen from the dead. But there will be no personality, no memory, not even the ability to speak. You'll have a living body without a soul. In other words, a zombie.

It's tricky, and not everyone agrees that this is the right procedure. So maybe you'd better leave it to a professional, an expert in voodoo known as a *bokor*. It is said that you'll find such experts in Haiti, the home of voodoo.

Once you have a zombie, you'll find lots of uses for it (no longer he or she). The zombie makes a fine slave, working indoors or out at whatever physical task you choose. It will obey without question and not talk back.

The word shows up in English in an 1819 history of Brazil, which says that Zambi "is the name for the Deity, in the Angolan tongue." In 1872 a dictionary of Americanisms includes a more familiar definition: "Zombi, a phantom or a ghost, not unfrequently heard in the Southern States in nurseries and among the servants."

Like *voodoo*, the word *zombie* has an African origin. It comes from a Bantu language of the Niger-Congo language family, either Kimbundu or Kongo. Here we will credit Kongo, also known as Kikongo, which is spoken in Congo, Democratic Republic of the Congo, and Angola by a total of more than three million people. One other well-known English word from Kongo is *chimpanzee* (1738).

∿DEMOCRATIC REPUBLIC OF THE CONGO

basenji *from Lingala*

If it says "Woof, woof," you know it's not a basenji, not by arf. Unlike most other breeds of dogs, the basenji can't bark.

Not that it keeps perfect silence. The basenji can growl and murmur, and it can express its happiness in what has

been described as a combination of chortle and yodel. But its larynx is too different from that of other dogs to allow it to raise a woof.

Staring silently from Egyptian drawings of more than 5,500 years ago, Basenjis are among the earliest domesticated breeds. Their homeland, however, is not Egypt but further south, in central Africa. There the Lingala people, among others, prize the Basenji as a hunting dog. It is smart, bold, fast—and silent. It can catch the scent of prey eighty yards away. Hunters tie a bell around its neck to keep track of it when silence is not needed.

The basenji is said to be happy, playful, and good-looking, with fine copper-colored fur. An adult stands sixteen or seventeen inches high and looks something like a small deer. It endears itself to owners by regularly licking itself clean.

Until the twentieth century, only Africans knew about basenjis. But the exploring English took an interest in them and after several unsuccessful attempts managed to bring basenjis back to England and breed them. Mrs. O. Burn, the dogs' first breeder in England, called them by a Bantu name meaning "bush thing" or "wild thing." In 1933 she wrote for a magazine, "Three years ago I imported to England five Beseiyis—the smooth-coated chestnut dog of terrier size used by the native chiefs for hunting antelope etc. on the Congo plateaux." The first English-born basenji puppies were such an attraction at a 1937 dog show that special police were needed to move crowds along.

It is difficult to determine which Bantu language to credit for *basenji*. Likely candidates include Lingala and Tshiluba, and we will credit Lingala here. This Niger-Congo language is spoken by more than eight million people in Democratic Republic of the Congo and another 300,000 in Congo. Lingala is also a possible source for *bongo* (1861) the antelope, which we have allowed Kélé to speak for in this book.

~DEMOCRATIC REPUBLIC OF THE CONGO

gumbo *from Tshiluba*

At first, *gumbo* was just another word for what we now generally call *okra*. Both are African words for the plant and its versatile, viscous pods; *okra* is most likely from the Ibo language of West Africa, while *gumbo* is from further south, probably the Tshiluba language spoken in Democratic Republic of the Congo (formerly Zaire). But something happened to the bland vegetable. It became the sturdy, unsung main ingredient of an increasingly palatable New Orleans dish that took the name *gumbo* in its honor.

Not that okra ever got top billing in a gumbo; it's too bland. Our earliest record of *gumbo* in the English language is an 1805 account of New Orleans that doesn't even mention okra: "Shrimps are much eaten here; also a dish called gumbo. This last is made of every eatable substance, and especially of those shrimps which can be caught at any time." John James Audubon wrote in 1835, "To me 'Ecrevisses' [crayfish], whether of fresh or salt water, stripped of their coats, and blended into a soup or a 'gombo,' have always been most welcome." Most of the time *gumbo* requires a modifier: shrimp gumbo, crab gumbo, chicken gumbo, wild duck gumbo, even gopher gumbo. Okra is always there, however, even though it always seems to come last, as in this recent description by food writer Elizabeth Hanby: "A standard, present-day New Orleans recipe for gumbo requires crab, shrimp, oysters, ham or veal, green pepper, celery, filé (powdered, dried sassafras leaves), thyme, bay leaf, salt, black pepper, cayenne pepper and—of course—okra!"

There is no question that *gumbo* comes from a Bantu language of the Niger-Congo language family. There is some question about which Bantu language, but it might well be Tshiluba or Luba, a national language of Democratic Republic of the Congo, spoken by more than six million of the population of forty-six million. Another

English word perhaps from Tshiluba, if not from one of the other closely-related Bantu languages, is *banjo* (1739).

∼Angola

marimba *from Kimbundu*

It sounds Spanish. It looks Spanish. The marimba has long been popular in Spanish-speaking Central America, and Mexico's southernmost province of Chiapas is said to be the "land of the marimba," with annual marimba competitions as fiercely contested as soccer matches. But at least its name, and quite likely its origin, is African.

There is no question that a musical instrument with the name *marimba* has deep roots in Africa. Like the present-day versions of the marimba, the ancestral African instrument was a kind of xylophone, but more resonant. On a marimba the bars, supported on cords, are made not of metal but of rosewood or a similar synthetic material; the mallets are covered rather than plain wood. Wooden "fingers" between the bars hold the cords up. Resonators may be metal or locally grown gourds.

The marimba was described in English as long ago as 1704 in a book about the Congo: "The Instrument most in request us'd by the Abundi . . . is the Marimba; it consists of sixteen Calabashes orderly plac'd along the middle between two side-boards join'd together, or a long frame, hanging about a Man's Neck with a Thong." Today's marimbas are larger and set on their own tables.

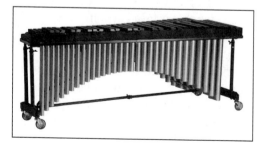

The marimba may have been brought to Central America by African slaves in the 1500s. Then again, perhaps Central Americans had already developed similar instruments to which the African name and perhaps details of construction and performance were applied.

In both places, now as earlier, each resonator of the marimba is covered with a membrane which buzzes when the key is struck. The Chiapas style involves teams of two, three, or even four performers at one instrument, while elsewhere each player has a separate marimba.

North of the border in the United States, and in Japan and Europe, there is generally no membrane and no buzz to marimbas. That allows the marimba to be accepted even in symphony orchestras, thanks to percussionist Keiko Abe, who worked with Yamaha to develop a clear-sounding symphonic version.

Kimbundu, the likely language of origin for *marimba*, is a Bantu language of the Niger-Congo language family. It is spoken by three million people in Angola, about a quarter of the population. Kimbundu may have had a hand in bringing us *banjo* (1739), and it could also be the source of *goober* (1833).

⁓BOTSWANA

tsetse *from Tswana*

One of the smaller creatures on the African continent is one of its bigger problems. By virtue of its harmfulness, the tsetse fly came to the attention of English speakers as early as 1849, when an Englishman in South Africa wrote of horses "killed either by lions or horse sickness, and the fly called tzetse." The tsetse likes blood. Some species of tsetse go for the blood of hoofed animals, others for the blood of humans. By carrying blood from one victim to the next, the fly spreads deadly parasitical diseases. To cattle it gives nagana, also called tsetse disease; to humans it gives trypanosomiasis, also known as sleeping sickness.

If you have sleeping sickness, you begin with something that feels like the flu and end up with parasites swelling your brain and causing bizarre changes in behavior before you lapse into apathy, a coma, and death. Vast areas of sub-Saharan Africa remain undeveloped because the tsetse keeps humans and their cattle away.

There are treatments, if not cures, for sleeping sickness, but they are expensive. Difluoromethylornithine or DFMO prevents the parasitical trypanosomes from multiplying, at a cost of $400 per person, far more than most African states can afford. Efforts to control the flies themselves have so far been unsuccessful, though research is being done to find environmentally benign natural controls.

The Tswana language, which is closely related to Sotho, belongs to the Bantu branch of the Niger-Congo language family. It is the national language of Botswana in southern Africa, where it has more than a million speakers, and it is also spoken by nearly three million people in South Africa. No other words from Tswana have immigrated into the general vocabulary of English.

~ SOUTH AFRICA

gnu *from Xhosa*

What's *gnu*? Nothing but one of the most famous of African animals and an indispensable three-letter word for crossword puzzles and Scrabble. The gnu is an antelope much bigger than its name, weighing four or five hundred pounds when grown. It looks something like an ox, with wide, smooth horns that curve down, then out, then up. It eats grass and is eaten by hyenas and lions. The black gnu is scarce and is found only in South Africa, but the blue gnu is abundant and ranges from South Africa to Kenya.

So we know where it's from. What about its name? That's something of a puzzle. We can easily trace it back to the German traveler Georg Forster, whose book *A Voyage Around the World,* published in English in 1777, is the first

English mention of the name. "There is another species of wild ox," he wrote, "called by the natives gnoo." The only problem is which natives he meant; several different native languages have the word. One possibility is Nama, a Khoisan language formerly called Hottentot, spoken by 90,000 people in Namibia. Equally likely, and with considerably more speakers nowadays, is Xhosa, a Bantu language of the Niger-Congo family spoken by nearly seven million residents of South Africa. Another kind of large antelope named in Foster's 1777 book, the kudu, seems also to derive its name from Xhosa.

Of course, the gnu is also known as a wildebeest (1824), a name that obviously means "wild beast" and comes from Afrikaans, a descendant of Dutch and a close relative of English. But that's not gnu, and it won't displace gnu in word games.

∼SOUTH AFRICA

trek *from Afrikaans*

English speakers had to go to South Africa to learn about *trekking*. They did this early in the nineteenth century, much to the annoyance of the people who taught them the word. These were descendants of the Dutch who had settled in South Africa as early as 1652; they had been there so long that their variety of Dutch went by the name *Afrikaans*. To these white Afrikaners, a *trek* was a day's journey by ox wagon. As Afrikaners had intruded on native black Africans, so the British began intruding on the Dutch-descended Afrikaners, claiming the land for their own. Finally, tired of British bullying, in 1835 the Afrikaners hitched up their oxen and journeyed far inland to establish independent communities. They left behind the name for this migration, the "Great Trek." With that, English speakers took possession of the word *trek* as well.

Recalling the Afrikaners' Great Trek, *trek* in English means not just a journey but a long and challenging one. So when an expedition attempts Mount Everest, it's a trek. And so in the last half of the twentieth century, when Gene Roddenberry sought a name for a television series about long journeys over astronomical distances, he decided on *Star Trek*. Devotees of that program are known as *Trekkies*, except in South Africa, where they are called *Trekkers*, the Afrikaans word for those who *trek*.

Today Afrikaans is spoken by about six million of the forty million inhabitants of South Africa. It is an Indo-European and West Germanic language, like English, by virtue of being descended from Dutch. In recent years, Afrikaans has lost favor because it was the language of the extreme racist *apartheid* (1947) policy. English has adopted about forty words from Afrikaans, including *commando* (1884) and wildlife terms like *springbok* (1775), *spoor* (1823), *aardvark* (1827), and *veldt* (1835).

⁓SOUTH AFRICA

indaba *from Zulu*

When the rest of the world goes to meetings and conventions, South Africa proclaims its African heritage by holding indabas.

English-speaking South Africans learned the word from Zulu chiefs, who would call their people together to discuss important issues at meetings called *indabas*. In the nineteenth century, when the word was first used in English, it always referred to the African tribes. An 1894 article, for example, reports that "a message was therefore conveyed . . . to the King, inviting Umtassa to come to an indaba at Umtali."

Not surprisingly, in the latter part of the twentieth century Nelson Mandela's African National Congress party used the word for its meetings. "More than three thousand delegates are expected at the African National Congress's fiftieth national conference to be held here next week," reported the *Klerksdorp Record* in December 1997. "This four-day ANC Indaba . . . will be officially opened by the provincial chairperson of the ANC." But today's pro-African South Africa has indabas for everyone. In recent years there have been a Dance Indaba, a Tourism Trade Indaba, an International Design Indaba, a Structural Chemistry Indaba, a Small-Molecules Indaba, and a Welding Indaba. The 10th Biennial Congress of the Hypertension Society of Southern Africa in 1996, with the goal of improving health care for all South Africans, was billed as the "Hypertension Indaba."

Also contributing to the spirit of the new South Africa are Cape Indaba Wines. Their maker explains that "a portion of the profits generated from the sale of the Cape Indaba Wines will be donated to the underprivileged for the purposes of education. This contribution, coupled with the ethnically styled label emphasizes our commitment to the upliftment and furtherance of our new nation."

Zulu is spoken by about nine million people in South Africa, nearly a quarter of the population. It is a Bantu language of the Niger-Congo language family. Other English words from zulu include *buchu* (1731), a medicinal shrub; *mamba* (1862), a poisonous snake; *impala* (1875), the famous antelope; and *nagana* (1895), a disease of cattle also called *tsetse disease*.

∼South Africa and Lesotho

milo *from Sotho*

What's a nice African grass like milo doing on the western plains of the United States? Well, it's at home in a dry land, and that's why it was imported. It's a sorghum grain that doesn't need nearly as much water and care as corn, yet its seeds contain more protein than corn and just as much starch. In addition to making feed for farm animals and flour or meal for people, milo has lots of industrial uses. The waxy coat of the seed is used for shoe and furniture polish. Milo also shows up in adhesives, laundry starch, and sizing for fabrics.

Milo usually goes by the full name *milo maize* because it is a kind of maize, closely related to corn. It was introduced to the United States from South Africa in the late nineteenth century. A circular of the Georgia Department of Agriculture in 1883 mentions it by name: "My attention was some time since called to the claims of 'Ivory wheat' and 'Millo Maize' to a place in our long list of profitable food crops." The milo that that writer planted grew to a height of twelve feet.

In South Africa, the name comes from the Sotho language, where the word is *maili*. Sotho is spoken in two versions, northern and southern, by well over six million people in South Africa. It is a national language there and in Lesotho, the land-locked kingdom surrounded by South Africa. There it is spoken by 85 percent of the population, about one and a half million people.

Sotho is a Bantu language of the Niger-Congo language family. Another English word imported from Sotho is *lechwe* (1857), the name of an antelope that likes to wade in water.

∾ZIMBABWE

mbira *from Shona*

For more than a thousand years the Shona people of Zimbabwe have played the mbira. Sometimes it just seems that long, because when you play it, you play it for a long time; mbira players are known not only for their skill but also for their endurance. The mbira is the instrument of choice for the lengthy ceremony known as Bira, in which an ancestral spirit, the Mudzimu, is called on to help the living in times of trouble. Songs of praise and supplication welcoming the spirits are sung to the accompaniment of the mbira, and the spirits speak through a medium.

The mbira of the ancestral spirits, or mbira dzavadzimu, consists of two dozen metal reeds or keys on a wooden board set inside a resonator made of a deze gourd. The musician plucks the reeds with the thumb and right forefinger. Attached to the board is a metal plate that formerly held snail shells but now usually has bottle caps. As the mbira is played, the shells or bottle caps buzz, forming a steady background for the melody. Each song is played on two mbiras, the melodies not only interlocking but producing overtones that "can be mesmerizing," explains Solomon Murungu, author of the Mbira Page on the World Wide Web. "It can establish, for the listener and player alike, a microcosm of serenity inducing a feeling of amazement, excitement and even a state of sheer catalepsy."

It is symbolic, too, of the Shona way of life. The metal keys personify the ancestral spirits, the board represents shelter and fuel, the gourd represents food and water. All are made of special local materials.

That is the traditional mbira, but in these days of world music, there are modern adaptations too. Thomas Mapfumo, for example, has developed a popular style using electric instruments and singing not the praises of ancestors but satirical remarks about politics and social issues. *Mbira* has been heard in the English language at least since 1951.

Aside from English, Shona is the principal language of Zimbabwe, spoken by more than six million of the population of eleven million. There are another three-quarters of a million speakers in Mozambique. It is a Bantu language in the Niger-Congo language family. No other words of Shona are part of the English general vocabulary.

∾ZIMBABWE AND SOUTH AFRICA

mbila *from Venda*

Do not confuse the *mbila* with the *mbira*, as some English writers regrettably have done. True, the mbila and the mbira are both musical instruments; they both are traditional and have deep cultural roots; both are handmade out of local materials; and they both come from southern Africa. But they come from different cultures and different languages. And musically the mbila is nothing like the mbira: the mbila is a kind of xylophone, while the mbira you hold in your hands and pluck.

An English-language book on the Bantu tribes of South Africa gave a proper description of the instrument in 1928: "The mbila, the finest and most perfect of the Venda musical instruments, consists of a number of carved wooden slabs of from three to four inches wide and of various thicknesses, which are beaten with india-rubber hammers by one or two players." Some thirty-five years later, another description makes it seem more like a marimba: "The mbila has resonator gourds with spider-web membrane covering a small hole bored in each one." Mbilas are played in ensembles of as many as thirty.

Until recently, English speakers writing about Africa sometimes used the name mbira to describe what is properly a mbila. The *Oxford English Dictionary* gives several examples of the misnaming, including a 1901 treatise on South Africa that says, "The best and most musical of their instruments is called the ambira. . . . It is composed of long gourds . . . held close together and arranged in order." Since the 1950s, however, a clear distinction seems to have been maintained.

Venda is spoken by 85,000 people in Zimbabwe and 666,000 in the adjoining northern part of South Africa. It is a Bantu language of the Niger-Congo language family. No other words of Venda are regularly heard in English.

ᔈMADAGASCAR

aye-aye *from Malagasy*

The zoo of the English language has a whole wing stocked with words from the Malagasy language. The words are needed to name the distinctive mammals of Madagascar island off the east coast of Africa, where Malagasy is spoken. There is the *tenrec* or *tanrec,* an insect-eating animal like a hedgehog but with a long snout and no tail. There is the *fossa,* a little meat-eating animal that is something like a cat. And then there are three kinds of lemurs.

The word *lemur* itself is Latin, from *lemures,* the name used in ancient Rome for the haunting spirits of the dead. Lemurs, found just on Madagascar and nearby islands, are indeed spooky, though they are harmless to humans. They are cat-sized, big-tailed, small-bodied, and large-eyed. They live on fruit and insect larvae. They live in trees and come out at night, looking like ghosts with their big eyes.

We call three species of lemur by their Malagasy names: the *sifaka,* the *indri,* and the *aye-aye.* The latter

was recorded in English as early as 1781. Though it is spelled like the sailors' way of saying "yes," this aye-aye is not a yes-sayer but simply a creature that cries "aye-aye" when it scampers around at night. In his 1993

book *The Aye-Aye and I: A Rescue Mission in Madagascar,* Gerald Durrell describes an encounter with one: "In the gloom it came along the branches towards me, its round, hypnotic eyes blazing, its spoon-like ears turning to and fro like radar dishes, its white whiskers twitching and moving like sensors; its black hands, with their thin fingers, the third seeming terribly elongated, tapping delicately on the branches as it moved along." The aye-aye uses that third finger to dig in rotten logs for its dinner of grubs. Its appearance is so haunting that it has a magical reputation among the Malagasy people and is said to bring death when it shows up in a village. Needless to say, the aye-aye is an endangered species.

Malagasy is the national language of Madagascar and is spoken by more than ten million people there. It is not a Niger-Congo language but belongs to the Malayo-Polynesian branch of the Austronesian language family.

~TANZANIA

Kwanzaa *from Swahili*

On the day after Christmas 1966 the Swahili word *Kwanzaa* entered the English language. It is possible to be so precise because *Kwanzaa* was no casual borrowing. Instead, it was a well-publicized adoption of a foreign word to designate a new cultural invention: a celebration of African American people, heritage, struggles, and hopes. Not a religious holiday and not intended to compete with Christmas, Kwanzaa is celebrated from December 26 through January 1. Its inventor, Dr. Maulana Ron Karenga, based Kwanzaa on African harvest celebrations. The name comes from Swahili *matunda ya kwanzaa*, meaning "first fruits."

Karenga devised seven symbols for Kwanzaa, naming them in Swahili. The symbols are *mazao* (crops), *mkeka* (a straw mat), *kinara* (candle holder), *mishumaa saba* (seven candles), *muhindi* (ears of corn), *zawadi* (gifts), and *kikombe cha umoja* (unity cup). Kwanzaa also has *nguzo saba* (seven principles): *umoja* (unity), *kujichagulia* (self-determination), *ujima* (collective work and responsibility), *ujamaa* (cooperative economics), *nia* (purpose), *kuumba* (creativity), and *imani* (faith).

In the Afrocentric 1960s, Karenga envisioned Kwanzaa as a means of furthering "social revolutionary change for Black America." In the less militant decades that followed, Kwanzaa developed a kinder, gentler image, to the point that beginning in 1997 it was celebrated, along with Christmas and Hanukkah, on a holiday stamp from the U.S. Postal Service.

The official Kwanzaa Song goes like this:

Kwanzaa is a holiday
Kwanzaa, Kwanzaa, Kwanzaa
Is an African holiday
Seven Principles
Seven Candles
Seven Black days for the African.

It can be sung "as often as is wished for elevation of the spirits." Kwanzaa yenu iwe na heri (Happy Kwanzaa)!

Karenga's choice of Swahili was no accident. It is a pan-African language, not restricted to one ethnic group or country but widely used for trade and official business throughout East Africa. It is one of the two official languages of Tanzania, where it originated, and also of Kenya. Nowadays it is the first language of more than a million Africans and a second language known by more than thirty million. A few other Swahili words of lesser note have also made their way into English: *topi* (antelope, 1894), *bwana* (boss, 1878), and *panga* (machete, 1925).

⟨~ TANZANIA

chikungunya *from Makonde*

Need another reason to hate mosquitos? One word: chikungunya. Like yellow fever, chikungunya is a virus carried by a gluttonous mosquito that has already dined on an infected person. The mosquito doesn't get sick but happily hosts the virus, nurturing it to greater strength before depositing some of the virus in the next victim.

Although widespread in tropical areas throughout the world, chikungunya is thankfully rather rare. You're more likely to be infected with the yellow fever virus or with filariasis, a disease caused by a roundworm that lives in your lymph vessels and tissues. But if you do get chikungunya, watch out. You will get a headache, fever, nausea, and perhaps a rash. The worst effect is sudden pain in the joints, like a severe case of instant arthritis. You aren't likely to die, but your joints can remain stiff for weeks or months after the mosquito bite.

There is no vaccine to prevent chikungunya, nor is there a cure. You just have to ride it out. Better still, you should try to avoid tropical mosquito bites in the first place by wearing clothing that covers most of your skin, by using mosquito nets, by staying in screened-in places, and by applying mosquito repellent with DEET. Or stay away from the tropics entirely and let the virus-free mosquitos of the north woods chew you up.

It was in Tanzania, in 1953, that chikungunya was first officially identified by the world medical community. That is how its name, published in English in 1954, happened to come from the Makonde language of southern Tanzania and northern Mozambique on the east coast of Africa. In Makonde, *chikungunde* is said to mean "that which folds up" and refers to the crippling of the joints.

Makonde is spoken by nearly a million of the thirty million people of Tanzania and by another 360,000 in Mozambique. It is a Bantu language of the Niger-Congo language family. No other word of Makonde has entered English.

⌒TANZANIA

suni *from Chaga*

If you don't find a suni when you're looking for it, that may be because you aren't looking low enough. A suni is an antelope, but pocket-sized. A full-grown suni, male or female, is only fourteen inches tall at the shoulder and weighs eleven pounds.

Furthermore, sunis are rare and shy. And since they're small, they like to hide in forests and brush. That makes them a threatened species because forests and brush are being cleared for agriculture in their native habitats in southeastern Africa. Sunis like to eat crops on the newly planted fields, so farmers like to get rid of them.

Fortunately, sunis breed well in captivity. In the United States you can see them, for example, at the San Diego Zoo in California, the Phoenix Zoo in Arizona, and the Birmingham Zoo in Alabama. For the $50 cost of a year's food and care, you can "adopt" a suni at the Hogle Zoo in Utah.

You can also arrange with Phillip Bronkhorst Safaris of South Africa to shoot one in Kwa Zulu Natal. Their trophy fee for a suni antelope is $850. That compares with $175 for a warthog and $3,000 for a giraffe.

Suni are found in the wild today in South Africa, Mozambique, Zimbabwe, and Tanzania. Their name comes from Chaga, a Bantu language of the Niger-Congo language family spoken by about one million of the thirty million people of Tanzania.

The Chaga word *suni* appeared in English in a scientific report as long ago as 1893, and has been mentioned regularly ever since, as in the 1942 *East Africa Annual:* "Any gap in the wire of the vegetable garden is found immediately by suni, duiker or bushbuck." No other words of Chaga have crept into English.

∼UGANDA

o'nyong-nyong *from Ganda*

The name means "joint-breaker." That is how the virus known as o'nyong-nyong acts. It hurts! Like chikungunya, it causes intense arthritis pains in the joints. For good measure, it also gives you a headache, a high fever, a rash, and a pain in the eyes. It is an equal opportunity disease, affecting all ages and both sexes.

O'nyong-nyong has the same source as chikungunya: the bite of a mosquito. In the case of o'nyong-nyong, it's the familiar Anopheles mosquito, and o'nyong-nyong is the only viral disease known to be spread by Anopheles. Symptoms show up two or three days after a bite. And there's no known vaccine or cure. If you get o'nyong-nyong, all you can do is take your choice of pain-relieving medication, lie down, and wait it out. It won't kill you, but it may make you wish it had.

O'nyong-nyong has one other connection with chikungunya. If you've been infected with chikungunya, you won't come down with o'nyong-nyong. The reverse is not true, so it is suspected that the new disease is caused by a mutant of the chikungunya virus.

Fortunately, o'nyong-nyong is rare and sporadic. It made its first known appearance in 1959 in Uganda, then circled through Kenya, Tanzania, and Zambia till it returned to Uganda again, affecting two million people or 60 to 80 percent of the population before it subsided in 1961. It reappeared in East Africa thirty-five years later, in 1996, in Uganda, Tanzania, and neighboring Malawi and continued into 1997, though a smaller population was affected this time. In the Nyanja language of Malawi, the disease is called *kabadula*, meaning "cut off at the knees."

Ganda or Luganda is the most widely spoken African language in Uganda, used by about three million people out of a population of twenty million. It is a Bantu language of the Niger-Congo language family. No other words of Ganda have reached the rest of the world in English.

∼Somalia

ouabain *from Somali*

Knock on wood, but be careful about knocking on the wood of the ouabaio tree. Aside from being the one-consonant botanical word with the greatest number of vowels, ouabaio is also the source of a deadly poison, ouabain.

Somalians have known this for a long time. In the Somali language, *ouabaio* means arrow-poison, and that's what they have extracted from the wood. But modern medicine has taken an interest too. The poison stimulates the heart, causing erratic heartbeats that can lead to quick death. Injected in very small doses, however, ouabain simply slows and regulates the pulse while it makes each heartbeat stronger. As the doctors say, that makes it cardiotonic; it's good for the heart. Its effects and chemical composition are like those of digitalis, which is extracted from the foxglove plant. Both are steroid glycosides with specific effects on the heart.

Ouabain is found not only in the ouabaio tree but also in the vine called Smooth Strophanthus. That plant has thick, glossy evergreen leaves and beautiful bell-shaped flowers, purple and white. They look like begonias, but at night they smell like roses. You can pick the flowers, but don't fondle the wood.

It was the French who helped the English language to the word *ouabain* and gave it its strange spelling; "wahbain" would be a more phonetic way to write it in English. "In the year 1882 some roots, stems, and leaves of the plant said to yield the ouabaio poison of the Somalis were sent from Africa to France by M. Revoil," says a report in the *Pharmacological Journal* of 1893.

Somali is the principal language of Somalia on the eastern peninsula of Africa, spoken by nearly seven million of the population of nearly ten million. It is also spoken by two million people in neighboring Ethiopia. Somali belongs to the Cushitic branch of the Afro-Asiatic language family. One other English word from Somali is *gerenuk* (1895), the name of an antelope.

∾ETHIOPIA

teff *from Amharic*

Now available at health food stores: a grain so fine that it takes 150 to equal a single grain of wheat. It is rich in protein, B vitamins, iron, and calcium. Its flavor is said to be

mildly nutty, mildly sweet, "molasses-like." Most of the world knows little about it, but in Ethiopia teff has been the main grain for many centuries.

Teff is the principal ingredient of injera, a sour pancake that is the basis for traditional Ethiopian meals. To make it, Ethiopians mix finely-ground teff flour with water and cover it with a cloth for several days until it ferments and develops bubbles like those in pancake batter. Stirring in a little salt, they then fry it in large cakes in a lightly oiled pan. A dish-sized injera is used in place of a serving plate at the dinner table, and diners tear off pieces of other injeras to pick up the food. When the injera plate has been picked clean, it too is eaten with all the drippings it has absorbed.

The name *teff* means "lost" in Amharic because grains spilled on the ground are so small that they are lost. Although teff has only recently been exported to English-speaking lands, it was noticed by English speakers more than two centuries ago. In 1790, writing about his travels through Ethiopia to discover the source of the Nile, James Bruce observed, "Teff is used by all sorts of people from the king downwards, and there are kinds of it which are esteemed fully as much as wheat."

Amharic is a Semitic language of the Afro-Asiatic language family, spoken by fifteen million people in Ethiopia and perhaps five million elsewhere. Two other Amharic words in English are *gelada* (1878), a kind of baboon, and *Negus* (1594), the official title for the ruler of Ethiopia (or Abyssinia) until the monarchy was abolished in 1975.

～EGYPT

oasis *from Egyptian*

Thousands of years before other parts of the world entered the pages of history, the ancient Egyptians created in the desert of North Africa an oasis not only of green fertile land but also of civilization. Their oasis was only as wide as the floodplain of a river, but the river was the world's longest, extending more than four thousand miles. The first Egyptian empire, encompassing the river from its delta to a thousand miles upstream, was founded there some five thousand years ago. Each year the river would flood, depositing new fertile soil on the farmland and making the desert bloom. In the idle farming time of the flood, rulers employed the farmers in public works like the building of the pyramids.

We think the Egyptians were the first to use the word *oasis*. It is not used in the written Egyptian records that have been preserved, but a word similar to *oasis* meaning "dwelling-place" is found in the descendant of Egyptian known as Coptic. From the Egyptians, Greek and Roman writers learned the word.

Its presence in English is much more recent, stemming from the time when English speakers were first becoming world travelers. In Samuel Purchas's 1613 travel book we find mention of Oasis as a fertile place in the Libyan desert. Nowadays we use *oasis* far from the deserts of Africa to mean a peaceful, flourishing place that makes a pleasant contrast to its surroundings, like an oasis of free time in the midst of a busy schedule.

Egyptian is a member of the Afro-Asiatic language family, cousin to Arabic and Hebrew. It is uniquely important to linguists and historians because its written records, beginning with the famous hieroglyphs, go back five thousand years. Through Latin and Greek it has given English a dozen or so other words that have stuck with us, including *ammonia* (1799) and *basalt* (1601), *ebony* (1382) and *ivory* (1300), and *gum* (1385)—the chewing kind. But there are no speakers of Egyptian today, the last having died about five hundred years ago. Arabic is now the language of Egypt.

～EGYPT

adobe *from Coptic*

In the American Southwest, adobe is a way of life, or at least a way of housing. The sun is bright enough, and the climate dry enough, that building blocks do not have to be baked in an oven. You can make bricks of clay mixed with straw and left to dry in the sun. With these adobe bricks, covered with an extra layer of adobe mud, you can build homes and churches that are thick-walled and cool against the desert heat. And you save the cost of lumber, which is not plentiful in the desert. Until the advent of modern transportation, construction methods, and air conditioning, adobe was the preferred way of dwelling in the Southwest. In English, references to *adobe* appear as early as 1748.

But the Coptic language, from which *adobe* apparently derives, is a world away in Egypt. How did *adobe* become so firmly planted in the distant North American desert? It came with the Spanish, who knew both the word and the technique. They, in turn, got it from Arabic, because for many centuries speakers of Arabic lived beside the Spanish in Spain. The Arabic word, in turn, seems to have come from Coptic *tobe,* the word for a similar kind of brick. Presumably Coptic got it from its ancestor, the Egyptian language, which has a hieroglyphic word of similar sound and meaning.

Coptic is the last living relic of ancient Egyptian. It was the language spoken by the small remnant of Egyptians who remained Christian after the Muslim conquest of the whole region. By the sixteenth century, the Copts had followed the example of the Muslims by switching to Arabic, but to this day Coptic is used in the liturgy of the Coptic Christian Church. Like its parent Egyptian, Coptic belongs to the Afro-Asiatic language family, along with Semitic languages like Arabic and Hebrew.

One other Coptic word in English is *berseem*, designating a kind of Egyptian clover, noted from 1902.

ASIA

*T*he next part of our tour of the world's contributors to English covers a greater distance and presents greater linguistic variety than Europe or Africa. It goes across Asia, the world's largest landmass, from the familiar land of the Bible to the remotest arctic corner of Siberia. From an English point of view, Asia is the East; it has been spoken of as the Near East and the Far East, and that is the route our tour will take, from near to far.

The ancient Bible lands of Israel, Syria, and Iraq provide the biblical words *shibboleth, mammon,* and *babel.* Other long-familiar words from the Near East are *arsenic, algebra,* and *paradise.*

Moving further eastward, to the neighborhood of Pakistan and India, we encounter more exotic immigrants to English. There we find everything from *polo* to *ginger, Aryans* and *gurus.* And there are exotic animals, not just the weasely *mongoose,* the pig-rat *bandicoot,* the snaky *anaconda,* the wild-dog *dhole,* and the goats *cashmere, tahr,* and *serow,* but even the elusive *yeti* of Nepal and Tibet, or at least its name. There is also the extinct *baluchithere,* of which a full-sized model exists only in Nebraska.

Further along, southeast Asia gives our language the polite *U,* the *bong* for pleasure, the *sampot* to wear, and *Tet* to celebrate. And in east Asia, we come upon the *gung ho* language spoken by nearly a billion people. We will stop long enough to take in two Chinese words, one from Mandarin and one from Cantonese.

There are only a few immigrants to the English language from Korean and one from Okinawan, but Japanese has hundreds, of which *bonsai* seems representative. The Asian tour concludes with Mongolian and single examples from each of three indigenous languages of eastern Siberia: *shaman, parka,* and *kamleika.*

Most of the languages of Asia are not related to English, but there is a major exception in the Indian branch of the Indo-European language family, as the "Indo" part of that name implies. Hindi, Urdu, and many other languages of India and Pakistan are Indo-European. They trace back to or are related to Sanskrit, the most ancient of the Indo-European languages for which a detailed written record exists. Of the forty-three languages in our Asian tour, sixteen are Indo-European. The other major language family in India, with four representatives on our tour, is the Dravidian.

Five languages in the Near East, including Hebrew and Arabic, are from the Afro-Asiatic family so dominant in Africa. There are six representatives of the great Sino-Tibetan family, including Chinese. Japanese and Okinawan belong to a language family of their own, possibly with Korean. And there are seven other language families that have contributed immigrants to English in this region. Asia is a vast place.

Many of the Near Eastern words have been in English a long time: *paradise* since the twelfth century, *mammon* and *arsenic* since the thirteenth. Even *ginger* managed to reach English, through intermediaries from India, as long ago as 1100. Further to the east, the imports are more recent, from the European "Age of Discovery" or later colonial and post-colonial times. Asian influence on the English language has remained strong in modern times, as evidenced by words as diverse as *yeti* and *bong, gung ho* and *tae kwon do.*

∾ISRAEL

shibboleth *from Hebrew*

Language can be a matter of life and death. This certainly was so in the case of the ancient Ephraimites, one of the twelve tribes of Israel, whose linguistic misadventure the Bible relates in the book of Judges. They had stood by while Jephthah took command of another tribe, the Gileadites, and routed their oppressors, the Ammonites. You would think the Ephraimites would have appreciated Jephthah's destruction of their common enemy, but in fact they were furious at being left out. "Wherefore passedst thou over to fight against the children of Ammon, and didst not call us to go with thee?" asked the Ephraimites in the accents of our King James version. "We will burn thine house upon thee with fire."

Jephthah, a mighty man of valor, didn't care for their attitude. He replied that he had called for them, but they hadn't come. With that, he gathered his Gileadites and smote the Ephraimites. After the battle, the surviving Ephraimites tried to sneak across the River Jordan: "And it was so, that when those Ephraimites which were escaped said, Let me go over, that the men of Gilead said unto him, Art thou an Ephraimite? If he said Nay, then said they unto him, Say now Shibboleth: and he said Sibboleth; for he could not frame to pronounce it right. Then they took him, and slew him at the passages of Jordan: and there fell at that time of the Ephraimites forty and two thousand."

To those of us who speak English, the *sh* of *shibboleth* is easy enough to pronounce. But there are many dialects and languages that do not have that sound. A speaker of Hawaiian, for example, or of Quechua, a major language of South America, could not come close.

In Hebrew, *shibboleth* means stream of water. But because of this biblical use, *shibboleth* has a different meaning in English: an arbitrary test or custom that distinguishes one group from another, or a word or slogan identified with a particular group or party. It appears in English as early as John Wycliffe's 1382 translation of the Bible.

Hebrew, like its close relative Arabic, is a Semitic language in the Afro-Asiatic language family. Until the present century it had survived for two thousand years only as a liturgical language for students of the Bible and for Jewish religious services. But the Zionist movement revived it for everyday use, and it has been the official language of Israel since that country came into existence in 1948. There are now nearly three million speakers of Hebrew in Israel.

Biblical Hebrew has had a strong influence on English. Hebrew words in English include *hallelujah* (1382) and *amen* (950), as well as *cherub* (825), *manna* (897), *behemoth* (1382), *cider* (1300), *messiah* (1300), *cabal* (1614), *schwa* (1895), and from modern Hebrew, *kibbutz* (1944). Other Hebrew words like *chutzpah* (1892) and *schmooze* (1897) have immigrated through Yiddish to English.

⌇SYRIA

mammon *from Aramaic*

"No servant can serve two masters," Jesus told his disciples. "For either he will hate the one and love the other, or he will be devoted to the one and despise the other. You cannot serve God and mammon."

These words are from the Sermon on the Mount, as recorded in Matthew 6:24. Of course, Jesus didn't say them in English. He spoke Aramaic, a Semitic language in the Afro-Asiatic language family. But thanks to what Jesus said and did, one of the words in this modern English translation is the same as in the original. A speaker of ancient Aramaic would recognize *mammon.*

The word was delivered unchanged from Aramaic to the Greek of the New Testament, from Greek to Latin, and eventually to English. Apparently there was nothing else in

Greek, Latin, or English that would exactly translate *mammon*, which means "wealth as an object of desire and false worship." Its earliest English appearance is as wealth personified in William Langland's allegorical *Piers Plowman* of 1362. The character named Dobet (that is, "Do Better") does what Jesus urged: "with Mammon's money he has made himself friends, has turned to religion, has translated the Bible, and preaches to the people St. Paul's words."

Aramaic is both younger and older than its close relative Hebrew. In Jesus' time it was a modern language, compared to Hebrew, but unlike Hebrew it has not been revived after it died out more than a thousand years ago with the spread of Arabic-speaking Islam. Although no one speaks Aramaic nowadays, one descendant, Assyrian Neo-Aramaic, is spoken by 30,000 people in Syria, another 30,000 in Iraq, and fully 80,000 in the United States, and another descendant, Chaldean Neo-Aramaic, is spoken by more than 100,000 in Iraq and 70,000 in the United States.

A few other biblical and religious words in English also come from ancient Aramaic, including *abbot* (880) from *abba* meaning "father" and *Pharisee* (897), as well as the Jewish *kaddish* and *tefillin* (both 1613).

∾TURKEY

arsenic *from Syriac*

As an element of the English language, arsenic made a modest debut in about the year 1386. It was a minor ingredient of a lesser-known story by a major author, Geoffrey Chaucer. In the Canon's Yeoman's tale, one of the last of the *Canterbury Tales*, the apprentice of a fugitive alchemist describes his master's laboratory. After inventorying the "vessels made of earth and glass" and other equipment used by the alchemist, the Canon's Yeoman lists his chemical supplies, including "waters rubifying, bull's gall, arsenic, sal ammoniac, and brimstone."

The *arsenic* mentioned by the Canon's Yeoman was probably what chemists nowadays call arsenic trisulphide, a bright yellow substance used as a pigment and for tanning. There was also the highly poisonous *white arsenic* or arsenic trioxide, mentioned in English as early as 1605. This is the arsenic used by murderers like the Brooklyn ladies in the Broadway play and 1944 Cary Grant movie *Arsenic and Old Lace.* White arsenic is slightly sweet, so the ladies masked its flavor in blackberry wine. Arsenic is not a wise choice if you wish to conceal poisoning, because it leaves traces that remain in the body of the victim for years. One mark of slow arsenic poisoning is "Mees' lines," white transverse lines on the fingernails.

In small amounts, though, white arsenic is said to be good for you; it stimulates the production of red blood cells. Once taken as a nutritional supplement in Alpine countries, it supposedly gave people ruddy complexions and increased their ability to work.

There is also just plain arsenic, which smells like garlic when it evaporates. *As* is the symbol for this semi-metallic element arsenic, No. 33 in the periodic table.

Linguistically, arsenic has a compound history too. English got the name from French; French got it from Latin; Latin got it from Greek. Greek seems to have taken it from Syriac *zarnika,* and though this word evidently goes back to Middle Persian and Old Iranian, Syriac is the oldest attested form.

Syriac is a language that became extinct a thousand years ago, although it is still used as a literary language by followers of the Syrian Orthodox and Syrian Catholic churches. It was spoken in a corner of present-day Turkey as well as Iraq and Syria. The alchemical name for mercury, *azoth* (1477), also traces itself back to Syriac. That language may also be the source, via Hebrew and German, for *schwa* (1895), the name given by linguists to an unstressed vowel, symbolized by an upside-down e.

∼TURKEY

divan *from Turkish*

Have a seat and make yourself comfortable. This explanation may take a while.

If the seat is a divan, you should be comfortable indeed. In fact, you might fall asleep, which would be easy enough to do on a divan; it's a name we use for a couch, usually without back or arms but furnished with pillows so that it can double as a bed. But a divan is no ordinary piece of furniture. It has connotations of romance, literature, and luxury, thanks to its Turkish and Persian heritage.

Divan can be traced back several thousand years to the Old Iranian language, where it probably began as a long word meaning "document house," a place to store written records. The Persians used a shorter version of the word to mean both a bundle of written material and a place where written documents were used, so it could mean a collection of poetry, a courtroom, or the activity that takes place in such a room. Speakers of Turkish got *divan* from the Persians and gave it the shape it now has in English. As early as 1586 a book in English describes a Turkish "council called divan."

But the Turks, and English travelers to Turkey, also used *divan* as the name of a cushioned bench, originally in a council room. A travel book published in 1702 explains: "Their greatest Magnificence consists in their Divans or Sofas." And a 1703 account of a journey to Jerusalem explains that divans "are a sort of low stages . . . elevated about sixteen or eighteen inches or more above the floor, whereon the Turks eat, sleep, smoke, receive visits, say their prayers, etc."

That is the divan with which the English language has been furnished ever since. It has always been more than a mere couch, as William Makepeace Thackeray in the nineteenth century implied in a poem about his attic hideaway: "No better divan need the Sultan require / Than the creaking old sofa that basks by the fire." The welcoming divan is both subject and title of a recent song by Smudge (Tom Morgan) performed by Evan Dando of The Lemonheads with the refrain, "You can crash out on my divan."

The Internet is stuffed with virtual divans couched in poetic language. Consider Saundra Mitchell's Web page poem "Crimson Divan," which ends with

> the hopes that
> we will soon lie together once more
> well met, well loved, well reckoned
> here on this crimson
> divan.

Or you can "Take a break from the fast-spinning light-flashing tyre-screaming chaos of the superhighway, and put your feet up with *Divan*, Australia's first national online poetry journal."

Divan is not the only Turkish delight in English. We have dozens of other delicious and exotic words imported from that language and culture, including *coffee* (1598), *sherbet* (1603), and *yogurt* (1625), *tulip* (1578) and *turban* (1588, related words), *dervish* (1585), *kiosk* (1625), and possibly even *yarmulke* (1903). Turkish is one of the world's major languages, spoken by about sixty-three million people in Turkey and another ten million or so in other countries. It belongs to the Altaic language family.

ARMENIA

shish kebab *from Armenian*

Does shish kebab ring a bell? Or perhaps even make your mouth water? If so, it's thanks to both the Armenians and the Turks. These two neighbors in the vicinity of Mt. Ararat, where Noah parked his ark, have had unfriendly relations, to say the least, and they have unrelated languages too. But both make shish kebab, and together they have made it

part of our language and culture.

In Turkish, the word is *siskebabiu*, where *sis* is a skewer or spit and *kebap* is roast meat. In Armenian, it's *shish kabab*, a little closer to our pronunciation. Apparently the word and the food originated long ago in Turkey and long ago became an Armenian favorite as well. The English-language version could well have come from Armenia along with the many Armenian immigrants to the English-speaking world in the twentieth century.

That is how Sinclair Lewis introduced it to Americans in 1914 in his first novel, *Our Mr. Wrenn.* The eponymous hero, having just inherited a thousand dollars, takes his landlady's daughter to an Armenian restaurant below 30th Street in Manhattan. "Shish kibub! Who ever heard of such a thing!" exclaims his guest. "What is that shish kibub?" "Kebab," Wrenn replies. "It's lamb roasted on skewers. I know you'll like it." Lee Theresa Zapp won't even try it, but that just shows her ignorance. Nowadays Miss Theresa would know better. She'd find Armenian restaurants even in Fresno, California, and West Bend, Wisconsin.

Armenia considers itself the first country to have converted to Christianity, some 1700 years ago. Its language belongs to our Indo-European family but in a branch by itself. Most of Armenia's population of three and a half million speak Armenian, and both Russia and Georgia have half a million Armenian speakers. No other Armenian words are in the general vocabulary of English.

⟅GEORGIAN REPUBLIC

zelkova *from Georgian*

In the early twentieth century, the streets of any American town that had pretensions to gentility would be shaded by elms. The elms grew bigger and shadier until, at mid-century, a little beetle killed off most of them by spreading a strangling fungus known as Dutch Elm Disease.

To shade the naked streets, horticulturalists looked around the world for replacements. In Japan they found one that had the elm's familiar vase shape. It was called the zelkova.

Though it grows more slowly than the elm, just twelve to eighteen inches a year, the zelkova will eventually become as tall, reaching sixty to a hundred feet high and spreading perhaps fifty feet wide. It withstands wind, drought, and cold winters. Depending on which authority you read, it is somewhat resistant or somewhat susceptible to Dutch Elm Disease.

And it inspires affection. "Overcoming many difficulties, the zelkova grows rich leaves and thick branches to offer spacious shade that people love," says the Zelkova Love Society of Korea. "This tree represents patience, tolerance, peace and harmony."

Although the zelkova is native to Korea and Japan, its name came to English (appearing in an 1893 book on ornamental trees) from the opposite corner of Asia, the present-day recently independent Republic of Georgia, where the zelkova also grows. Georgian, a member of the South Caucasian language family, is spoken by nearly four million people in that country, where it is the official language. Zelkova is the only word of Georgian in the general vocabulary of English.

∼IRAQ

babel *from Akkadian*

It's in the Book: the story of why we use *babel* to mean a noisy clash of languages and speakers, all striving in vain to be heard and understood. According to the Hebrew Bible, God was worried that humans communicating with one another would get too uppity, so He split up their language in a place called Babel. In the King James Version, here is the gist of the story from Genesis 11:

> And the whole earth was of one language, and of one speech. . . . And they said, Go to, let us build us a city and a tower, whose top may reach unto heaven; and let us make us a name, lest we be scattered abroad upon the face of the whole earth. . . . And the Lord said, Behold, the people is one, and they have all one language; and this they begin to do: and now nothing will be restrained from them, which they have imagined to do. Go to, let us go down, and there confound their language, that they may not understand one another's speech. So the Lord scattered them abroad from thence upon the face of all the earth: and they left off to build the city. Therefore is the name of it called Babel; because the Lord did there confound the language of all the earth.

The last sentence suggests that the name Babel means "confusion" in the original Hebrew. But it doesn't, except in this sentence. It is simply the Hebrew name for the city of Babylon. Perhaps that was enough; Babylon must have had a noisy variety of languages in biblical times. In any case, Babel came to Hebrew from Akkadian, the chief language of Babylon. The Akkadian *Bab-ilu* means "gate of God" and is probably a translation from an earlier Sumerian term, *Ka-dingir*.

The ancient city of Babylon, on the Euphrates River about fifty miles south of present-day Baghdad, exists only in ruins today, and there are no speakers of ancient Akkadian left. It was a Semitic language, related to Arabic and Hebrew, and spoken thousands of years ago in the land now known as Iraq. Another Akkadian word in English is *ziggurat* (1877), the name for a style of step pyramid used by the Babylonians as a temple.

In English, the name *Babel* was used as early as 1382 by John Wycliffe in his translation of the Bible. By 1529 it also was being used with today's broader meaning of any incoherent collection of noise or speech. Strangely enough, the word with two *b*'s, *babble*, is not related but goes back to a common Indo-European word imitating the sound to which it refers.

⁓IRAQ

algebra *from Arabic*

In about the year 830, Mohammad ibn-Musa al-Khwarizmi of Baghdad wrote a book with the Arabic title *Hisab al-jabr w'al-muqabala*, which may be translated as *Science of the Reunion and the Opposition*. The reunion, or *al-jabar*, became our *algebra*, which deals not so much with numbers themselves (that's arithmetic) but with relations among numbers, relations such as equation. The notion of algebra goes back to the Hindus; Al-Khwarizmi was the man who synthesized their knowledge for the Arabic, and in due course the European, world.

It was much later than the ninth century, of course, when the notion and the name of algebra reached the English language. Italian was the first of the European languages to use *algebra*, in 1202; English finally got it in 1551 in Robert Recorde's *Pathway to Knowledge*, which treats of "the rule of false position, with divers examples not only vulgar, but some appertaining to the rule of Algeber." During that century English was also using *algebra* to mean bonesetting, the "reunion" of bones, another meaning of the word that the Spanish had learned from the Arabs.

Al-Khwarizmi was so influential that has own name, warped a little in translation, also has became a European and an English word, *algorithm* (1699), which now means any mathematical procedure. Other words attesting to the importance of Arabic scholarship in mathematics and science include *alchemy* (1362), *elixir* (1386), *zenith* (1387), *nadir* (1391), and *cipher* (1399). The Arabic language has given several hundred significant words to English, including *admiral* (1205), *syrup* (1392), *cotton* (1400), *crimson* (1440), *alcohol* (1543), *jasmine* (1548), *magazine* (1583), *monsoon* (1584), *sash* (1590), *hashish* (1598), *coffee* (via Turkish, 1598), *ghoul* (1786), and of course *Islam* (1613).

Arabic, a member of the West Semitic branch of the Afro-Asiatic language family, is one of the world's major languages. Like Spanish, French, and English, it has different national varieties in many countries, but there is also a common Standard Arabic, which is the language of schools. Throughout North Africa and the eastern Mediterranean, there are now about two hundred million speakers of Arabic. Iraq deserves credit as the country of origin for *algebra* in honor of al-Khwarizmi's presence in Baghdad, a renowned center for scholars in his day.

⌒IRAN

satem *from Avestan*

English has not needed to import numbers from any other language. We still count *one, two, three . . . one hundred* as the Angles and Saxons did, and before them our Germanic ancestors. Yet one of the words of English is *satem,* the word for "one hundred" in Avestan, the ancient language of Zoroastrianism.

It's not because any ancient Persians have opened currency exchanges or schools of mathematics in English-speaking countries. Nor have English speakers been listening to Zoroastrians counting aloud. Instead, *satem* was imported by scholars who study the history of the Indo-European language family. Shortly before 1900, a German scholar named von Bradke observed a neat geographical division among Indo-European languages. Western Indo-European languages used words beginning with a *k* sound, like Latin *centum*, for the number 100, while Eastern languages of the Indo-European family named their hundreds with words beginning with *s*, like Avestan *satem*. The pairing of western *k* and eastern *s* was also found in numerous other words. Von Bradke called the two branches *centum* and *satem*, respectively. The centum languages include the Celtic, Germanic, Italic, and Greek branches of Indo-European; the satem ones include Slavic and Indo-Iranian. (In the Germanic languages, including English, the *k* sound developed into *h*, as in *hundred*.) Scholarly discussion of centum and satem languages took place in English as early as 1901.

Unfortunately, this perfectly neat division was spoiled by the discovery of records of an ancient and very far eastern Indo-European language, Tocharian, which is somewhat like centum languages and somewhat like satem. But it is still convenient to be able to label the two major branches as centum and satem.

Avestan is the language of Avesta, the scripture of the ancient Zoroastrian religion founded more than three thousand years ago by Zoroaster or Zarathustra. It was the dominant religion of the Persian empires and is still practiced nowadays in Iran and India. The Zoroastrian writings keep Avestan alive, but it is no one's native language nowadays. The only word that has come direct from Avestan into English is *satem*, but it is also possibly the source of Persian words that have made their way into English, including *baksheesh* (1775), a tip, *kiosk* (1625), and *paradise* (1175).

∿IRAN

paradise *from Persian*

Biblically speaking, the first paradise was the Garden of Eden. But linguistically speaking, it was a Persian amusement park. Or more precisely, it was the walled park of a Persian ruler or noble, observed more than two thousand years ago by a young Greek named Xenophon, who was serving as a soldier in Persia (modern-day Iran). After Cyrus, Xenophon's leader, was killed in the battle of Cunaxa in 401 B.C., the ten thousand Greek troops had to fight their way through hostile Persian territory to get home. Xenophon made it back and lived to tell about it. His telling, called *Anabasis,* established his reputation as one of the greatest historians of all time. And in *Anabasis* he used the Persian term *pairidaeza* to describe the great parks of the Persian rulers. *Pairi* means "around," and *daeza* means "mound" or "wall," so *pairidaeza* is a place that is walled around.

The actual origin is more complicated than that, but suffice it to say that Xenophon's history brought the ancestor of our word *paradise* into Greek. From thence, several centuries later, it became the word used for the Garden of Eden in the Septuagint, the Greek translation of the Hebrew Bible. So the great parks of the Persian kings became the great garden of God, the earthly paradise. Of course, the first humans in that park were expelled and the place shut down after they violated a park regulation against eating the fruit of a certain tree.

From Greek to Latin to French to English, our language got its first paradise of this sort in about the year 1175. Since then, English speakers have liberally applied the term to all sorts of real and imagined places of happiness. Nowadays it is often a name for a gambling casino, symbolized by a pair of dice.

Persian is an Indo-European language belonging to the Indo-Iranian branch. Modern Persian is known as Farsi and is spoken by more than twenty-five million people in Iran, about half of that country's population. Perhaps a hundred other words have also made the long trek from Persian to English, including *azure* (1325), *spinach* (1530), *jasmine* (1562), *caravan* (1588), *bazaar* (1612), *mummy* (1615), *seersucker* (1722), and *serendipity* (1754).

⌁TURKMENISTAN

Akhalteke *from Turkmen*

In 1935, when Stalin ruled the old Soviet Union, the ancient Akhalteke horses of the Soviet-governed republic of Turkmenistan were threatened with extinction. To prove the worth of keeping them as a separate breed, twenty-eight riders took Akhaltekes from the Turkmen capital of Ashkabad to Moscow, a distance of more than 2,500 miles, in eighty-four days, including three waterless days across the Kara Kum desert. The Akhaltekes proved their worth; the only horses that arrived in bad condition were Anglo-tekes, Akhaltekes that had been crossbred with modern English thoroughbreds.

Horses, however, were not a priority of the Soviet Union. A tractor was said to be worth a hundred horses. Under the Soviets, the size of the Akhalteke herd in Turkmenistan dwindled to about 700. But Akhaltekes once again became the pride of Turkmenistan with the collapse of the U.S.S.R. and the arrival of independence in 1991. The "golden horse" is on the currency and the state emblem. The herd now numbers well over 2,000, and international auctions of Akhaltekes are now a major annual event in the country.

The Akhaltekes are known as "horses that sweat blood." They aren't as big, as strong, or as fast as the Arabian and English horses that are their descendants and that dominate horse breeds in the world today. But they have intelligence and unsurpassed endurance. Like camels, they are not daunted by extreme temperatures and salty water. For thousands of years they have been bred to thrive and move fast on the desert that occupies more than three-quarters of Turkmenistan.

The horse is named for a famous place in Turkmenistan, the Akhal Teke oasis of the Teke Turkmens. It was first bred nearly 2,500 years ago, and it is said that Bucephalus, the horse of Alexander the Great, was an Akhalteke.

Turkmen belongs to the Turkic branch of the Altaic language family. It is spoken by about three and a half million people in Turkmenistan, three-quarters of the population, and by an additional million in Iran. *Akhalteke* is the only word of Turkmen that has been imported into English.

∽PAKISTAN AND IRAN

baluchithere *from Baluchi*

"There is no *there* there," said the writer Gertrude Stein about Oakland, California, her hometown. She wouldn't have said that about Gering, Nebraska, population 7,946, located twenty miles from the Wyoming border on

State Route 71, because there is a '*there* there: the world's only authentic replica of a baluchithere.

And what is a baluchithere? Why, it's the world's largest prehistoric land mammal, a kind of maximum rhinoceros measuring nineteen feet tall and thirty feet long. It's on display in the Wyo-Braska Museum of Natural History at 10th and U Streets in Gering, along with a prehistoric triceratops, hyracodon (another prehistoric rhinoceros), and dinohyus (a prehistoric pig eight feet high and twelve feet long), plus over two hundred specimens of present-day animals from around the world. Hand-painted dioramas show the animals in their native habitats.

How did the baluchithere end up in Gering? Wyo-Braska director Ron Kephart explains that it is a copy of an extinct model baluchithere at the University of Nebraska. That one had to be destroyed because it contained asbestos. Aside from the Wyo-Braska Museum, the only place you can find baluchitheres nowadays is in the role-playing game RuneQuest.

The baluchithere flourished twenty-five million years ago on the other side of the world from Nebraska, in the region known as Baluchistan, where the Baluchi language (or Balochi, the official spelling) is spoken today in three variants by about five million people. This includes parts of present-day Pakistan, Iran, and Afghanistan; nearly four million of the Baluchi are in Pakistan. In 1913 an English naturalist named the animal *baluchitherium* in recognition of the place where its bones were found.

Baluchi is a member of our Indo-European language family, in the Indo-Iranian branch, a close relative of Farsi or Persian. No other words of Baluchi have made their way into English, in Nebraska or anywhere else.

∾PAKISTAN

dhandh *from Sindhi*

Is it a lake or a swamp? That's the advantage of calling it a *dhandh:* you don't have to make up your mind. In the Sind province of Pakistan, *dhandh* means something that is a lake or pond in one season but less in another. Back in 1851, the famous English explorer and translator Sir Richard F. Burton, in a book about Sindh, discussed channels that "carry off the surplus water, feeding and refilling the lakes and dandhs, whose moisture has evaporated during the cold season." A British magazine in 1928 extended the definition: "Any swamp or overflow water or tank or jhil in Sind is a dhand." (A *tank*, in Pakistan and India, is a pond, natural or artificial. A *jhil* is a large pool or lake formed by heavy rains.)

We could apply the word to our own disappearing lakes. Maybe even the Great Salt Lake, which becomes pretty shallow at times, could be characterized as a dhandh.

But it isn't. The most recent dictionary evidence for *dhandh* is dated 1928 and still confined to watery places in Sind. But despite these limitations, *dhandh* deserves a stop on our tour because it is apparently the only word of the Sindhi language that found its way into English. And Sindhi is one of the world's major languages, at least in number of speakers. Of some six thousand languages the world over, Sindhi is fiftieth. Nearly twenty million people speak Sindhi, seventeen million of them in Pakistan and another two and a half million in India. It is a member of the Indo-Iranian branch of our Indo-European language family.

∼PAKISTAN

polo *from Balti*

It's the sport of kings—and of horses, bicycles, elephants, and Ralph Lauren. For perhaps two thousand years it has been played in Asia, as both recreation and training for cavalry. Six hundred years ago, Tamerlane, the Mongol conqueror, had his own polo field, still visible today in his capital city of Samarkand in present-day Uzbekistan.

The U.S. Polo Organization says polo may be the oldest of team sports. It certainly is one of the most demanding, because each of the four humans on a team has

charge of a thousand-pound horse trained to charge at thirty-five miles an hour, then stop on a dime. A polo match is divided into six "chukkers" (a Hindi word meaning circle or turn) of seven minutes each, and a chukker is so exhausting for the horses that they cannot play two in a row. In championship polo, each human will have a different mount for each chukker.

If you're not near the stables, you can always play polo in the water, or on a bicycle. Bicycle polo was supposedly invented in Ireland in 1891, and like the original form of polo it is now played worldwide. It is not only an inexpensive alternative to playing with horses but also good practice for the equestrian game; the Indian Army polo team includes bicycle polo in its weekly training schedule.

Those who want something more substantial can join the World Elephant Polo Association at Tiger Tops Jungle Lodge in Meghauly, Nepal, where a championship has been held every year or so since 1982. The playing field is an enormous 140 by 70 meters, with only three players on each side and two chukkers of ten minutes each. The nature of the beast requires special rules, including these: "No elephants may lie down in front of the goal mouth. An elephant may not pick up the ball in its trunk during play. Sugar cane or rice balls packed with vitamins (molasses and rock salt) shall be given to the elephants at the end of each match and a cold beer, or soft drink, to the elephant drivers and not vice versa."

Polo was known all over Asia long ago, but the word came to English back in 1842 from the Balti language, spoken today by nearly 300,000 people in Pakistan. Balti is a Sino-Tibetan language closely related to Tibetan. No other words of Balti are in common use in English.

∼PAKISTAN AND INDIA

cheese *from Urdu*

You might expect the big cheese to come from Wisconsin. Or, viewed historically, it might be considered a nickname for the twelve-hundred pound "mammoth cheese" presented to President Thomas Jefferson on New Year's Day 1802 by the Republican farmers of Cheshire, Massachusetts. But in fact it seems to have come from the other side of the world, from the Urdu language of Pakistan.

That's because this is not the same cheese as the milk product that serves as a topping for pizza, the main ingredient of fondue, or headgear for fans of the Green Bay Packers football team. It's a *cheese* that means "thing" in Urdu and has been imported into English spoken in the Indian subcontinent with the meaning "thing" or "the real thing." Salman Rushdie, in his 1995 novel *The Moor's Last Sigh,* uses *cheese* with that meaning.

English has had this special meaning of *cheese* since at least 1818. "You look like a Prince in it," says a character in William Makepeace Thackeray's *Codlingsby* (1850). "It *is* the cheese," replies the other. In the twentieth century this became the *main cheese* (1903), the *real cheese* (1914), even the *head cheese* (1914); and then, from as early as 1914, the *big cheese,* which is the current favorite. In his famous 1914 short story "Haircut," Ring Lardner has one character saying, "They was one big innin' every day and Parker was the big cheese in it." At the end of the twentieth century, the term was well established. You could find a site on the Internet proclaiming, "Yes, this year, 1998, we are going to see some manifestation of THE Antichrist, the big cheese himself."

Urdu, a member of the Indo-Iranian branch of the Indo-European language family, is the national language of Pakistan, where it is spoken by more than ten million people, and it has nearly fifty million additional speakers in India. It is a Muslim language closely related to the Hindu language Hindi. Because Urdu and Hindi are so similar, it is often difficult to tell which one has contributed a word to English. Other possibilities from Urdu include *nabob* (1612) or *nawab* (1758), an important person; *chador* (1614), the modest robe that conceals Moslem women, and *purdah* (1865), the policy that requires the concealment; *howdah* (1774), a saddle for an elephant, and *khaki* (1857), which needs no introduction.

⌇India

cashmere *from Kashmiri*

It is the name of a valley, of a high-altitude goat that lives in this valley, and of the ultrafine wool that grows under the outer hair of this goat. It is also the name of the principal language spoken by people who live in the valley. English has developed two different spellings that try to approximate its sound in its native language. In English, the place and the language start with a *K*, but the goat and its wool with a *C*.

The cashmere goat now lives in other places too. Today sixty percent of the cashmere wool in the world is produced in China, including Tibet; other major producers are Nepal, Afghanistan, Iraq, Australia, and New Zealand. With the price of cashmere wool nearing $200 a pound, a few growers in the United States have also begun to raise cashmere goats. But the weavers of Kashmir first brought the wool to the attention of the English, so cashmere remains our name for it. It is recorded in English as early as 1822.

To get the cashmere wool from under the goat's outer hair, you can comb it out, gently, during the two times a year when the goat is shedding. Each goat produces less than three ounces of this wool in a year, so it takes three goats to make even a small scarf and thirty or more to make a blanket. Cashmere is said to be the finest and lightest wool in the world, except for the rare shahtoosh wool from the serow goat-antelope of Tibet.

The Kashmiri language belongs to the Dardic branch of the Indo-Iranian branch of our Indo-European family. There are more than four million speakers of Kashmiri in Indian Kashmir. Aside from the name itself, no other Kashmiri words have been imported into today's English.

✎ PAKISTAN AND INDIA

bhangra *from Punjabi*

Where do you go for the annual Bhangra Blowout™, a dance competition celebrating the music of the Punjab region of Pakistan and India? To Washington, D.C., of course, on the campus of George Washington University. And where do Bhangra Blowout champions come from? Texas, of course, at least in the sixth annual competition in 1998; the team from the University of Texas at Austin won the $1,000 first prize.

Where did these American competitors learn about bhangra? Probably from London, where bhangra has been big since the 1980s, or New York, a bhangra scene in the 1990s. Bhangra is so much at home in England and America that its popularity here has revitalized it back in India.

It's not what it used to be. The original bhangra, which goes back at least five hundred years, is folk music and men's dance celebrating the harvest and the new year.

Strong rhythms for the music are provided by two-sided drums called the dholak, tabla, and dhol, all played with hands, and the dhol also with a stick. Those instruments are still the basis of bhangra, but the international version has added many more. Bhangra recently became a sensation in London thanks to a performer who called himself "Apache Indian" and his music "bhangramuffin" because it mixed bhangra with reggae. Since then bhangra has been combined with rock, pop, soul, rap, hip-hop, and ska, among others. The lyrics, though, are still mostly in Punjabi.

And Punjabi is one of the major languages of the world. In its western (Pakistani) and eastern (Indian) versions, it is spoken by about sixty-five million people, forty million in Pakistan and twenty-five million in India. It belongs to the Indo-Aryan branch of our Indo-European language family but has not had as much influence on English as the related Hindi, Urdu, and Sanskrit. Bhangra has been spoken of in English at least since 1965. One other Punjabi word in English is *tope* (1815), the local name for a low dome that sometimes functions as a religious shrine.

∼INDIA

ginger *from Pali*

What's life without ginger? Not very spicy. Consider Ginger Spice, the former Spice Girl who once was "naughty, bossy, totally independent, excellent fun," not to mention the subject of provocative nude photos. After she left the group in 1998 to became plain Geri Haliwell again (and a United Nations "ambassador for good will"), you could find the BBC describing her as "demure." *Allure* magazine admiringly said she "looks like a schoolgirl."

And what would the English language be without the spice of ginger? Fortunately, for the past millennium that

has been only a hypothetical question. You can read about ginger in English medical treatises of about the year 1000. Here's one prescription: Take white gum, aloe, myrrh, ginger, and cumin; grind them together and add honey, as much as needed. Put this on a cloth, fasten it over your stomach, and your weariness will go away. Or, if you really really want a cure for a pain in the thigh, mix a drink of ginger spiced with appletree, thornbush, ash, aspen, thistle, elecampane, bishop's wort, ivy, betony, ribwort, radish, alder, white gum, costmary, nettle, and a couple of other plants which we can't identify today. By the time you find all those, your pain will likely be gone.

Not many cures involved ginger, since it had to be imported from warmer climes. In those days, a pound of ginger would cost you the price of a sheep. Much later, we learned to speak *gingerly* (1519), a word that seems to come from an unrelated French source meaning "delicate" but which took its English shape and spelling from the well-known spice.

Ginger now is grown around the world in tropical and subtropical areas. Its slightly sweet, slightly sharp, slightly citrusy rhizome is packed with nutrients, and ginger is used as a remedy for fever, nausea, arthritis, heart problems, and ulcers.

Like ginger itself, our word for it came from India. We can trace it back from English to French, from French to Latin, and from Latin to Greek, which got it from one of the ancient Indo-Iranian languages of our Indo-European language family, which in turn seems to have obtained it from a non-Indo-European language of the Dravidian family. Of the many languages in this chain, we will allow credit here to Pali, an Indo-Iranian descendant of Sanskrit which is still used in India, Myanmar, and Sri Lanka for Buddhist scriptures but is otherwise no longer spoken.

Also possibly from Pali are the gem *beryl* (1305) and the *palanquin* (1588) for transportation.

∼INDIA

Aryan *from Sanskrit*

Despite the propaganda of Adolf Hitler and the posturing of white supremacist groups in the United States, the true Aryan nation is to be found not in the woods of Idaho but in the words of ancient India.

Aryan comes from Sanskrit, the sacred and carefully preserved language of the Vedas, the oldest scriptures of Hinduism. *Arya*, the Sanskrit word, is not a racial designation but a term of respect, meaning "excellent, worthy, honorable, noble" or "lord, master, friend." Before a person's name it is used like "Sir," as in Aryaputra or Aryakanya.

Sanskrit is of great interest to linguists and historians, because it is the oldest preserved language of the Indo-European family. It is now thought to date back at least six thousand years. A word similar to *Aryan* is found in other Indo-European languages; from it developed Persia's modern name, *Iran*. Following this clue, linguists in the nineteenth century decided that the noble name *Aryan* was probably what the original Indo-Europeans called themselves before they split into different tribes speaking different languages. They also used *Aryan* to designate the branch of Indo-European that we now call Indo-Aryan. In English these usages appear as early as 1839.

In the twentieth century, the Nazis applied the designation *Aryan* to their own "race" far to the north and west of the original Aryans. As the century ended, certain spiritual descendants of the Nazis continued that tradition, calling themselves the Aryan Nations. Their leader, Pastor Richard G. Butler of California, declared that "the true, literal children of the Bible are the twelve tribes of Israel, now scattered throughout the world and now known as the Anglo-Saxon, Germanic, Teutonic, Scandinavian, Celtic peoples of the earth," proclaiming them "the Aryan Race, the true Israel of the Bible." There is just one problem with this: the word *Aryan* never appears in the Bible. And Pastor Butler makes no mention of the Vedas.

No one today speaks Sanskrit as a native language, but many people learn it for religious, historical, or linguistic purposes. A 1961 census of India counted nearly 200,000 speakers of Sanskrit as a second language. Many words of modern Indo-Aryan languages like Hindi and Urdu can be traced back to Sanskrit, so it is the ultimate origin for words like Hindi *guru*, Gujarati *banyan*, and Bengali *jute*.

∼INDIA

guru *from Hindi*

If you want just an ordinary leader or guide, the ordinary words *leader* and *guide* (from Old English and French respectively) will do. But an extraordinary mentor requires a passage to India.

As long ago as the seventeenth century, English travelers to India brought back reports of gurus. In 1613 Samuel Purchas, the most famous travel writer of his time, first mentioned them in English: "They have others which they call Gurupi, learned Priests." He also tells of "A famous Prophet of the Ethnikes, named Goru."

In the Hindu and Buddhist religions, the guru is not merely a priest, nor merely a teacher, but a combination of the two. The relationship of guru to disciple is more intense and all-encompassing than that of teacher to student, more educational than that of priest to parishoner. A guru provides not just instruction but "guidance, protection, and grace." Until *guru* came into our language, we had no word for that most intense of leaders and teachers.

And it was not until 1940 that *guru* was exported from India to use in an English context. H. G. Wells wrote then,

"I ask you, Stella, as your teacher, as your Guru, so to speak, not to say a word more about it," and in 1949 Arthur Koestler wrote, "My self-confidence as a Guru had gone."

Nowadays gurus and would-be gurus are plentiful in the English-speaking world. There are, for example, hardware gurus, magic gurus, game gurus, fantasy football gurus, and of course Internet gurus. For Yellowstone National Park, you can find a geyser guru.

Hindi is the official language of India, spoken by about one-third of the population of nearly a billion. Like many other languages of India, it belongs to our Indo-European language family. Thanks to British trade relations with India and then nearly two centuries of British rule, several hundred Hindi words have come into the English language, including familiar ones like *bungalow* (1676) and *veranda* (1711), *jungle* (1776) and *juggernaut* (1841), *loot* (1788) and *thug* (1810), *shampoo* (1762) and *pajamas* (1800).

⌒INDIA

mongoose *from Marathi*

It's not a goose but a small meat-eating mammal, something like a weasel or ferret, about a foot long with a tail of equal length. Since it's not a goose, its plural is not *mongeese* but *mongooses*. It's native to southern Asia and Africa.

You won't have any mice if you have a pet mongoose. But then you might not have any kittens or puppies either. Mongooses are so effective in getting rid of small mammals that they are household pets in India. They are banned from import into the United States because they would destroy too many of our native creatures.

From a mongoose you can learn how to catch a snake. First, get its attention and dare it to strike. Second, jump out of the way. Third, repeat steps one and two till the snake is worn out. Then grab the snake's head in your mouth, crush it, and enjoy your meal at leisure. During steps one, two, and three you do have to watch out, because if a poisonous snake bites you while you're taunting it, you're dead. But if you're a mongoose, once the snake is dead you can eat it, venom and all, without the slightest indigestion.

In number of speakers, Marathi is one of the world's major languages, spoken by about sixty-five million people in western India. It belongs to the Indo-Iranian branch of our Indo-European language family. *Mongoose,* a word Marathi obtained from a non-Indo-European Dravidian source, showed up in English, in a book about India, as early as 1698. From Marathi we also have *carambola* (1598), an evergreen tree and its star-shaped fruit, and *bummalo* (1673), also known as *Bombay duck* (1860), not a duck but a kind of fish.

⁓INDIA

vindaloo *from Konkani*

You want hot? Vindaloo is for you. Speakers of English have known about this hot curry dish at least since 1888, when W. H. Dawe explained it in *The Wife's Help to Indian Cookery,* published in London: "Vindaloo or Bindaloo—A Portuguese Karhi. . . .The best Vindaloo is prepared in mustard-oil. . . . Beef and pork, or duck can be made into this excellent curry."

The basic component of a vindaloo is the vindaloo paste, often made separately ahead of time. This paste is a mixture of hot spices and vinegar, cooked in oil over low heat for a few minutes. One recipe calls for cayenne, cumin, turmeric, ground coriander, black pepper, hot mustard powder, ground ginger, and cinnamon. You can make a vindaloo by adding this paste to any meat or vegetable dish, such as mutton, lamb, chicken, prawns, or peas pulao. Or how about Goanese Fiery Duck Curry in Vindaloo Sauce?

In contemporary English, vindaloo can mean more than food. A hot young Japanese politician, Ms. Makiko Tanaka, was described by an Australian newspaper as "all vindaloo." And for the World Cup soccer tournament of 1998, a British group calling itself "Fat Les" supported their team with a hit song: "Vin-da-loo! Vin-da-loo! And we all like vin-da-loo! We're gonna score one more than you!" Alex James, one of the singers, declared that it was "a post-modern tribute to multiculturalism."

As Dawe stated in 1888, vindaloo is actually Portuguese in origin, though it comes from the Indian subcontinent. The name too is ultimately Portuguese, from the phrase *vinho de alho* or "wine of garlic." Portuguese sailors brought their garlic-flavored vinegar stew to Goa, which from 1510 to 1961 was a Portuguese colony on the southwestern coast of India. The Goans spiced up the recipe and the name, making it *vindaloo* in their Konkani language, a member of the Indo-Iranian branch of the Indo-European language family. The English tongue has only *vindaloo* from Konkani.

∼India

banyan *from Gujarati*

"Brahma-shaped at the root, Vishnu-shaped in the middle and Shiva-shaped at the top, we salute you, the king of all trees." So says the ancient Sanskrit verse in regard to the tree called in English *banyan*.

The banyan is a fig tree and a botanical wonder. It starts its life on another plant, subsisting on sun, air, and rain, and gradually taking over from its host. Once established, it sends down auxiliary roots from its branches, which become auxiliary trunks sending out new branches sending down more auxiliary roots. Spreading in this way, a single banyan tree can eventually cover several acres of ground. It can provide a shaded place for a village meeting or for merchants to show their wares.

And that is how it got its modern English name. In the Gujarati language, *banyan* means not "tree" but "merchant." The Portuguese picked up the word to refer specifically to Hindu merchants and passed it along to the English as early as 1599 with the same meaning. By 1634, English writers began to tell of the *banyan tree*, a tree under which Hindu merchants would conduct their business. Eventually *banyan* came to mean the tree itself.

Even today, we are told, the banyan is considered sacred in India and Pakistan. A recent Indian almanac, for example, says that on Vata Pournima, June 20, women worship the banyan tree. They supposedly use the day to fast and to pray to the tree that they will get the same husband in every rebirth.

Gujarati is spoken by more than forty million people in the Gujarat region of western India. Like Hindi, it is an Indo-European language of the Indic or Indo-Aryan branch. No other words of Gujarati have established themselves in English.

∿INDIA

bandicoot *from Telugu*

Not every animal is a friend to humankind. There is a particularly unappetizing little mammal in the southeast of India known as the "pig-rat" or *pandikokku* in the Telugu language spoken there. In 1789, an English writer called it a "troublesome animal" because of "its offensive smell." In 1813, another complained that "bandicoote rats frequently undermine warehouses and destroy every kind of merchandise."

Meanwhile, another kind of bandicoot was in the making. Australia was beginning to swarm with English explorers and settlers. As early as 1799, someone familiar with the bandicoot of India saw something that looked like it in Australia and gave the latter that name. It has stuck with the Australian creature ever since.

Later observers realized that the Indian bandicoot and the Australian one are quite unrelated. What's more, the Australian bandicoot is cute. Or at least comical. It is the size of a rabbit but with a long nose and long legs. Like a kangaroo or opossum, it is a marsupial and sleeps during the day. Also like a kangaroo or opossum, it has a combing toe on each hind foot for grooming and scratching. Its main foods are roots, bulbs, and insects, but it also occasionally eats lizards or other small animals.

Australian bandicoots come in several species, but there aren't as many as there used to be. The desert bandicoot and the pig-footed bandicoot are extinct. The golden bandicoot and barred bandicoot are rare, and even rabbit bandicoots are not plentiful. According to the *Australian National Dictionary,* since the 1830s the bandicoot has been spoken of "as an emblem of deprivation" in phrases like "miserable as a bandicoot" and "poor as a bandicoot." To *bandicoot,* in Australian English, is to surreptitiously dig potatoes, leaving the tops behind.

The language from which *bandicoot* came, Telugu, is spoken by nearly seventy million people in southeastern India. It is an official language in the state of Andhra Pradesh and has the greatest number of speakers of any of the Dravidian languages. The *pitta* (1840), a bright-colored bird, also has a Telugu name in English.

∼INDIA

dhole *from Kannada*

It's a dog, about the same size as a border collie, but if you think it's an ordinary dog you're barking up the wrong tree. In fact, the dhole doesn't bark at all. It whistles, it screams, it clucks. And it runs wild. Nobody likes it very much, and because its habitat is being destroyed, the World Conservation Union classifies it as a "vulnerable" species.

You wouldn't want a dhole as a pet, and a dhole

wouldn't want you; it needs its own kind. Dholes live in packs of about ten and raise their offspring communally. When they hunt, even more dholes may gather, in packs of as many as thirty or forty. A pack can bring down an animal thirty times the weight of an individual dhole, including deer, boar, and wild ox.

The dhole is a dog of a different color. Its coat varies from gray to yellow but is generally a rusty red. It has rounded ears and hooded amber eyes. Among the family of canids, it belongs to neither the wolf nor the fox branch but to an ancient sub-family of its own, named by biologists *Cuon*, the dhole being *Cuon alpinus*. As *alpinus* implies, dholes thrive in high-altitude forests, but they also roam lowlands from rain forest to open plains. Dholes used to range all over Asia, from Russia to China to India, but they are now found mostly in central and southern India. If you're a tourist in India looking for dholes, you can find them in Kanha National Park in Madhya Pradesh and Corbett National Park near the Himalayas in Uttar Pradesh.

The earliest mention of the dhole in English is a description by Colonel Hamilton Smith in an 1827 book on the animal kingdom: "The Dhole, or Wild Dog of the East Indies, is made like the Dingo, but the hairs of the tail are not bushy. It is of a uniform bright red colour."

Kannada is spoken by forty-four million people, mainly in the state of Karnataka in India, where it is an official language. It belongs to the Tamil branch of the Dravidian language family. Nothing else from Kannada has entered the general vocabulary of English.

∼INDIA

mango *from Malayalam*

As early as 1582 English speakers were tasting mangos, if only in print. Nicholas Lichefield, translating Lopes de Castanheda's account of *The Historie of the Discouerie and*

Conquest of the East Indias, mentioned Mangas as one of the fruits of India. In 1598 another translation, this one of John Huighen van Linschoten's *Discours of Voyages into ye Easte & West Indies*, informed English readers that "The Mangas is inwardly yellowish, but in cutting it is waterish. . . . The season when Mangas are ripe is in Lent."

It would be several centuries, however, before fresh mangos could be imported to English-speaking countries. Until then, the only way they could travel to England and America was as pickles. Prepared Indian style, a mango is not just an ordinary pickle but an experience. *Saroj's Cookbook* from present-day India has a recipe for Spicy Mango Pickle that starts with three mangoes chopped into chunks and adds mustard, fenugreek, aniseed, turmeric powder, a half cup of salt, and a half cup of red chili powder, topped off with a cup of oil. According to Saroj, "This pickle will not go bad for over a year even at room temperature."

Because mangos were first known to Americans in this pickled form, *mango* was sometimes used to mean any pickled fruit, even if not from the mango tree or from India. An American recipe from 1847 noted in the *Dictionary of American Regional English* calls for "melon mangoes" to be stuffed with horseradish, cucumbers, green beans, nasturtiums, onions, mustard seed, peppercorns, cloves, and allspice before being pickled. Muskmelons, cucumbers, and green peppers were all made into "mangoes." Even today green peppers are sometimes called *mangoes* or *mango peppers* in the middle of the United States because they used to be pickled that way.

Malayalam is one of the major languages of India, and indeed one of the most populous in the world. About thirty-five million people in southwestern India speak Malayalam, a Dravidian language. Malayalam has also given us *copra* (dried coconut meat, 1584), *teak* (1698), and *jackfruit* (1830), which remains less known and less appreciated than the mango.

∽INDIA

catamaran *from Tamil*

The English adventurer and pirate William Dampier, traveling around the world in the 1690s in search of business opportunities, once found himself on the southeastern coast of India, in Tamil province on the Bay of Bengal. He

was the first to write in English about a kind of vessel he observed there. It was little more than a raft made of logs. "On the coast of Coromandel," he wrote in 1697, "they call them Catamarans. These are but one Log, or two, sometimes of a sort of light Wood . . . so small, that they carry but one Man, whose legs and breech are always in the Water."

The name came from the Tamil language of India. But the catamaran as we know it came from a different part of the world, the South Pacific. English visitors applied the Tamil name *catamaran* to the swift, stable sail and paddle boats made out of two widely separated logs and used by Polynesian natives to get from one island to another.

It was too good an idea to leave to the Polynesians. In the 1870s an American, Nathanael Herreshoff, began to build catamaran boats to his own design. The speed and stability of these catamarans soon made them popular pleasure craft in America.

In the twentieth century, the catamaran inspired an even more popular sailboat. A Southern California maker of surfboards, Hobie Alter, came up with the idea for "a small catamaran that you could easily take out into the water and sail and take back in." In 1967 he produced the first 250-pound Hobie Cat 14, and two years later the larger and even more successful Hobie 16. That boat remains in production, with more than 100,000 made in the past three decades.

Tamil is spoken by more than sixty million people in southern India. It is the source of *pariah,* first recorded in English in 1613, more emphatic than its synonym *outcast.* About a dozen other Tamil words have found their way into English, including *cheroot* (1679), *curry* (1681), the soup *mulligatawny* (1784), and the perfume *patchouli* (1845).

⌁Sri Lanka

anaconda *from Sinhala*

Boa o boa! You wouldn't want to exchange hugs with an anaconda. Your lifespan would be constricted—not to mention your ribcage. That's how an anaconda prepares you for dinner; it sinks its teeth into you, then wraps itself around your chest so tightly you can't inhale to shout "Down, boa."

It's the terror of the Amazon, or at least of the Amazon as depicted in the 1997 movie *Anaconda,* where special-effects imitation anacondas writhe and gobble up the bad guys and some of the good. South America is its only native habitat. But it has a name from the other side of the world, from the Sinhala language of Sri Lanka, formerly Ceylon. How come?

The *Oxford English Dictionary* provides us with a reasonable explanation, namely, that it was a mistake. At first, the name from Ceylon was properly applied to a snake from Ceylon. In 1693, in a list of snakes from India in the Leyden (Holland) Museum, the Englishman John Ray wrote of "anacandaia of the Ceylonese, i.e. he that crushes the limbs of the buffaloes and yoke beasts." And for more than a hundred years afterwards, in English eyes, the anaconda was indeed a resident of Ceylon. But nineteenth-century experts unaccountably began using the same name for the snake residing in the Amazon basin. An 1849 British Museum Catalogue of Snakes lists "The Ancondo, *Eunectes murimus* . . . Brazil . . . Tropical America."

There are indeed constrictor snakes in Sri Lanka. Schoolchildren in a remote part of the country even found a double-headed one in 1997. Since the nineteenth century, however, the constrictors of Sri Lanka and elsewhere in Asia have been called *pythons*, a name the ancient Greeks used for a mythical monster.

Sinhala is the national language of Sri Lanka, spoken by more than thirteen million people there. Like English, it is a member of the far-flung Indo-European language family; Sinhala belongs to the Indo-Aryan branch along with Hindi, Urdu, and Romani. One other word from Sinhala that is known in English is *ambarella*, not a special kind of umbrella but a tropical tree with an egg-shaped yellow fruit also called the Otaheita apple.

∼NEPAL

tahr *from Nepali*

Halfway around the world from England and America is the habitat of an animal halfway between a goat and a sheep. Actually, it has several different species and habitats, but the animals all belong to the the same genus. That's *Hemitragus* for the naturalists and *tahr* for the rest of us.

There's an Arabian tahr, *Hemitragus jayakari;* a Nilgiri tahr, *Hemitragus hylocrius*, named after a region in southern India; and the Himalayan tahr, *Hemitragus jemlahicus*, that comes from the Himalayas, where we get the name *tahr*. Tahrs now also flourish in other parts of the world. On the central coast of California, Himalayan tahrs roam the hills of the Hearst Ranch. In New Mexico, they have been seen west of Albuquerque in the vicinity of Mount Taylor, perhaps escapees from a wild animal park.

Down in New Zealand, Himalayan tahrs have become pests, so numerous that they are crowding out other wildlife. You can help reduce the population by hiring a guide to put you on the track of a solitary trophy bull. If you get one, you pay a trophy fee of NZ $1,000. You'll also have to pay for a helicopter to get you into the mountains and back, at NZ $1,050 an hour.

The two other kinds of tahr are much scarcer than the Himalayan. There are said to be only about 2,000 Nilgiri tahrs left.

Lifelong companionship isn't the custom for tahrs. Grownup males will join the herd of women and children for a few months each year to help make tahr babies, then go off to live by themselves for the rest of the year.

Since 1835 English has had the word *tahr*. It comes from Nepali, the national language of Nepal, spoken by ten million people there and by six million more in India. Nepali is a member of the Indo-Aryan branch of our Indo-European language family. A well-known word of obscure origin that may also have come from Nepali is *panda*, another word that made its English appearance in 1835.

⚬INDIA AND BHUTAN

serow *from Lepcha*

From the foothills of the Himalayas to a sanctuary in Japan, the serow has leaped into the English language. In the Himalayas this mountain goat innocently masqueraded as a yeti; on the island of Formosa it leaps twenty feet at a bound, and in Japan it's endangering another species.

In 1960, Everest summiteer Sir Edmund Hillary led a Himalayan expedition to look for the yeti, the larger-than-human "abominable snowman." His quest led him to a Tibetan monastery that displayed a rounded skin described as a "yeti scalp." But a Dutch zoologist, asked to examine the find, was reminded of something else: the serow. Comparing the skin with that of a specimen serow in Brussels, the zoologist concluded that the "scalp" was in fact a hat made of stretched serow skin. Its origin had probably been forgotten and then imagined to be the scalp of a yeti.

On Taiwan, the island formerly known as Formosa, nobody mistakes the serow for a yeti. The Formosan serow is a natural wonder in its own right, a goat that likes living in trees and easily jumps twenty feet from tree to tree. "No other animal anywhere can match their agility," says one authority. They are easy to track, however, because they make a point of marking their territory with their urine. They eat grass and plants, enjoying the leaves of cypress, fir, hemlock, and spruce.

As for the Japanese serow, not only is it an endangered species, so are baby trees in the serow's protected habitat. The Japanese version of this animal has been designated a national natural monument. In the Wakayama Experimental Forest of Hokkaido University, fences had to be put up around newly planted cypress trees to keep Japanese serow from damaging them. Cheesecloth over the fences hid the view so the serow would not try to break through.

Though the serow is found throughout eastern Asia, its name probably comes from the Lepcha language of the Sino-Tibetan language family, spoken by the Lepcha people of India and Bhutan. There are about 36,000 Lepchas in India, 24,000 in Bhutan. The name *serow* is attested in English as early as 1847 in the *Journal of the Asiatic Society of Bengal.* No other words of Lepcha are common to English.

∼ BANGLADESH

jute *from Bengali*

Only three languages in the world are spoken by more people than Bengali. And Bengali-speaking Bangladesh leads the world in exporting jute, our most important import from that language.

Jute entered English in the eighteenth century when English trade began in earnest with India and Bengal. The log of the English ship *Wake* notes at 8 A.M. on September, 22, 1746: "Sent on shore 60 Bales of Gunney belonging to the Company with all the Jute Rope . . . 20 Ropes in all, 116 Bundles."

Jute is a natural fiber, made from the bark of a tree also known as *jute* that grows especially in the Brahmaputra River valley of present-day Bangladesh. The "gilden fiber" makes not only ropes, yarn, and twine but also mats, rugs, bags, shoes, and clothes. As it became known and widely traded, jute displaced flax as the chief plant fiber of the English-speaking world. Flax mills in Dundee, Scotland, for example, converted to jute in the nineteenth century.

With nearly two hundred million speakers, Bengali is the fourth most populous language in the world, behind only Chinese, English, and Spanish, and ahead of Russian, Japanese, German, French, Arabic, and all others. It is an Indo-European language belonging to the Indo-Iranian and Indic branches. Other English words from Bengali include *chaulmoogra* (a tree, 1815) and *gavial* (a crocodile, 1825). The word *bungalow* (1676) comes from the name *Bengali* but is actually a Hindi word meaning "of Bengal."

⌇TIBET

yeti *from Tibetan*

In 1953 England's Sir Edmund Hillary made history by leading an expedition that took him, along with Tenzing Norgay of Nepal, to the top of Mount Everest. On the way up he noticed giant footprints in the snow that were said to belong to an apelike creature called a yeti. Curious about this elusive animal, Hillary returned to Tibet in 1960 and tried to make natural history by leading an expedition in search of the yeti. The second expedition failed as completely as the first had succeeded. Not only did he not see an actual yeti, alive or dead, but even the relics shown him proved to be something else. A shaggy fur hide came from a Tibetan blue bear; a supposed scalp of a yeti came from a serow. And it was noticed that footprints in the snow, over time, tend to grow much larger than the original foot that made them, thus accounting for the "yeti tracks" he had seen. Hillary returned an unbeliever.

Other observers are said to have been more fortunate. In 1938 a certain Captain d'Auvergue, curator of the Victoria Memorial in Calcutta, said that during a trek alone in the Himalayas he was rescued from death by a kind yeti nine feet tall. And in 1974 a Sherpa girl told police that an apelike creature broke the necks of two of her yaks and tried to drag her off before she started screaming.

Whatever the truth, you can definitely find a *yeti* in the Tibetan language. In Tibetan, *yah* means rock and *ti* means animal, so a yeti can be called an animal of the rocks. Alternatively, the first syllable of yeti may be a version of *mi,* the word for person. Another name for the creature is *metoh-kangmi,* which has been roughly translated as "abominable snowman."

A little more than a million people speak the Tibetan language, which belongs to the Sino-Tibetan language family, along with Chinese. For most of its history, Tibet remained a hidden realm, high above and far beyond the reach even of the expanding English language, and disinclined to spread its language to the rest of the world. Since 1951, Tibet has been a remote province of China. Despite this isolation, a few words of Tibetan have immigrated into English, mostly designating distinctive animals of the Himalayas. These include *goa* (1846), a gazelle or antelope; *kiang* (1869), a red and white wild ass; *Lhasa apso* (1935), a breed of dog; and of course the *yak* (1795), beloved of animal alphabet books for beginning with the letter Y. There is also the *lama* (1654), the Tibetan Buddhist monk.

∽MYANMAR

U *from Burmese*

How are U? No, that's not what you'd say in Burmese, even though *U* is a polite word to say when you're addressing a man by name. You use it when addressing a social superior. Someone who is your equal would be *Ko*, and a subordinate would be *Maung*. For a woman, the idea of politeness is the same but the words are different. *Daw* is the polite prefix for the name of a woman who is your social superior, *Ma* for an equal or subordinate.

All well and good, but what does this have to do with English? Well, one of these honorifics was introduced to the whole world in 1961, when U Thant, an educator and head of the Burmese delegation to the United Nations, was appointed U.N. Secretary General after the death of Dag Hammarskjöld of Sweden in an airplane crash. Thant went on to serve two full terms as Secretary General, retiring in 1971. His name was always given simply as "U Thant," and the world was given to understand that "U" meant something like "the honorable Mr."

In referring to Burmese gentlemen, U has been used in English since at least 1930. It is still used today, as in a 1998 news story referring to a member of the executive committee of the opposition National League for Democracy in Myanmar, U Hla Pe.

Burmese belongs to the Tibeto-Burman branch of the Sino-Tibetan language family. It is the official language of Myanmar, the Burmese word for a country known until 1989 as Burma. About twenty-two million people speak the language. One other Burmese word in English is *padauk* (1839), the name for a tropical tree with reddish wood. There are also names for local animals like *tsine* (1880), a wild ox; *thamin* (1888), a deer; and *tucktoo* (1896), a lizard.

By the way, to ask "How are you?" in Burmese you say "Nay kong ye' lah?" And the reply is "Nay kong bar te'," "I am fine," or "Ma soe ba boo," "Not too bad."

⌇THAILAND

bong *from Thai*

As if they did not have satisfaction enough from home-grown hallucinogenics like jimsonweed (named for Jamestown, Virginia) and cannabis, speakers of English have turned for inspiration to Asia. In the nineteenth century the English fought wars to keep China open to opium. In the twentieth, marijuana users enhanced their experience with a device from Thailand known as the *bong*.

For those who missed the psychedelic trips of the 1960s and 1970s and who just say No nowadays, *bong* may need explanation. It is a water pipe designed to cool the smoke from a substance (like marijuana) burned in a bowl by routing the stem through a vertical tube or bottle partly filled with water or other liquid. The word is a recent import to English, noted in dictionaries only as far back as 1971.

Bong comes from Thai, the most widely spoken of the languages in the Tai-Kadai language family. It has about twenty-five million speakers in Thailand, where it is the national language. One other word from the Thai or Siamese language is the word *Siamese* itself. It designates a blue-eyed breed of cat from Thailand, mentioned in English as early as 1871, and a bright-colored tropical fish known as a *Siamese fighter*, mentioned as early as 1929. But the most famous phrase using this name is *Siamese twins* (1829). The first Siamese twins were really twins from Siam (now Thailand): Chang and Eng, who lived from 1811 to 1872 and traveled for many years as prime exhibits in P. T. Barnum's circus. Now that term is used for any twins who are born with their bodies joined.

∼CAMBODIA

sampot *from Khmer*

You can see the importance of the sampot, the Cambodian national garment, by looking at ancient Cambodian sculptures. Consider, for example, the thousand-year-old Khmer statue of the god Vishnu, six feet tall in polished sandstone and now at the Norton Simon Museum in Pasadena, California. The bare upper body is plain; the elaborate detail and beauty of the statue are in the crown and the sampot around the figure's thighs. A sampot is just a rectangular piece of cloth wrapped into a skirt, but it is a focus of traditional Cambodian culture.

Until the French made Cambodia a colony in the nineteenth century, the sampot was the chief national garment for both men and women. Then, following European custom, it began to be seen as a women's dress, and men began to wear pants or shorts except on traditional ceremonial occasions. During the brutal Khmer Rouge regime of the late 1970s, in a campaign to wipe out education and traditional culture altogether, the sampot was banned, and men and women alike were required to wear black jackets and pants. Today, with the Khmer Rouge mercifully gone, the sampot is back in fashion, although it is now considered a woman's garment.

Khmer, a member of the Austro-Asiatic language family, is the national language of Cambodia. It is spoken by about six million people there, 90 percent of the population. There are another 700,000 speakers of Khmer in Vietnam, 100,000 in Thailand, and 50,000 in the United States.

Speakers of English have marveled at sampots at least since 1931, when an article in the journal *Notes & Queries* commented: "The women of Cambodia make sampots. These are the long and wide sashes of silk of many colours which they bind around their waists." One other Khmer word in English is *kouprey* (1937), the name of a wild ox native to Cambodia.

ᕦ Vietnam

Tet *from Vietnamese*

Since 1885, speakers of English have known about the biggest annual celebration in Vietnam. In a book called *France and Tongking: A Narrative of the Campaign of 1884*, published in London that year, Sir James George Scott wrote: "The especial great season for every one, rich and poor, is the new year, the Tet."

Tet starts in January or February at the time of the full moon before spring planting. Officially it lasts three days, but since advance preparations are important, it often requires a week or more away from everyday activities like school and work. Houses are cleaned (so that the Kitchen God can give an approving report to the Jade Emperor) and decorated with gold banners, red ribbons, and colored lights. Food and wine are placed at the family altar to please the spirits of dead ancestors. The community celebration can include a parade with elaborate floats, and fireworks, song and dance.

It is said that the first visitor on the first day of Tet brings luck, good or bad, so many people take care to invite the right person to make that visit. Whatever happens that first day is said to set the pattern for the whole year.

With close to a million ethnic Vietnamese now living in the United States, Tet is now a more familiar celebration in this country as well.

We also have a grimmer reason to speak of Tet. Just as the first mention of Tet in English was related to the French military conquest of Vietnam in 1884, so the word gained military prominence in English in January 1968 when the Viet Cong and North Vietnamese attacked South Vietnamese cities in what was called the "Tet Offensive." They didn't succeed in overwhelming the South Vietnamese and U.S. forces, nor did they cause a "general uprising" of the southern population, but the Tet Offensive did turn the tide of the war and was a major step toward the ultimate North Vietnamese triumph.

Vietnamese is a Mon-Khmer language of the Austro-Asiatic language family. It has sixty-five million speakers in Vietnam, more than 85 percent of the population, and nearly a million more speakers each in Cambodia and the United States, the final resort of many refugees from the Vietnam War. Although the United States was deeply involved in Vietnam in the 1960s and 1970s, no other words of Vietnamese have managed to become part of the general vocabulary of English.

∼CHINA

gung ho *from Chinese*

It was the best of translations; it was the worst of translations. It showed American admiration for the Chinese; it showed American misunderstanding of them. In any case, it was adopted into English with gung-ho enthusiasm.

We know exactly who was responsible for our *gung ho:* Lt. Col. Evans Carlson of the U.S. Marines. And we know when he first used it in English: during World War II, early in 1942, in China, to the troops of his newly formed Second Raider Battalion, which fought against the Japanese invaders alongside the Chinese 8th Route Army. Carlson told *Life* magazine in 1943: "I was trying to build up the same sort of working spirit I had seen in China where all the soldiers dedicated themselves to one idea and worked together to put that idea over. I told the boys about it again and again. I told them of the motto of the Chinese Co-operatives, *Gung Ho.* It means Work Together—Work in Harmony."

Well, it doesn't quite mean that. *Gung Ho* is simply the third and fifth syllables of *Chung-Guo Gung-Yeh Ho-Tso She,* the name of the Chinese Industrial Cooperatives Association. *Gung* and *Ho* were used together as an abbreviation of the name and on signs designating the cooperative. It is true, however, that *gung* means "worker" or "work," and *ho* means "to agree," "joined," or "the whole," although the two together do not make a sentence or phrase in Chinese. As the exploits of Carlson's raiders became known, they filled America with gung ho enthusiasm. The term became an enduring part of the English vocabulary.

Chinese is the Number 1 language of the world, with nearly a billion speakers of its various dialects. It belongs to the Sino-Tibetan language family, to which Tibetan and Burmese also belong. *Gung ho* is from the dominant Mandarin dialect, spoken by more than seven hundred million people. English has imported about a hundred Chinese words, everything from *ginseng* (1654) and *tea* (1655) to *yin* and *yang* (1671), *kowtow* (1804) and (in a literal translation) *brainwashing* (1950). The word *china* itself, which derives from the name of the Chinese *Qin* dynasty, has been used in English since 1579 to mean fine porcelain.

∼CHINA

yen *from Cantonese Chinese*

If you have a yen, you may have a unit of Japanese currency equivalent to a hundred sen and worth about one 130th of a dollar. Or you may just have a craving, in which case your word is not Japanese at all, but Chinese of the Cantonese variety.

Nowadays in English our yens are mild, compared to desires and cravings, and they are generally directed to benevolent ends; but when we first got the word, in 1876, a yen was specifically a desire for opium. A book on China published that year explained that a person will "ask if an opium-smoker has the *yin* or not, meaning thereby, has he gradually increased his doses of opium until he has established a craving for the drug." But English speakers soon began to yen more widely, and today in English you can have a yen for anything, from gambling to horticulture, from exercise to classical music. In 1961, for example, *Time* magazine even discussed "the yen of Christian churchmen for achieving church unity."

In numbers of speakers, Cantonese or Yue is one of the second-rank dialects of Chinese, having a mere fifty million or so. That compares with more than seven hundred million for Mandarin, the dominant dialect. But Cantonese is the form of Chinese spoken in Hong Kong, where it has interacted with speakers of English for more than 150 years; Cantonese is also the variety spoken by the majority of Chinese immigrants to the United States, so it has had a disproportionate influence on English.

Thus it is, also, that Chinese cooking in America has a Cantonese accent with words like *kumquat* (1699), *chop suey* (1888), *chow mein* (1903), *won ton* (1934), *bok choy* (1938), *subgum* (1938), *dim sum* (1948), and *wok* (1952). Other English words from Cantonese include *sampan* (boat, 1620), *typhoon* (1771), *tong* (secret society, 1883), *cheongsam* (dress with slit skirt, 1952), and *shar-pei* (dog, 1975).

∾KOREA

tae kwon do *from Korean*

The XXVII Olympiad in Sydney, Australia, in the year 2000, marks the inauguration of a new Olympic sport: *tae kwon do*. That is the ultimate recognition for a martial art that did not even exist fifty years earlier.

In Korean, *tae* is to kick, jump, or strike with the foot; *kwon* is fist, or to strike with the hand; *do* is the way or the art. Together they became *tae kwon do*, the art of kicking and punching, using bare feet and hands as weapons.

The art derives from Japanese karate, which was a strong influence during the Japanese occupation of Korea

from 1910 to 1945. After independence from Japan, South Koreans developed in the 1950s a variety of karate that emphasized high spinning kicks. In 1957 they agreed to call it *tae kwon do*, echoing the name of a martial art called *taek kyon* that seems to have been practiced in Korea two thousand years earlier. Interest became international in 1961, when the general who had required tae kwon do for the South Korean military and police came to the United States. By 1963, there was an International Taekwondo Federation and by 1973 a World Taekwondo Federation. In 1988 tae kwon do was an Olympic demonstration sport, and it was granted full status at the Olympics for 2000.

Korean is one branch of the Korean-Japanese-Okinawan language family, although it is so distantly related to Japanese and Okinawan that some experts consider Korean an entirely separate language. It is spoken by about forty-six million in South Korea and twenty-four million in North Korea, as well as more than two million elsewhere in the world. From Korean English has also imported *kimchi* (1898), a seasoned vegetable pickle that is the Korean national dish, and *hangul* (1946), the name for the style of alphabet in which the Korean language is written.

⁓ JAPAN

bonsai *from Japanese*

In recent history, war and peace have brought Japanese and English together. Until the middle of the nineteenth century, Japan had closed itself off from conversation with  other parts of the world, but after the American Matthew Perry opened the country to foreign trade in 1854, the Japanese began to take an intense interest in learning from speakers of languages like English. By 1900 Japan was a world power, imitating the European powers in establishing its own empire. The climax and collapse of Japanese imperialism came in World War II. Afterwards, occupying Americans took charge in rebuilding a peaceful, democratic Japan. The two countries have kept close ties ever since, exchanging many words along the way.

One of these words is *bonsai,* the art of making much of little, noted in English as early as 1900 but popularized after the war. The word means "planted in a tray." The art of bonsai involves choosing a seedling tree or other plant that would naturally grow large, planting it in a container, and cultivating it to develop its full natural shape and beauty in miniature. "The difference between bonsai and ordinary potted plants," says a Japanese authority, "is that the latter are usually plant species in which the flowers or leaves are the focus of appreciation, while with the former, the beauty of the entire tree and its harmony with the container in which is planted is the matter of esthetic concern." Sometimes the container will create a whole harmonious landscape of trees, shrubs, earth, and rocks.

Bonsai is now an international art. The American Bonsai Society was founded in 1967, and many American cities have bonsai clubs. Bonsai growers sometimes also take an interest in the related arts of *suiseki* or viewing stones and *ikebana* or flower arrangement.

The hundred or so words of Japanese that have entered English express a wide variety of customs and attitudes. We have learned more than a *skosh* (1959) of Japanese: to eat *sushi* (1893) and plant *kudzu* (1876), write *haiku* (1902) and sing *karaoke* (1982), wrestle with a *sumo* (1880), become *tycoons* (1857) and *honchos* (1947), wear *zori* (1823), sleep on *futons* (1876), and say *sayonara* (1875). There is the old warrior spirit in *samurai* (1727) and a newer one in *kamikaze* (1945).

Thanks to the importance of Japan in the world's economy, Japanese today is one of the world's leading languages. Well over a hundred million people speak it. Although its writing system comes from Chinese, Japanese belongs to an entirely separate language family known as Korean-Japanese-Okinawan.

∿Japan

nunchaku *from Okinawan*

How do you arm yourself when you're disarmed? How do you defend yourself when you can't even have a knife around the house? For several hundred years, the people of Okinawa needed to find answers to those questions. It is said that under the Ryukyu Kingdom, which began in the fifteenth century, only soldiers and nobles were allowed to carry weapons. Under Japanese rule, which began in 1609, even iron household tools were supposedly prohibited. Each village was allowed only one knife, which was kept at the town square and lent for short periods to individual households. How could citizens defend against robbers and worse?

Their response, we are told, was to fight barehanded (a skill that developed into today's karate) or make weapons out of household implements. They learned to fight with a staff (*bo*), a sickle (*kama*), even the handle of a millstone (*tonfa*). And then there was the lowly *nunchaku*, two curved sticks tied together as the bit for a horse. The descendant of the original nunchaku, now made of straight rather than curved wood, has become one of the major martial arts weapons. In the 1970s Chinese-American actor Bruce Lee spread its popularity far beyond Japan and east Asia, demonstrating in his action movies the awesome efficacy of nunchaku in the hands of a skilled fighter. The word was used in English as early as 1970.

The nunchaku has advantages over the traditional police baton, not the least that it's folded over and thus easier to carry. In the United States, more than two hundred police departments now use the Orcutt Police Nunchaku system, developed by police sergeant Kevin Orcutt in the 1980s.

Okinawan is spoken by about 900,000 people on Okinawa and the other Ryukyu Islands to the south of Japan. Though Okinawa, now a Japanese possession, has early historical ties to China, its language is closely related to Japanese, not Chinese, and belongs to the Japanese-Okinawan branch of the Korean-Japanese-Okinawan language family. No other Okinawan words are widely used in English.

∼MONGOLIA

mogul *from Mongolian*

The original Mogul was Babur the Lion, otherwise known as Zahir ud-Din Muhammad, who lived from 1483 to 1530. From his kingdom in Afghanistan, he invaded and conquered the northern part of India. The empire he established lasted more than three hundred years. It produced not only great wealth but also great works of art and architecture, most memorably the Taj Mahal, finished in 1648.

The name *Mogul* is simply a version of the name *Mongol* in the Mongolian language. It was used for the empire Babur established because he was of Mongolian ancestry, having both Genghis Khan and Tamerlane as forebears. But the empire was in fact Persian and Muslim rather than Mongolian.

The wealth and splendor of the Mogul empire gave the name *Mogul* a wider meaning in English. The word was used in English as early as 1588 for the ruler of the Indian empire, the "great Mogul." By 1678 it could be used, often humorously, to designate any magnificent ruler, even of a household. The *New York Daily Tribune* could declare in 1877 that "John A. Logan [Civil War general and U.S. Senator] is the Head Center, the Hub, the King Pin, the Main Spring, Mogul, and Mugwump of the final plot," while Mark Twain wrote in 1902 of a railroad station-master being a "great mogul."

Today we have media moguls, net moguls (Internet millionaires), and a computer game called Baseball Mogul, in which you act as both manager and general manager of a team. A famous type of steam locomotive built early in the twentieth century is called a mogul. But the Mongolian *Mogul* is not the bump on a ski run; that kind of *mogul* comes from an unrelated Scandinavian word.

Mongolian is the national language of Mongolia, spoken by more than two million people there. It is an Altaic language. Also from Mongolian in English is *argali* (1779), the name of a large wild sheep with curved horns.

⌒RUSSIA

shaman *from Evenki*

In the morning of June 30, 1908, the most powerful explosion in recorded human history took place in the sky over the Tunguska region of central Siberia. According to eyewitnesses, its cause was the wrath of a shaman.

A shaman is a person with exceptional powers over nature. The Tungus people, as they are known to outsiders, or Evenki, as they call themselves, use *shaman* as both a noun and a verb, and their practice of shamanism has given this word to anthropologists and comparative religionists the world over.

Magankan, the Tunguska shaman, had already demonstrated his powers by catching a bullet shot at him and by stabbing his own chest without leaving a scratch. But his greatest feat was summoning a huge flock of *agdi*, the birds that produce the thunder, for the explosion over the land of a rival Evenki clan. It flattened nearly a thousand square miles of forest and started a fire that burned for weeks, sending ash so high that it circled the Northern Hemisphere, making sunsets bright. Needless to say, it scared away his rivals for good.

This is the story they told some twenty years later to the first scientist to reach the remote, swampy, mosquito-ridden site. Since then, the scientists have given other explanations. The forty-megaton explosion, two thousand times as powerful as the bomb dropped on Hiroshima, is now generally thought to have been caused by a meteorite or comet that exploded in the Earth's dense atmosphere. But there are still Evenki who think differently.

Long before that big bang, English speakers had taken note of shamans. A book published in 1698 explains, "If five or six of the Tonguese families happen to live near one another . . . they maintain betwixt them a Shaman, which signifies as much as Sorcerer or Priest."

The Tungus or Evenki are found over a wide area of both Siberia and northern China, though they are not particularly numerous. There are about 30,000 in Siberia, about one-third of them speaking Evenki as a native language, and another 10,000 in China who speak Evenki. It is an Altaic language. One other Evenki word in English is *pika* (1827), the name of a little round-eared rabbit with a squeaky voice.

∼Russia

parka *from Nenets*

If you want cold, go to Siberia. If you want really cold, go to the treeless tundra in the far north of Siberia and spend a winter herding reindeer with the Nenets. There your only shelter will be a tent covered with reindeer skin. It's a good thing they invented parkas.

Many of the Nenets still enjoy their traditional nomadic life. Their culture centers on reindeer, which provide food, clothing, and shelter, and are their only kind of wealth; a family is rich depending on the number of reindeer in its herd. During the arctic winters, a hooded pullover parka made of reindeer skin is a necessary part of a man's winter clothing. (Nenets women traditionally wear something different: a long overcoat that fastens in the front and has no hood.) "Thanks to the reindeer skin," notes a recent visitor, "the Nenets wearing it can do without washing for months."

The name *parka* comes from the Nenets language, which belongs to the Uralic language family, along with Finnish, Estonian, and Hungarian. No English speakers were around to hear the Nenets speak of parkas, but the Russians did, and they passed the word on to native peoples in Alaska, who in turn gave it to us. The first English use of the word is in William Coxe's 1780 *Account of the Russian Discoveries Between Asia and America:* "The inhabitants of Alaxa, Umnak, Unalaksha . . . wear coats (parki) made of bird skins."

Today there are about 27,000 speakers of Nenets in northern Russia and Siberia. They have not yet given our language any other words.

⌒RUSSIA

kamleika *from Chukchi*

If you can't find a parka for your trip to the far north, try a kamleika. It comes from about as far north as you can get, the Chukchi Peninsula of northeast Siberia, just across the Bering Strait from Alaska. When they went hunting for seals and sea lions, men of the Chukchi traditionally wore the kamleika, an overcoat made of skin or fur and decorated to honor the spirits of the animals they hunted as well as to show off their accomplishments.

Only men wore the kamleika. A woman would dress in a kerker, described as "a kind of one-piece jumpsuit."

The Chukchi are reindeer herdsmen who have not changed their life much to accommodate the outside world. One source notes, "Although those under fifty speak Russian with varying proficiency, nomadic groups resist Russian language and culture. Difficult access." There are about 16,000 of them, and most still speak the Chukchi language. It belongs to a language family called Chukotko-Kamchatkan, which includes the closely related languages of three other small indigenous populations, Alutor, Kerek, and Koryak.

The English language acquired *kamleika* in Alaska in the nineteenth century, by way of Russian fur traders. That is why it has a Siberian name instead of one from the native languages of Alaska. In 1866, a year before the American purchase of Alaska from Russia, an American traveler in Alaska noted in his journal, "Bought a comleka to-day." An 1870 guide to Alaska describes the "Kamláyka" as "A water-proof shirt, made of the intestines of the seal or sea-lion, and used while travelling in their kyaks, or in rainy weather, by the Aleuts and Esquimaux."

The Chukchi word behind our *kamleika* is *kemlilyun*. Not surprisingly, no other words of Chukchi have made their way into English.

OCEANIA

Oceania, the gem of the earth, sparkles in the blue Pacific. If that's over the edge, so is Oceania, by which we mean the islands of the world's biggest ocean. For our purposes, we include Australia, which is either the world's biggest island or the world's smallest continent, as part of Oceania. It's mostly water, this region, which is why it's called Oceania and not Landia. It covers part of what has recently been called the Pacific Rim, but instead of just the rim Oceania includes what's inside.

And what gems English speakers found when they at last reached this region halfway around the world from the homeland of the language! They went for science; they stayed for pleasure—or so we might say with just a little exaggeration in the case of Captain James Cook's eighteenth-century voyages. From Tahiti to Australia, from *tattoo* to *kangaroo*, Cook's first expedition in the *Endeavour* garnered new knowledge, new words, and new notions of how to enjoy life to the fullest. Even his ship contributed to our language, becoming the namesake of an American space shuttle two centuries later.

They went for knowledge; they stayed for conquest and profit, we might also say. And there is the peculiar case of Australia, which once was the designated place of remotest exile for English criminals and then a great contributor to the British commonwealth of language as well as territory.

Our tour of the linguistic innovations of Oceania takes us across vast stretches of water to surprisingly related languages. Leaving behind the cold Chukchi Peninsula of Siberia in farthest mainland Asia, we warm ourselves first in the *boondocks* of the Philippines. In Indonesia we run *amok;* in Singapore we chat, *lah*. Indonesia feeds us with *tempeh* and entertains us with the *muntjac*, a barking deer, while bringing us a cup of *java* under the *ailanthus* tree. The rain forests of Papua New Guinea teach us the perils of *kuru*.

And then comes Australia, mate. Before the English began to settle in, a little more than two hundred years ago, there were hundreds of aboriginal languages in Australia. From the Aborigines who lived closest to the early English outposts came many words to describe the continent's distinctive flora, fauna, natural features, and customs: the pocketed *kangaroo*, the foolish *galah*, and the spooky *bunyip*; the *billabong* to sit beside under the shade of a *coolibah* tree, and to *yabber* about afterwards. There's also a *nugget* from the English language itself, transformed to gold in Australia.

East of Australia, in the South Pacific, we encounter the *kiwi* of New Zealand, wear the *bikini* of the Marshall Islands, observe the *taboos* of Tonga, *tattoos* of Tahiti, and bring to our California culture the *tiki* of the Marquesas Islands. In Samoa we wear the *lavalava*, called elsewhere everything from *pareo* (Tahiti) to *kikepa* (Hawaii). And in Hawaii, a very Pacific part of the USA, we say *aloha*.

Except in Australia, the dominant language family in Oceania is the Austronesian. Its dominant branch is Malayo-Polynesian, which includes the languages of the Philippines and Indonesia in the west and those of Polynesia in the east, from New Zealand to Hawaii. The Australian aboriginal languages are in an independent family by themselves, and Fore of Papua, New Guinea, is unrelated to the other languages we will visit here.

∾PHILIPPINES

boondocks *from Tagalog*

If you're out in the boondocks, linguistically speaking, you're much more distant than the sticks, the backwoods, the hinterland, or the bush. In fact, you're in the Philippines. That's where the boondocks came from, during the American occupation that began with the defeat of Spain in 1898. In Tagalog, the national language of the Philippines, *bondoc* means "mountain," and the term was used first by the occupying U.S. military to mean the Philippine mountains . . . or jungle . . . or remote area of any sort. By 1909 it was already in *Webster's New International Dictionary* with those meanings. But in English it remained largely military slang until the 1960s. The Marine Corps especially made use of *boondocks*. During World War II the Marines began calling their heavy combat boots *boondockers*, and they have worn that name ever since.

About fifteen million people, one-quarter of the population of the Philippines, speak Tagalog natively. It belongs to the Malayo-Polynesian branch of the Austronesian language family. The official language of the Philippines is a version of Tagalog with a more inclusive vocabulary, called Pilipino or Filipino. Pilipino, introduced in the 1970s, was so close to Tagalog that speakers of other Philippine languages protested. In response, in the 1980s the government allowed more non-Tagalog words and changed the name. Filipino's broader scope is indicated by its initial F, which was not in the original Tagalog alphabet but imported from Spanish.

Another English word from Tagalog is *yo-yo*, now the universally accepted name for a toy formerly known in English as a *bandalore* (1824, of unknown origin). Pedro Flores of the Philippines brought the name and the idea for a superior yo-yo (with string looped around the center rather than tied to it) to California in the 1920s. Donald Duncan bought him out, copyrighted the name *yo-yo* in 1932, and made it world famous. Tagalog has also given English some plant and animal names: *abaca* (1818, banana plant and fiber), *ylang-ylang* (1876, tree, perfume), *lauan* (1894, timber), *cogon* (1898, coarse grass), *tamarau* (1898, buffalo), *atemoya* (1914, fruit), and *calamondin* (1928, citrus).

⌇PHILIPPINES

carabao *from Cebuano*

What the ox was to the American pioneer, the carabao is to farmers of the Philippines. Gentle and slow, it is the engine for pulling plows and carts and vehicles for riding, and when its working days are over, it is a store of meat and hide.

The name *carabao* is unique to the Philippines, but the creature itself is not. Elsewhere English speakers call it by the generic name *water buffalo*. This animal is found in parts of Asia, from India eastward. It looks something like our cattle but has horns that curve back to form a crescent. It is a true buffalo, known to scientists as *Bubalus bubalis*, not the shaggy bison of North America.

In the Philippines, the carabao is central to play as well as work. Every May 15, for example, a carabao festival is held in the town of San Isidro. Farmers groom and dress their carabaos, bring them for a blessing to the church, and parade them through town. Although the animals are not particularly noted for their speed, the festival culminates with a carabao race across the fields. At the finish line, the carabao kneel and receive another blessing.

The name *carabao* comes from the Cebuano (or Visayan or Bisayan) language, a close relative of Tagalog, the dominant language of the Philippines. Cebuano apparently got the word from Malay. Like Tagalog, Cebuano is from the Western Malayo-Polynesian branch of the Austronesian language family. It is spoken by some fifteen million people in the Philippines, about one-quarter of the population.

∾MALAYSIA

amok *from Malay*

European travelers sometimes encountered less than friendly people. Among the Malays of southeast Asia, according to an English translation in 1518 of a book by the Portuguese Duarte Barbosa, there are people called "Amuco," who "go out into the streets, and kill as many persons as they meet." Sometimes, it appears, the Amuco were soldiers. Another Portuguese account, translated in 1663, says that "all those which were able to bear arms should make themselves Amoucos, that is to say, men resolved either to dye, or vanquish." Captain Cook, in his account of his voyages in the 1770s, offers that "To run amock is to get drunk with opium . . . to sally forth from the house, kill the person or persons supposed to have injured the Amock, and any other person that attempts to impede his passage."

Although the English first recorded "running amok" as a trait of the Malay temperament, they readily noticed that it could apply to more familiar instances of murderous frenzy. So before the 1600s were over, "run amok" could refer to an English-speaking madman as well as a Malay one. In the nineteenth century, the writer of *The Mind in Lower Animals* identified "running amok" as "a peculiar form of human insanity."

Our century has defined *amok* as a psychological state of unprovoked, extremely destructive behavior followed by amnesia, exhaustion, or even suicide. In the 1980s and 1990s Amok was also a fitting name for a Los Angeles bookstore and press that published a "Sourcebook of the Extremes of Information in Print," including *The Sniper's Handbook* and *The Color Atlas of Oral Cancers.*

The Malay language is spoken by more than seventeen million people in present-day Malaysia. Some sixty words from Malay have become significant additions to the English vocabulary, including foods, plants, animals, and fabrics: *ketchup* (1690), *agar* (1889), *bamboo* (1586), *rattan* (1660), *cockatoo* (1634), *gecko* (1774), *orangutan* (1691, meaning man of the forest), *cootie* (1917), *gingham* (1615), *sarong* 1830, [rice] *paddy* (1623), and *caddy* (1792, a container).

∼Singapore and Malaysia

lah *from Singaporean and Malaysian English*

"Steady lah, life is just a series of experiences." So says the congenial Mr. Lam Kuen Tat George of Singapore on his résumé. If you ride a cab in Singapore, chances are the driver will say "Okay lah?" at the end of a sentence. On Date Trader.net, Cindy of Singapore, a "fun, humorous gal," writes, "Anybody also can, ugly, fat, handsome, pretty, all also can talk to me. 100% reply. don't shy lah." Welcome to Singapore lah!

Or perhaps you're in Malaysia. Here are some words of Malaysian English conversation, according to the girls of Bukit Bintang Girls School, 5 Science 2, Batch of 1996:

> "Wah, so expensive-lah."
> "You know-lah, she's always like that one-lah. Everything also this-lah, that-lah, mine-lah, yours-lah. Aiyah, I don't know-lah!"

It's like, *like*, you know, or *you know*, but with a Singaporean or Malaysian flavor. As one Malaysian writes, "If you are walking the streets of London or sipping coffee at a sidewalk cafe somewhere in Paris, and you hear in plain English, 'So expensive-lah' or 'So hot-lah,' just turn around in the direction where the voice comes from and I guarantee you that ten out of ten, that person who just dotted his or her sentence with a lah is a Malaysian . . . or Singaporean, which is close enough!"

It's not surprising that Malaysian and Singaporean varieties of English are similar, since the city-state of Singapore is next to Malaysia at the tip of the Malay peninsula. The word *lah* was adapted from a southern dialect of Chinese, which is widely spoken in both countries. About one-quarter of the population is literate in English in both countries, although the number of native speakers of English is small: about a quarter of a million or less than 10 percent of the population of Singapore. In that country purists sometimes complain about the "corruption" of the English language in Singapore English or "Singlish," but they enjoy it too much to lay down the lah.

∾INDONESIA

tempeh *from Indonesian*

What happens when you ferment soybeans? No, you don't get soy wine. If you skin soybeans, split them, and cook them thoroughly, add a strain of bacteria known as *Rhizopus oligosporus* after they cool, and then wait a day, you'll get firm little cakes with streaks of white and sometimes black mold. Cut off the black mold, cook, and serve. You can stir fry, steam, or marinate the cakes, and cut them in strips or cubes to mix with sauces or other food. The result tastes and feels something like mushrooms.

It's called *tempeh* by the Indonesians, who may have invented this use for the soybean by accidentally leaving a pot of cooked soybeans sitting for a day. And what an invention! High in protein and fiber, low in saturated fats—an excellent meat substitute not just for vegetarians. Soybeans are the only food containing isoflavones, which are said possibly to reduce the risk of cancer. But soybeans also contain phytates, which prevent the absorption of minerals. Cooking doesn't get rid of the phytates, but the fermentation of tempeh does. And unlike most beans, including soybeans prepared in other ways, tempeh won't disturb anyone's intestines because fermentation gets rid of the oligosaccharides that can produce gas.

One caution, courtesy of *The New Joy of Cooking*. If your tempeh is slimy, smells like ammonia, or has mold in color rather than black-and-white, it's not good for you. Throw it out.

Indonesian is the national language of Indonesia. It is spoken natively by twenty to thirty million people there and used by well over a hundred million more. Belonging to the Western Malayo-Polynesian branch of the Austronesian language family, it is very similar to Malay. Many Malay words have immigrated to English, but *tempeh* is the only well-known Indonesian import.

⌇INDONESIA

muntjac *from Sundanese*

They are deer, but not the kind of deer we're used to. Full-grown muntjacs stand barely two feet high and weigh only about fifty pounds. They have tusks, too, and upper canine teeth. They bark and meow. And they make good pets. Maryann Nash of Mom's Critters in Mantua, Ohio, explains: "Muntjacs have a high-pitched bark and may bark up to an hour or more if they sense a predator or other threat. I have yet to hear mine bark. They also make a 'mewing' sound. My tame male often talks to me that way, especially when he wants something." She also notes that their tongues are long enough to reach up and clean their eyes. They love to eat apples, raisins, and carrots, as well as grasses and leaves.

What is especially newsworthy about muntjacs is that there are more kinds of them than we had thought. Nowadays the report of a new mammal is a rare event. In the 1990s, however, in the forests of Vietnam, two new species of muntjac were discovered. One was bigger than any muntjac previously known; one was smaller. There was the "giant muntjac," giant at least in muntjac terms, weighing perhaps a hundred pounds. And there was the little Truong Son muntjac, named for the place where it was found. It weighs about thirty pounds and is half the ordinary muntjac size.

The muntjac ranges widely throughout Asia, from India to the Malay peninsula and Indonesia. Its name comes from Indonesia, from Sundanese, a Malayo-Polynesian language spoken by twenty-seven million people in the western part of Java Island. No other Sundanese words have made their way into English.

∼INDONESIA

java *from Javanese*

There is coffee, and then there is java. Since 1850, *java* has been the nickname for the real thing, as opposed to the substitutes that sometimes go by the name of coffee. We find it that year in a book by Lewis Garrard called *Wah-to-yah and the Taos Trail:* "To secure the good will and robes of the sensitive men, we had to offer our dear-bought Java at meal time." A character in a *Harper's Magazine* story of 1886 remarks, "I should admire to know what your coffee is made of. Reel old Javy don't make no brown stain."

Not that every cup of java is premium coffee. The nickname is widely applied to coffee of any sort, sometimes ironically. But it is always a reminder of the highly regarded coffee grown on the island of Java in Indonesia.

Coffee has its origin on the other side of the world from Indonesia, in Ethiopia, where the beans were mixed with fat as a day's meal for nomads a thousand years ago, and in Arabia, where coffee roasting was invented. But it was the Dutch in the seventeenth century who brought coffee to Indonesia because of its ideal climate: high altitudes, rainfall, and lack of frost. The coffees of Java became renowned the world over for their earthy, full-bodied taste.

Centuries later, in the computer age, Java and the reputation that comes with it were borrowed to name an innovative programming language.

Javanese, from which *java* comes, is one of the world's major languages. It is spoken by seventy-five million people in Indonesia, most of them on the island of Java. Javanese belongs to the Western Malayo-Polynesian branch of the Austronesian language family. Other words that have immigrated to English from Javanese include *junk* (ship, 1555), *palanquin* (1588), *gong* (1600), and *batik* (1880).

⁓INDONESIA

ailanthus *from Ambonese*

Although the ailanthus is the Tree of Heaven, it also grows in Brooklyn. It is prized for its shade and condemned as a weed, valued for its medicinal properties and shunned for its smell, admired for its looks and cursed for its messy winged seeds. Thriving on city streets where other trees wither, with an exotic, almost tropical look, the ailanthus has been called the "tenement palm."

The tree is said to have almost heavenly curative powers. Leaves, fruits, bark, and roots are variously reported to be remedies for asthma, cancer, diarrhea, dysentery, dysmenorrhea, dysuria, epilepsy, eruption, fever, gonorrhea, hematochezia, leucorrhea, malaria, metrorrhagia, premature ejaculation, sores, spasms, spermatorrhea, stomachic tumors, and wet dreams.

It can also be used for wood or for raising silkworms, a thriving industry in the Williamsburg section of Brooklyn, New York, around the turn of the last century. Caterpillars of the cynthia moth fed on ailanthus leaves and wove cocoons that were processed into silk in Paterson, New Jersey. The ailanthus was the centerpiece of Betty Smith's 1912 book, *A Tree Grows in Brooklyn,* and of the 1945 movie based on the book, which won an Academy Award for James Dunn as best supporting actor.

Ailanthus glandulosa, to give it its botanical title, is an import from Asia. Missionaries brought it to Europe in 1751 and to the United States in 1784. Our use of the name *ailanthus* is attested as early as 1807. Although the tree is native to China, the name comes from Ambonese, a dialect of the Malay language spoken by about 200,000 people on Ambon and neighboring islands in Indonesia. Ambonese belongs to the Malayo-Polynesian branch of the Austronesian language family. From Ambonese we also have the name *amboyna* (1879) for a tropical tree with reddish wood that we also know by the Burmese name *padauk* (1839).

～PAPUA NEW GUINEA

kuru *from Fore*

Some of the remotest civilizations on earth live in the hilly rain forests of eastern New Guinea—hundreds of separate cultures and tribes, speaking hundreds of separate languages. Although "Coca-colonization" by Western popular culture is beginning to have an effect even there, for the most part these New Guinea villagers and their languages have remained out of touch with the rest of the world. How, then, did a word from the Fore language of Papua New Guinea leave its remote mountain hideout and travel round the world, earning a Nobel Prize for the man who explained it?

The world's attention was drawn by a terrifying disease suffered by the Fore people, a disease they called *kuru*. Over a period of fifteen years or so, kuru can turn the brain to mush. Victims gradually lose the ability to walk, talk, or eat. In an autopsy, the brain looks something like a sponge or Swiss cheese, hence the term "spongiform encephalopathy."

There was no known cure, and for a long time there was no known cause. The Fore thought the disease might be caused by sorcery. Outside researchers thought it might be genetic, since it resembled the inherited Creutzfeld-Jacob Disease. What stopped the kuru epidemic was the discovery by Carleton Gajdusek of the U.S. National Institutes of Health that kuru is infectious. Chimpanzees can be given the disease by injection of kuru-infected brain tissue.

That discovery ended the Fore custom of showing respect for their ancestors by eating them after they died. The widow had the honor of preparing the brain for her children to eat, and only women and children who had participated in such feasts suffered from the disease. Once they learned of the connection with kuru, the Fore quickly stopped this practice. And for his work with kuru, Gajdusek shared the Nobel Prize for Medicine in 1976.

What has made kuru more than a historical footnote is its association with Creutzfeld-Jacob Disease and with scapies or "mad cow disease," more formally known as Bovine Spongiform Encephalopathy. Kuru was the first known human version of spongiform encephalopathy, but there have been others since. When another infection of humans was found in what is now Slovakia, it was given the name Oravske Kuru.

The Fore language is spoken by some 17,000 residents of 170 villages in the Eastern Highlands Province of Papua New Guinea. It is among more than 500 little-known languages of the Trans-New Guinea group, none with more than 100,000 speakers and most with just a few thousand. English has no other words from Fore.

∼AUSTRALIA

kangaroo *from Guugu Yimidhirr*

It was a hop, a skip, and a bump on the Great Barrier Reef in the night of June 12, 1770, that brought Captain James Cook to an unplanned sojourn of nearly two months on

the northeast coast of Australia. While carpenters and black-smiths repaired the gaping hole in the hull of the *Endeavour*, Cook's sailors and scientists went hunting for food and exotic flora and fauna. They found wolves, mosquitos, and bats as big as partridges, as well as an animal as big and fast as a greyhound, as gray as a mouse, and with a very big tail. It had the astonishing property of raising its young in a pouch on its mother's abdomen. And it made fine eating.

What was that? the English asked after dinner. *Gangurru*, said the local inhabitants, speaking Guugu Yimidhirr. "The animals which I have before mentioned [are] called by the Natives Kangooroo or Kanguru," Captain Cook wrote in his journal for August 4, as he was at last departing from what he named the Endeavour River. Thus *kangaroo* entered the English language. And the captain got it right; the story that *kangaroo* means "I don't know" in Guugu Yimidhirr is just a bit of nonurban folklore.

Later, as English speakers expanded their knowledge of Australia, the meaning of *kangaroo* in English expanded as well. The Guugu Yimidhirr word referred to the large gray kangaroo found at the place where Captain Cook repaired his ship. In English, the word was soon generalized to refer to any of the fifty different species of the marsupial, including the red kangaroo and the wallaroo.

Guugu literally means "speech, voice, or word" and *Yimidhirr* means "this way," so the name *Guugu Yimidhirr* means "speaking like this." Guugu Yimidhirr belongs to the Pama-Nyungan branch of the Australian Aboriginal language family. It is said that in Guugu Yimidhirr the notions of "left" and "right" are much less important than absolute directions like "north" and "south." The language is still spoken in Hope Vale, thirty miles north of Cooktown, the place where the *Endeavour* was repaired. But Guugu Yimidhirr is endangered; it has only about a hundred speakers in the ethnic group of about four hundred. *Kangaroo* is the only contribution of Guugu Yimidhirr to the general English vocabulary.

~ AUSTRALIA

boomerang *from Dharuk*

It all comes back to you, doesn't it? That's the beauty of the boomerang, a hunting tool, weapon of war, and toy invented by resourceful aborigines in Australia. Invented long ago, too; a preserved boomerang recently recovered from Wyrie Swamp in South Australia dates back some 10,000 years, or 9,800 years before anyone spoke English in Australia. Just a simple crescent of wood, but it gets around.

In recent years, the boomerang has gone around the world, starting with the first international competition between Australia and the United States in 1981. Ten years later the World Boomerang Association was founded. There is a United States Boomerang Association and three dozen U.S. clubs. Competition events now include throwing for accuracy, distance, speed, and MTA or "maximum time aloft." A different kind of boomerang is used for each event. The record set by John "Air" Gorski for an MTA throw and catch is a full seventeen minutes. Materials come from around the world, too, the current favorite being aircraft-grade Finnish birch plywood. The 1998 world championships, held near St. Louis, Missouri, involved eighteen teams from a dozen countries on five continents. The next world championship was scheduled for Melbourne, Australia, in 2000.

The name *boomerang* comes from the Dharuk language, once spoken along the southeast coast of Australia, where Sydney now stands. The first English notation, in

1798, renders it as *wom-ur-rang*, but by 1827 it was the now-familiar *boomerang*.

Nowadays you will search in vain for a speaker of Dharuk. Even when Dharuk was spoken, there were few speakers of that language. But it was from the Dharuk that the English learned names for many of the exotic Australian creatures: *dingo* (1789), *wallaby* (1798), *wombat* (1798, not a bat, but a bearlike marsupial), *koala* (1803), *wallaroo* (1827); the *kurrajong* tree (1823); the *corroboree* (1811, a nighttime festival); and two kinds of weapon, the *waddy* (1790, a stick that doesn't come back when you throw it), and the boomerang.

∾ AUSTRALIA

billabong *from Wiradhuri*

It's an endangered species. There are only half as many billabongs in Australia now as there were in 1895, when they were immortalized in the first line of the song that was destined to become the country's unofficial national anthem. The song begins like this, in the original version by Andrew Barton "Banjo" Paterson:

> Oh, there once was a swagman camped in the billabong,
> Under the shade of a coolibah tree,
> And he sang as he looked at the old billy boiling,
> Who'll come a-waltzing Matilda with me?

A *swagman* was an itinerant sheep shearer, a *coolibah* a eucalyptus, a *billy* a tin can, and *waltzing Matilda* going on a walking journey with just your pack on your back. But the *billabong*? No, it's not a name for the great Australian desert, nor a sacred place where ancient rituals once were performed. The last stanza of "Waltzing Matilda" translates it simply as "waterhole." A billabong is a still backwater next to a river. When the river floods, it fills the billabong and flushes it out. The dams used in modern flood control have cut off and dried up more than half the billabongs in Australia, according to one estimate.

The word *billabong* is consequently endangered too, except for its good fortune in being enshrined in a happy song with a sad story about a swagman who commits suicide rather than give up the sheep he bagged when it came to drink at his billabong. *Billabong* is attested in English as early as 1865, thirty years before "Waltzing Matilda" was written.

The language from which it came is almost extinct; a 1981 survey located only three speakers of Wiradhuri, an aboriginal language belonging to the Pama-Nyungan branch of the Australian language family and spoken just over the mountains in New South Wales. In the nineteenth century, Wiradhuri also gave English the name *kookaburra* (1890) for a peculiar bird, a kingfisher with a cry that earned it the nickname "laughing jackass."

∾ AUSTRALIA

galah *from Yuwaalaraay*

In Australia, to be told that you've made a galah of yourself is not a compliment. And you wouldn't want to belong to a pack of galahs. But there's nothing wrong with taking part in a galah session, if you have the time.

It all goes back to a bird called a *galah* by the Yuwaalaraay people, a name learned by English speakers as long ago as 1862. The bird is found almost everywhere in Australia. It is a cockatoo with a pink breast and a gray back, used for food in earlier times and known for gathering in large flocks and calling raucously to one another. It seems foolish and talkative. From those habits came the twentieth-century application of *galah* to humans and their activities. A *galah*, as explained by the Australian National Dictionary Centre, is a fool, as in this statement from 1960: "The bloke on the other end of the line is only some useless galah tryin' to sell a new brand of dip."

A *galah session*, on the other hand, is just a gabfest. It has specific application to an hour allotted for women isolated in the outback to talk with each other over a radio network, but it also can mean any long chat.

The Yuwaalaraay lived in the east of Australia, in northern New South Wales. Their language, one of about two hundred in the Australian language family, is apparently no longer spoken. One other word of Yuwaalaraay is *coolibah* (1893), a type of eucalyptus whose name is notable in English because it is in the first stanza of "Waltzing Matilda."

∼AUSTRALIA

bunyip *from Wemba*

Everywhere in the English-speaking world, children snuggle up with books about bunnies—or Barneys. But Australian children get even more; they have books about bunyips.

Once upon a time, adults in Australia believed in bunyips too. The aboriginal inhabitants told the first English-speaking settlers about menacing creatures that lived in rivers, lakes, and billabongs. Bunyips would lurk in these waters, devouring stray kangaroos and sheep but even hungrier for humans, especially women and children. They would come out at night, bellowing with a voice described as booming, and both the Aboriginals and the English settlers knew better than to approach a bunyip-haunted waterhole after the sun went down.

Descriptions of bunyips varied because anyone who ventured close enough to get a good look wouldn't be likely to return to tell about it. But many observers said that bunyips were bigger than humans, fat and ugly, with plentiful dark hair or fur. Their adaptation to water was marked by scales and webbed hands. Such bunyips were mentioned in English as early as 1848. Other witnesses saw a huge bearded snake, but they called that a *wanambi*, which is from a different language.

In the nineteenth century, when English-speaking scientists began poking around Australia, they found bones of a recently extinct two-ton marsupial that they named the diprotodon. Although it was a vegetarian, the diprotodon looked menacing enough; imagine a kangaroo as big as a rhinoceros. This, they hypothesized, might have been the creature that encouraged a belief in bunyips.

Nowadays everyone agrees that bunyips are extinct. Being safely dead, they make good monsters for children's stories, scary but often harmless and misunderstood. The State Library of Victoria recently exhibited some of them: "Fierce, scary bunyips that bellow in the night; timid, docile bunyips; black bunyips; pink bunyips; animal bunyips; spirit bunyips; bunyips from swamps and waterholes; bunyips from outer space. What a range of bunyips there are in picture books, poetry and fiction written for Australian children!"

Bunyip is just one of the aboriginal names for the monster, but it is the one that has become the norm in English. It comes from the Wemba language of western Victoria in the southeast of Australia. Like most aboriginal languages on that continent, it belongs to the Pama-Nyungan branch of the Australian language family. There are no speakers of Wemba left, and no other Wemba words have migrated to the English language.

∾AUSTRALIA

yabber *from Wuywurung*

G'day! At the September 2000 Olympics in Sydney, with the world's attention on Australia, what do you get from media commentators? Yabber, yabber, yabber. In other words:

talk, talk, talk. Every collection of Australian slang agrees that *yabber* is the Australian name for talk, chat, or conversation. It's not as if we haven't occasionally heard *yabber* in other parts of the English-speaking world, but non-Australians tend to use it harshly: "Stop your yabbering!" In Australia, on the other hand, yabber is what you do to pass the day. And if you can't yabber with a mate face-to-face, you can always send a *paper yabber*—a letter.

English-speaking Australians have been yabbering about yabber since the mid-nineteenth century. In 1855, regarding an uprising of gold miners at the Eureka Stockade near Melbourne, Raffaello Carboni wrote, "There was further a great waste of yabber-yabber about the diggers not being represented in the Legislative Council."

Yabber may seem to have derived from *jabber*, which has been in English since 1500 (apparently imitating the sound of speaking), and in any other part of the world that would be a good guess as to its origin. But *yabber* seems to have originated in Australia with *yaba* meaning "speak" in the Wuywurung aboriginal language. The similarity to *jabber* undoubtedly helped its migration to English.

Another English word from Wuywurung is the name of a tree, the *mallee* (1845). It is a slow-growing eucalyptus with wood so heavy it doesn't float and stems that grow from water-filled underground roots.

But Wuywurung itself is extinct. It was a member of the Pama-Nyungan branch of the Australian language family and was spoken in western Victoria, in the southeastern part of the country.

⟿ AUSTRALIA

nugget *from Australian English*

During the California gold rush of 1848 and 1849, no one found even a single nugget. They found pieces of gold that we would now call nuggets, but there were as yet no such *nuggets* in the English language. That discovery was made at the other end of the earth, in another gold rush just a few years later. Australian speakers of English were able to turn dirt into gold, linguistically speaking.

Before the Australian gold rush of the early 1850s, *nug* was an obscure dialect word in England referring to a lump of dirt or other material. Someone must have transported it to Australia, added a second syllable, and applied it to the visible pieces of gold found by miners. In Australia, the term was used in print as early as 1851, when the gold rush in Victoria began.

George Francis Train, a "Yankee merchant" who went to Australia for the gold, wrote home to the *Boston Post* just two years later, in October 1853: "They have a slang language at the gold fields peculiar to that district. Tea and coffee are 'slingings,' 'swags' is the term for luggage and 'shiser' for an unprofitable hole. I believe 'nugget' is peculiarly Australian."

The English language of Australia arrived directly from the mother country, halfway around the world, starting with a shipload of criminals in 1788. The language that developed into present-day Australian English was somewhat disreputable, as were many of the early colonists, who were sent from England to Australia as punishment for their crimes.

Other Australian contributions to the English language include the *Australian ballot* (1888), so called because Australians were the first to use a secret ballot printed with all candidates' names. There are also many Australian terms having to do with bush life, including *Aborigine* (1864) for the original native peoples, *bushed* (1885) meaning "lost in the bush," and *walkabout* (1828), an Aborigine's temporary return to the bush after living in the English-speaking world. Australia's present population of nearly twenty million is mostly English speaking.

∽NEW ZEALAND

kiwi *from Maori*

It's a bird. It's a fruit. No, it's a person, at least in New Zealand. If you say you're taking a bite of a kiwi, you might just get bitten back.

The first mention of the Maori word *kiwi* in English was back in 1835, in a description of "the most remarkable and curious bird in New Zealand." It was given the scientific name *apteryx*, or "wingless," because its wings are so stubby it can't even think of flying. It hardly has a tail, either, and its vision is poor. But it has sturdy legs and a pointed bill, some six inches long, with which it grubs at night for its dinner of grubs and worms. And it burrows underground for its nest; the male takes care of hatching the eggs the female has laid. The bird has a cry that sounds like "kiwi, kiwi"—which may be how the Maori gave it its name.

The kiwi is a relative of the ostrich and emu, and also of the moa, another wingless bird of New Zealand whose name comes from the Maori language. Only bones and feathers of the moa remain; it has been extinct for some time.

New Zealand has adopted the kiwi as its symbol on stamps and money. From this has come the use of *kiwi* to mean an inhabitant of New Zealand. The Maori are the original native population, and *paheka* is the Maori term for a white person, but the designation *kiwi* encompasses them both.

The most familiar kiwi in recent years is neither fowl nor human, but a little brown fruit grown in New Zealand and shipped worldwide, otherwise known as the Chinese gooseberry.

About 100,000 of the more than three million inhabitants of New Zealand speak Maori, a Malayo-Polynesian language of the Austronesian family. A few other Maori words are also current in the English of New Zealand, for example *kauri* and *kowhai,* both trees; *kahawai,* a fish; *kumara,* a sweet potato, and *kai,* a general word for food.

ᕽMARSHALL ISLANDS

bikini *from Marshallese*

Four days after an atomic bomb exploded on little Bikini Atoll in the remote Pacific Ocean, the little *bikini* exploded  into the French language and then into English. On July 5, 1946, Louis Reard revealed to the fashion world of Paris a shockingly skimpy swimsuit he had designed, consisting merely of four triangles of material strategically placed on the female body and held in place by thin straps. No decent woman would think of wearing one; Reard couldn't get any fashion models in town to show it off. But he was able to recruit a nude dancer from the Casino de Paris to pose in the garment, and the rest was front-page history throughout the civilized world.

The French couturier called his sensation a *bikini*, shamelessly appropriating the name of a place half a world away that had just been the site of an equally sensational news event: the first peacetime explosion of a nuclear weapon. That event was the first of twenty-three American nuclear tests that would extend more than a decade, including a fifteen-megaton H-bomb explosion on March 1, 1954. The tests contaminated Bikini with so much radiation that the survivors and descendants of the 167 pre-bomb inhabitants are still exiles, having been shuttled from island to island while the cleanup of their homeland continues.

Meanwhile, although the *bikini* was an instant success in the English language, it took much longer to become acceptable beachwear. Brian Hyland's 1960 hit song "Itsy-Bitsy-Teenie-Weenie-Yellow-Polka-Dot Bikini" helped it along, as did the beach movies and liberated styles of the

1960s. Nowadays Bikini itself is visited by tourists wearing bikinis. The food produced at the Bikini Atoll is still too contaminated for permanent residents, but because of the warships sunk there in the first two bomb tests, the Bikini lagoon is now rated among the top scuba diving destinations in the world.

The name *Bikini* is from the Marshallese language, spoken by about 30,000 people in the Marshall Islands. It belongs to the Micronesian subgroup of Eastern Malayo-Polynesian. No other words from Marshallese have made their way into present-day English.

⌇TONGA

taboo *from Tongan*

If it's taboo, maybe we shouldn't discuss it. But we find it the world over, each culture having its own particular version. The English language acquired its *taboo* in the eighteenth century, from people who would seem least likely to have it, the inhabitants of the South Pacific kingdom of Tonga. The English explorer Captain James Cook, visiting Tonga in 1773 and 1777, received such a welcome that he called these the Friendly Islands. But he also noted that they observed strict prohibitions. In his account of his 1777 visit, Cook wrote: "Not one of them would sit down, or eat a bit of any thing. . . . On expressing my surprise at this, they were all taboo, as they said; which word has a very comprehensive meaning; but, in general, signifies that a thing is forbidden. . . . When any thing is forbidden to be eat, or made use of, they say, that it is *taboo*."

It was too good a word to leave to the Tongans. Thanks to the Friendly Islanders, English acquired a word to characterize anything prohibited not by the laws of nature but by the laws of custom or religion. And the word allowed us a certain scientific detachment; we could discuss taboos without violating them. Scholars observed that there were two kinds of taboo, things to be avoided because they were too sacred and things to be avoided because they were too profane. Many languages have such taboos; the name of God may be too sacred to mention, while the names of certain body parts may be too vulgar. And taboos, we discover as we study them, may change over time. In present-day America, the taboo against discussion and depiction of sex has diminished, while the taboo against derogatory names for groups has increased.

Taboos can be extreme. Until recently, the entire Dyirbal language, spoken in Australia, was taboo in the presence of certain relatives: a parent-in-law or child-in-law of the opposite sex or a cross cousin of the opposite sex. Under those circumstances, speakers of Dyirbal had to use a "mother-in-law language" similar to Dyirbal but with an entirely different vocabulary.

Tongan, from which we got the first taboos, is spoken today by about 100,000 people in Tonga, the last remaining Polynesian kingdom. Like Tahitian and Hawaiian, Tongan is in the Oceanic subbranch of the Eastern Malayo-Polynesian language family.

The only other word from Tongan that has found its way into English is *kava* (1810), the name of a plant whose root makes a drug and a drink also known as kava. The beverage is said to have a mildly psychedelic effect. "Unlike most herbs you don't wonder if it's working," says a Texas company, Better Living Products, which sells kava powder: "Almost immediately one feels a slight numbing in the mouth followed by a feeling of relaxation and stress reduction. These benefits occur without intoxication or hang over."

⌇Samoa

lavalava *from Samoan*

How will you make yourself at home when you visit Samoa? Try etiquette tip No. 7 from the Western Samoa Visitors Bureau: "As a sign of respect to our village chiefs, please be seated (cross-legged) and be clad in our traditional lavalava (wrap-around waist cloth)."

The lavalava is just that: a piece of cloth, decorated in your favorite pattern, that becomes a skirtlike garment for the lower half of the body. You put it on by holding the square of cloth behind you, pulling the two ends together in front of you, folding the doubled material in zigzag fashion till it reaches your waist, rolling the top edge into a waistband, taking a deep breath, and tucking the waistband in. Both men and women can wear it.

The Samoan word *lavalava* has been noted in English since 1891. Elsewhere in the South Pacific a similar garment is called a *sulu* (Fiji), *pareu* (Tahiti), *sarong* (Malaysia), or *kikepa* (Hawaii). According to a 1997 article in the *Honolulu Star-Bulletin*, the lavalava is increasingly popular with both residents and tourists in Hawaii. Haunani Kay Trask explained why to reporter Burl Burlingame: "The perfect clothing to wear in a hot climate. And not just because it makes a political statement—I'm pretty political, you know—because the muumuu is an imposed clothing style. The kikepa ties us in with the South Pacific.

"And it's just cloth! No zippers, no buttons, incredibly inexpensive, and you don't have to accessorize. There's something about the way they fit—their fluidity of line that goes with the body. It's why Polynesian women look so good in them."

Samoa is another of the Eastern Malayo-Polynesian languages of the Austronesian language family. It is spoken by more than 300,000 people in Western Samoa, American Samoa, Hawaii, the west coast of the United States, and New Zealand. One recent English word from Samoan is *faamafu* (1934), the name for a home brew made of potato peels, malt, and sugar. Samoan culture was made world famous by anthropologist Margaret Mead in her *Coming of Age in Samoa* (1928), though Rule No. 3 from the Western Samoa Visitors Bureau is "Margaret Mead was wrong (just ask Derek Freeman)."

～TAHITI

tattoo *from Tahitian*

On April 11, 1769, at the opposite end of the earth from England, an expedition sent by Britain's Royal Geographic Society arrived in Tahiti and found a way of life quite

opposite from the English way. Captain James Cook and the crew of the *Endeavour* had a happy reception in a land where nature and culture made life easy. The English were welcomed with open arms (and their pockets were sometimes picked) by the friendly, uninhibited Tahitians. And the English noticed that, since the climate made clothing optional, the Tahitians made sure to look their best by decorating their bodies as well as their clothes.

They drew on their bodies the same patterns with which they decorated their possessions: tools, weapons, bowls, and canoes. Joseph Banks, naturalist on the *Endeavour*, wrote in his journal in August 1769: "I shall now mention their method of painting their bodies or *tattow* as it is called in their language. This they do by inlaying the color black under their skins in such a manner as to be indelible; everyone is marked thus in different parts of his body according maybe to his humor or different circumstances of his life. Some have ill-designed figures of men, birds or dogs, but they more generally have this figure 'Z' either simply, as the women are generally marked with it, on every joint of their fingers and toes and often round the outside of their feet, or in different figures of it as squares, circles, crescents, etc. which both sexes have on their arms and legs."

The application of tattoos was painful, accomplished by dipping a sharp-pointed comb into lampblack and then hammering it into the skin. But Banks noted that everyone did it.

As word of tattooing in Tahiti and other Polynesian islands spread, European sailors began to get tattooed themselves. The low reputation of sailors kept tattooing in low repute among English speakers for the next two centuries. Recently, however, it has gained favor as an art form, with renewed respect for the talent of its Polynesian progenitors. In Tahiti it was done between ages fourteen and eighteen, and it seems to have an appeal for youth today. Like nose and navel piercing, tattooing has become a means for contemporary teenagers to enhance their bodies and appall their elders.

Tahitian is still spoken by the inhabitants of Tahiti, who now number more than 100,000. It is a Malayo-Polynesian language in the Austronesian family. From Tahitian we also have the *pareu* (1860), a wraparound skirt worn by both men and women that covers up the tattoos.

⌇MARQUESAS ISLANDS

tiki *from Marquesan*

Art and religion, past and present combine in the Polynesian figure of the tiki. It is a stone or wood carving in simplified human shape, sometimes small enough to be worn as an ornament, sometimes so large as to tower over a human visitor. In the Marquesas, tikis were carved on bowls and dishes, clubs and canoe paddles, as well made into separate statues and amulets. The typical tiki is a powerful figure with hands clasped over its stomach, a large flat nose, round eyes, and an elliptical mouth. Tiki is said to be the ancestor and creator of humans.

English speakers first learned of tikis from accounts of Captain James Cook's eighteenth-century expeditions to the South Pacific, where tikis are mentioned as early as 1777. Two centuries later, in a twist of cultural history, tikis conquered California. In their new habitat they may be tacky, but tiki is now alive and well among the natives of the west coast of the United States.

The first wave of the tiki invasion came between 1945 and 1965, when bars and family rooms added bamboo and copies of the Polynesian stone tikis. The second wave is now. "In the United States," explained a 1996 article by Richard von Busack in a Silicon Valley newspaper, "tiki can refer to a whole range of popular ersatz exotica that some aficionados claim represents a form of suburban rebellion. Throughout the valley, look hard enough and you can find old bachelor apartments with names like The Palms and Moana Lei. These relics are adorned with features that turn up again and again: dead sockets that once held colored floodlights, surrounded by unkillable palms; the Tiki Rooms for cocktail parties; the peculiar lagoon-like curve of the kidney-shaped swimming pool." There are collectors of the tiki mugs that were once given out by tiki bars, and there is a "suburban art" movement called Polynesian Pop.

The original tiki came to the English language from two Malayo-Polynesian languages: Maori, spoken in present-day New Zealand, and Marquesan, spoken in the Marquesas Islands by about 10,000 people nowadays. Marquesan is a close relative also of Tongan, Samoan, Tahitian, and Hawaiian, and along with them shares the honor of introducing to English words like *tapa* (1823, cloth) and *mahi-mahi* (1943, fish).

⁓UNITED STATES (HAWAII)

aloha *from Hawaiian*

Hawaii's best-known export is not sugar, pineapples, or Kona coffee, but a word: *aloha*. It is much more than a greeting; on the islands, it is a way of life. Hawaii's businesses include Aloha Fresh Flowers, Aloha Surfboards, Aloha Bicycle Tours, Aloha Quilts, Aloha Spirit Coffee,

Aloha Candy and Card Company, and Aloha Beautiful Hawaii Weddings. There is an Aloha United Way, a football game called the Aloha Bowl, and a shirt and a day of the week dedicated to aloha. Summing up, one islander says *aloha* means "Hello, goodbye, love, compassion, welcome, good wishes. It means belonging to others with a common humanity. It's defined better as a feeling in the heart than by words."

How can you get the feeling? The "Live Aloha" website offers these practical suggestions:

- Respect your elders and children.
- Leave places better than you find them.
- Hold the door. Hold the elevator.
- Plant something.
- Drive with courtesy. Let others in.
- Attend an event of another culture.
- Return your shopping cart.
- Get out and enjoy nature.
- Pick up litter.
- Share with your neighbors.
- Create smiles.
- Make a list of your own.

A colorful manifestation of the aloha spirit is the aloha shirt, a short-sleeved work of art distinguished by its bold print and worn untucked. Derived from the simple worker's shirt of a century ago, the aloha shirt became popular in the 1920s and 1930s. Frustrated that the shirt was not considered proper business attire, the Hawaii Fashion Guild in 1966 began a successful campaign to designate every Friday as "aloha Friday," a day to wear aloha shirts to work. Aloha Friday may have been the inspiration for the "casual Friday" instigated on the mainland a few decades later.

Hawaiian is a member of the Malayo-Polynesian language family, related to Fijian, Samoan, Maori, and Tahitian. Although Hawaiian is well known and studied, only about a hundred people still speak it as their first language.

Aloha, the most famous word of the Hawaiian language, was recorded in English as long ago as 1820, in a traveler's report. Nowadays a hundred words or so from Hawaiian are used in the English of Hawaii, and some are world-famous, including *hula* (1825), *lei* (1843), *luau* (1853), *muumuu* (1923), and *ukulele* (1896).

THE AMERICAS

*F*rom Polynesia we cross the Pacific to South America, reversing the path of Thor Heyerdahl's *Kon Tiki* raft voyage of 1947, undertaken to show how humans could have reached the South Sea islands. The ancient civilizations of South America will concern us briefly, then the Caribbean, where Europeans first encountered the languages of the Americas, but we will devote most of our attention to the continent where more languages have contributed to English than any other on earth, North America. We will visit fifty languages there, compared with forty-five in Europe, forty-five in Asia, thirty-eight in Africa, twenty-three in Oceania, and thirteen in South and Central America and the Caribbean.

In 1491, not a word of any American language had immigrated to English. The New World was undreamed of by Europeans, even by Columbus, who was looking for a direct route to India. In 1492—well, that was too early, too. English was not the language of Columbus or his sailors, and for the next half-century England was too busy ushering in its Renaissance and deciding whether to be Catholic or Protestant to pay much attention to the world across the Atlantic.

But by 1550 the immigration was ready to start: American words started coming to the English language, and in the 1600s speakers of English started landing in the Americas, where their language absorbed much from the natives.

In the 1500s, news of the Spanish discoveries stimulated both the imagination and the vocabulary of England. From the West Indies came *cannibal* (Carib) and *hurricane* (Taino), from Guyana *cacique* (Arawak). Like most of the other words from Central and South America, these came to us courtesy of Spanish. Spanish-assisted additions to the vocabulary continued in the seventeenth century with *chocolate*

(Nahuatl) and *jaguar* (Guaraní). Portuguese and French helped with the import of *buccaneer* (Tupí).

Later additions from the languages of Latin America, brought to us with the help of Spanish, include the *poncho* (Mapudungun), sometimes made of *alpaca* (Aymara) wool, the game bird *guan* (Panama), the *dory* (Miskito) for transportation, the water-filled *cenote* (Maya) of Mexico, and something extra, *lagniappe* (Quechua).

Meanwhile, with the founding of Jamestown in 1607, the English language began to make itself at home in North America and no longer needed an intermediary to import words. Because of the great variety of native languages, and because of the extended contact of English-speakers with speakers of these languages over the next centuries, North America became the most diverse source of all for the English language today.

Direct from the Algonquian languages that predominated in eastern North America at the time of the first English settlements came numerous words like *moccasin* (Virginia Algonquian) and *sea puss* (Unquachog). Moving westward over the next centuries, speakers of English heard not only from Algonquian but from numerous languages unrelated to that family. Indian languages gave us names of plants: the *catalpa* (Muskogee) and *hackmatack* (Western Abenaki) trees, medicinal *mechameck* (Menominee), cure-all *cohosh* (Eastern Abenaki), and out in Utah, the *sego lily* (Southern Paiute). There were numerous new animals: the noble *wapiti* (Shawnee), the swift *appaloosa* (Choctaw), the chubby *chuckwalla* (Cahuilla), and the pesky *punkie* (Munsee). Fish leapt into our language, from *squeteague* (Mohegan) and the rare *cui-ui* (Northern Paiute) to the several kinds of salmon. Foods included *succotash* (Narragansett) and *pemmican* (Cree), and beverages included *hooch* (Tlingit).

The *tepee* (Dakota), *wickiup* (Sac and Fox), and *hogan*

(Navajo) were built into English, and we learned about the leader known as *mugwump* (Massachusett), the party called a *potlatch* (Nootka), and the creature called *Sasquatch* (Halkomelem).

The Indians had names for distinctive kinds of weather, like the *chinook* wind (Chehalis) and the fog called *pogonip* (Shoshone). They had clothing for North American conditions, from the *moccasin* to the waterproof *shoepac* boot (Unami). The northernmost regions of North America had their own wintry vocabulary, from the *toboggan* (Micmac) to the *husky* dog (Montagnais), with clothing that includes the foot-warming *mukluk* (Yupik).

In the Americas in 1492, the number of distinct native languages was about a thousand. Today, despite the devastating inroads of European population and culture, perhaps seven hundred of the American Indian languages are still spoken, though many are nearly extinct. For some like Powhatan and Massachusett, borrowings into English are the only way the language still lives.

The Americas also provided the opportunity for a few words to enter English from sources other than the Indian languages. Pennsylvania German gave us *dunk*, Yiddish gave us *maven*. We learned to dance the *merenge* from Haitian Creole French, and Lesser Antillean Creole French gave us the popular music known as *zouk*.

Nowadays, half a millennium after Columbus, we may claim that the center of the English-speaking world has shifted from England to North America, the source of the language's greatest variety. Canadian and American English have each developed distinctive words, and we'll give each an entry, eh? OK?

⌢CHILE

poncho *from Mapudungun*

In the southern regions of Chile live a people, the Mapuche, who managed to avoid Spanish conquest and have held on

to their culture and language under the independent Chilean government as well. The Mapuche learned military tactics from the Spanish so that they could fend them off; the Spanish learned from the Mapuche to fend off the rain with an ingenious garment they called a *poncho*.

To make a poncho, the Mapuche take a watertight wool blanket and make a slit in it so it can be worn as a cloak. It was discussed in English as early as 1717: "The Spaniards have taken up the Use of the Chony, or Poncho . . . to ride in, because the Poncho keeps out the Rain." As that remark indicates, it is through Spanish that *poncho* came to English.

The Mapuche invention is used by soldiers, campers, and other outdoors people the world around. Now sometimes equipped with a hood, it serves not only as a cloak but also as a pillow and blanket. When it isn't needed for protection against the elements, a wool poncho makes a fine wall decoration.

Mapudungun or Araucano is spoken by 400,000 people in Chile today and 40,000 more in Argentina. It is in a language family by itself. The Mapudungun language has also given us the *coypu* (1793), an otter-like rodent also known as the *nutria* (a Spanish word). Valued for its fur, the coypu has been imported into North America along with its name, where it has escaped from fur farms and become a pest.

~PARAGUAY

jaguar *from Guaraní*

Since their creation in 1936, Jaguars have increased their numbers in the United States from zero to hundreds of thousands. Dealers who sell them are found in practically every state. But these are the British variety. The original American jaguar, the inspiration for the motor vehicle, has experienced a population decline corresponding to the increase for the car.

Centuries ago there were many thousands of jaguars in the southern parts of what is now the United States. In the mid-twentieth century, a few were still to be seen in Arizona. Nowadays there are not even a hundred live jaguars in the United States, and all of them are in zoos. In 1997, the U.S. Fish and Wildlife Service declared the jaguar an endangered species. If any should show up in Arizona again, they'll be protected.

Fortunately, only a small part of the jaguar's original habitat was north of the Rio Grande. It ranged from the United States all the way south through Latin America, so there are still some wild jaguars left. But it is greatly endangered even in those places where it is still found: Mexico, Central America, Venezuela, Belize, the Amazon rainforest of eastern Brazil, Patagonia, and Argentina. It faces the danger of being hunted by humans for its spotted fur, and the even greater danger of destruction of its habitat. Jaguars prefer rain forests and swamps.

They are solitary, fast, and nocturnal, often surprising their prey with a leap in the dark. The speed, agility, and fierceness of the jaguar are commemorated in the hood ornament of the Jaguar, the "leaper" first displayed in 1937 and now standard on all XJ Series Jaguar sedans sold in North America.

The word *jaguar* came into English as long ago as 1604, in a book on the West Indies. It immigrated directly from the Guaraní language, spoken today by more than three million people in Paraguay. Guaraní is the principal member of the Tupí-Guaraní language family. In Guaraní, *jaguara* apparently is the general name for any kind of carnivore; the animal we call jaguar is their *jaguareté* or "true jaguar." Aside from jaguar, Guaraní has also given us the names of two wading birds, the *jacana* (1753) and *jabiru* (1774).

⌒PERU

lagniappe *from Quechua*

It's a gift. *Lagniappe* is a word well known in New Orleans and vicinity, and it means just that: a gift given with a purchase, or anything extra, like a toaster with a bank account. In English, it is recorded as early as 1849, spelled *lanyope*. Mark Twain discussed it in his 1883 *Life on the Mississippi:*

> We picked up one excellent word—a word worth travelling to New Orleans to get; a nice limber, expressive, handy word—"Lagniappe." They pronounce it lanny-*yap.* It is Spanish—so they said. . . . It has a restricted meaning, but I think the people spread it out a little when they choose. It is the equivalent of the thirteenth roll in a "baker's dozen." . . . The custom originated in the Spanish quarter of the city. When a child or a servant buys something in a shop—or even the mayor or the governor, for aught I know—he finishes the operation by saying—"Give me something for lagniappe."

Twain's sources were right; the word came from the Spanish. But it belonged to two other languages as well. The modern spelling *lagniappe* looks French. And indeed *lagniappe* is from the French creole spoken in Louisiana, "la ñapa" or "the gift." In turn, *ñapa* comes from the Spanish, and the Spanish got it from the Quechua Indian language of South America.

It is not surprising that Quechua has made some contributions to English. It was the language of the great Inca empire of South America. And of all the Indian languages of the all the Americas, Quechua is the most widely spoken today. There are more than eight million speakers of Quechua, including more than three million in Peru, nearly three million in Bolivia, a million in Ecuador, and nearly a million in Argentina. The different regional varieties of Quechua form a separate language family, though some scholars believe Quechua belongs with Aymara in a larger family they call Quechumaran.

We can thank Quechua, always courtesy of Spanish, for the English words *coca* (1577, the source of cocaine), *condor* (1604), *guano* (1604), *pampa* (1704), and *quinine* (1826); the camelids *llama* (1600), *vicuña* (1604), and *guanaco* (1604); and even *jerk* (1707) and *jerky* (1848) referring to dried meat.

∼BOLIVIA

alpaca *from Aymara*

Camels in South America? Yes, llike llamas, vicuñas, and guanacos, alpacas are members of the camel family adapted for the high altitudes of the Andes. They are not the spitting image of Middle Eastern camels, but like other camels they do spit, though usually at each other rather than at people. About half the size of llamas, alpacas grow to three feet tall and about 150 pounds. They are cute and cuddly, we are told, and make good pets.

They also make good profits for their owners, who are located in places like Ohio and Vermont, as well as in Bolivia. It is the alpaca fleece that is especially valuable: softer, lighter, and stronger than wool; warmer than cashmere and just as comfortable; and with a greater variety of natural colors than any other fiber. There are eight basic alpaca colors: black, white, silver, piebald, caramel, coffee, fawn, and red, and many variations of each.

The fine quality of alpaca fiber comes from five thousand years of careful breeding. Along with llamas, alpacas were the mainstay of the Aymara civilization which flourished in present-day Bolivia from about 400 to 1000. The Incas, who conquered them, also bred alpacas, reserving their fleece for royalty.

Our English language began using the name as early as 1604, when a writer about the West Indies calls them *pacos*. (The prefix *al* was a later addition.) We got the name from the Spanish, who got the name from the Quechua spoken by the Incas, who got it from the Aymara. Alpaca is apparently our only word from the Aymara language. The other camelids, llama, vicuña, and guanaco, have Quechua names.

Aymara is still spoken by nearly two million people in Bolivia and some 400,000 in Peru. It is in a language family nearly by itself, along with the Jaqaru language spoken by a few thousand people. About one-quarter of its vocabulary is the same as that of Quechua, so some experts consider it and Quechua to belong to a family they call Quechumaran, but it seems more likely that the similarity results from borrowing, just as English has borrowed one-quarter of its vocabulary from French.

⌁Brazil

buccaneer *from Tupí*

If the word had kept its original meaning, many law-abiding Americans of today would be proud to call themselves buccaneers. That's because *buccaneer* originally meant nothing more or less than "barbecuer."

The word came from Brazil hundreds of years ago. There the invading Portuguese observed Tupí Indians smoking meat on a wooden frame the natives called a *mocaém* or *bocaém*. Their reports about this practice carried the word into other European languages. And European adventurers carried the word back to the Caribbean island of Tortuga, near Hispaniola (present-day Haiti and the Dominican Republic), in the 1660s. There they went into the business of selling smoked or barbecued meat to passing Spanish ships, advertising it as cooked on the *boucan* (as they said in French), a word known in English since 1611. They may not have advertised that they obtained their meat free by raiding the cattle of Hispaniola. Soon these *boucaniers* became more adventurous, sailing out to capture not just the trade of the passing ships but their cargoes as well. And thus *buccaneer* came to mean "pirate," recorded in that meaning in English as early as 1690.

Tupí is not a single language but an entire family of closely related languages spoken by Indians in Brazil. Tupí, in turn, belongs to the larger Tupí-Guaraní family. Tupí peoples are still to be found in Brazil today, but many of their languages are extinct. Because the Portuguese had extensive dealings with the Tupí in the early days of European exploration, many Tupí names for American flora and fauna have come to us through Portuguese. These include the animals *cougar* (1774), *tapir* (1774), and *piranha* (1869); the birds *toucan* (1568) and *tanager* (1688); and the plants *cashew* (1598), *ipecac* (1682), *tapioca* (1707), *cayenne* (1756), and *petunia* (1825).

∼Guyana

cacique *from Arawak*

Among the first American peoples encountered by Columbus and his successors in the Caribbean were the Arawak. They and their linguistic cousins the Taino, now extinct, called their leaders by the name that has come to us via Spanish as *cacique* (with the pronunciation ka-*seek*). The word was noted in English as early as 1555. Since the North American Indians used different titles for their chiefs, *cacique* is not commonly heard in the United States or Canada, but it still is common in the Caribbean. The Bahamas, for example, have annual Cacique Awards for leadership in promoting tourism.

And *cacique* has become more than just the title of an Indian chief. Where Spanish is spoken, both in Spain and elsewhere, *cacique* was imported as a name for a nearly autonomous local political boss under a feudal national government. In Mexico down to the present day, power has frequently been in the hands of local self-appointed bosses, often wealthy landowners, who are called *caciques*. In the Philippines, some analysts have argued that the American occupation of the early twentieth century fostered "cacique democracy."

Meanwhile, back in North America, in 1988 the Limited Company began a chain of boutiques known as Lingerie Cacique, "a world of singular, sensual lingerie and gifts with a distinctly Parisian point of view." Unable to compete with the company's Victoria's Secret division, Lingerie Cacique's 118 stores were closed in 1998.

In earlier times, Arawak was spoken in the Bahamas and Trinidad as well as on the north coast of South America, but it is now limited to a few thousand speakers in Guyana, Suriname, French Guiana, and Venezuela. Arawak belongs to the Caribbean branch of the Maipúrean language family. Another English word from Arawak, also via Spanish in 1555, is *iguana*.

∼GUADELOUPE

zouk *from Lesser Antillean Creole French*

Want to have a party? Music, please!

That seems to be the way the word *zouk* developed in the special variety of French spoken in the French Antilles of the West Indies. *Zouk* means "party," but it also means a kind of dance music developed for partying. It is light and lively, blending modern technology with traditional instruments, rhythms, and melodies.

Zouk music took a roundabout way to reach English. Musicians from Guadeloupe started zouk not in the West

Indies but in France. In the late 1970s, the group known as Kassav began playing what they called zouk in Paris. In the late 1980s, zouk became known in England and in the United States. By 1993, it was well enough known that the University of Chicago Press could publish a scholarly book on zouk, by Jocelyne Guilbault, asserting that zouk is an important component of world music.

Like any other music, zouk is hard to describe in words. "It is based on interlocking rhythmic and melodic patterns rather than a dense sound where all instruments play simultaneously," says the All-Music Guide on the World Wide Web. "A basic rule of zouk is to create space in the music by avoiding an overwhelming density of simultaneous parts, allowing the insertion of interesting sounds into the 'holes' that are created." "Driving tempos, layered percussion (and lots of it), sizzling brass sections, and smooth vocal harmonies all go into the mix," adds Tom Pitmon, a California enthusiast.

The language of zouk music is Lesser Antillean Creole French, a long name referring to a mixed language, based on French, that developed for trade purposes centuries ago. It is spoken by the 350,000 people of the French possession of Guadeloupe in the French Antilles, as well as by more than half a million others in nearby Martinique, Grenada, and other islands, and in France itself. The word *zouk* may have originated in the Bambara word *juke* discussed in the African section of this book. No other words of Lesser Antillean Creole French are widely current in English.

∼Haiti, Puerto Rico, and Cuba

hurricane *from Taino*

Among the wonders of the new world encountered by Columbus were storms different from any seen in Europe or the Mediterranean. These were not little tempests but huge cyclones of wind and rain that developed, moved, and faded over many days. They were distinguished by a

clear, calm space at the center, and so the Taino Indians who lived in what is now Haiti, the Dominican Republic, Cuba, and Puerto Rico called the storms *huraca'n* or "center of the wind," where *hura* means "wind" and *ca'n* means "center." Columbus's expeditions captured *huraca'n* and made it a Spanish word; it found its way from Spanish to English as early as 1555. A similar storm in Asia is called a *typhoon*, deriving from words in both Greek and Chinese that happened to sound the same.

We know all about hurricanes now, or at least we know a lot. We know that they are centers of low air pressure and that the lower the pressure, the more intense they are. We track them by radar, by satellite, by airplane, and on the Internet. We have even turned them into a kind of sporting event, with season counts and records for intensity and damage, and with the players named in advance each season. Thanks to the National Hurricane Center, we know that the total number of hurricanes in the past century was 23 in June, 25 in July, 152 in August, 196 in September, 96 in October, and 22 in November. We know that the deadliest was Hurricane Mitch in October and November 1998, which killed 10,000 people in the Central American countries of Honduras, Nicaragua, Guatemala, and El Salvador. We know the costliest was Andrew in Florida and

Louisiana in 1992, causing $26.5 billion of damage.

Every hurricane is now named in advance, thanks to a practice that began with George Stewart's novel *Storm* fifty years ago, in which a California weatherman called a storm Maria. The names used to be all female, but now they alternate between male and female, going down the alphabet each year. Particularly strong storms are honored by having their names retired.

Taino is a member of the Caribbean branch of the large Maipúrean language family. *Hurricane* is also found in the related Carib language, so some sources derive it from that. The Taino language and people are extinct today, thanks to the European invasion, but they left us, via Spanish, three of the most important ingredients of their lifestyle and ours: *potato* (1565), *tobacco* (1577), and *barbecue* (1709). From Taino we also have *hammock* (1555), *savanna* (1555), *cassava* (1555), *guava* (1604), *mangrove* (1613), and *key* (island, 1697).

∿Haiti

merengue *from Haitian Creole French*

Not only can you eat merengue, you can dance it off. It's a simple step that has been described as going up the stairs sideways: you step on one foot and pull the other to it, again and again.

The dance is known as the *merengue* to English speakers and to the Spanish speakers of the Dominican Republic, and as *meringue* to the French speakers of Haiti. The two nations, which share the island of Hispaniola, share an enthusiasm for the dance too, and both claim to have originated it.

The merengue is a lively dance, but when you dance it you look like you're limping, which is an explanation the Dominicans give of its origin. In the nineteenth century, they say, a hero returned home from battle wounded in the leg, and the townspeople celebrated his victory by limping with him. Or, some say, it's the limping movement slaves made when chained together and working in the fields to the beat of a drum. Haitians simply say the Dominicans got it from them.

Whoever started it, merengue is now said to be the most popular dance music in all of Latin America, and it has been noticed by English speakers too, at least since it was mentioned in a book in 1936. Traditionally in merengue, saxophones play very fast percussive notes, and the basic rhythms come from two West African percussion instruments, a two-ended drum known as the tambora and the guiro, a gourd scraped by a stick. Modern merengues make use of a great variety of instruments and styles, traditional and modern, including hip-hop and rap.

If merengue came from Haiti, which was the dominant country on Hispaniola at the time of the dance's origin, we can credit the word to Haitian Creole French, which is an official language of the country, along with French. There are about seven million inhabitants of Haiti, and while perhaps 5 percent of them speak French, they all speak the French-based, African-influenced Creole. The word merengue comes from the familiar French confectionery word and suggests the lightness and quickness of the dance. No other words of Haitian Creole French have stepped into English.

∼ JAMAICA

labrish *from Jamaican Creole English*

In the rest of the English-speaking world, it's gossip or chitchat. In Jamaica, it's labrish. Or so the dictionaries say. But if you look at what Jamaicans call labrish in their particular variety of English, it turns out to be a whole attitude as well. Louise Bennett, who in the 1940s was among the first authors to write in Jamaican Creole English, entitled one of her collections of poems *Labrish*. "Miss Lou" uses the word in a poem about Liza, a chatty woman who ought to be required to pay "mouth taxes." Here are some excerpts:

> An wen we try fe warn you Lize,
> Yuh always chat we out,
> Yuh chat an chat till govament
> Come income-tax yuh mout!
> . . . .
> Start a-talk yuh neighbor business,
> Form a labrish committee!

Labrish is a broad enough word to include "sweet memories of primary and high school, 'crude jokes,' songs and rhymes, tall tales, an' a whole heap more," according to a description of an "authentic compilation of Jamaica labrish." And on the World Wide Web, a Jamaican online chat is called "Jamaica Labrish."

The English spoken in Jamaica ranges from standard British to the creole exemplified by Miss Lou's poems. In Jamaica, although standard English is used in the schools, 95 percent of the population of two and a half million speak Jamaican Creole English. There are many distinctive words of Jamaican Creole, but *labrish* is the only one that has talked its way into being one of the new additions to the *Oxford English Dictionary*, with examples as early as 1942.

～CUBA

cannibal *from Carib*

Talk about misunderstandings. The terrible word *cannibal* is just a variation of the innocent name *Carib*, which we remember today in the name *Caribbean*. And when Columbus, exploring Cuba, heard the name *Canib*, he was thrilled. It was proof that he was near China, Columbus thought, because the natives were named after the

Chinese ruler. "Caniba no es otra cosa sino la gente del Gran Can," he declared, that is, the "Canibs are nothing other than the people of the Grand Khan."

By the time that misconception was cleared up, another was in the making. These *Caribs* or *Canibs*, known to be warriors, were said to be eaters of human flesh: anthropophagi, to use the scientific term then current. And though later historians doubt the truth of that report, *cannibal* gradually became the everyday word in Spanish, and then in English, for anyone thought to eat humans. An English version of *cannibal* appears as early as 1553 in a translation from the Spanish. The generalization of a local name to a descriptive quality is similar to what happened centuries later in the United States when *bunkum* developed from Buncombe County, North Carolina, and *piker* from Pike County, Missouri.

The warlike Caribs came from northern South America, where there are 20,000 speakers of a language called Carib today. But the Carib language Columbus encountered was entirely different. It is sometimes called Island Carib to make the distinction clear. Island Carib belonged to the Arawakan or Maipúrean family of Central and South America. It got the name Carib because these Arawakan people were conquered and ruled by Caribs.

There are still some Island Caribs on the islands of Dominica and St. Vincent, but their language was last heard in the 1920s and is now extinct. Before its extinction, Carib gave us, through Spanish, such words as *canoe* (1555), *caiman* (crocodile, 1577), *peccary* (a piglike mammal, 1613), *pirogue* (canoe made from a hollowed tree, 1666), and *curare* (1777).

~PANAMA

guan *from Kuna*

Guans are not the stuff of epics. There is no *Guan with the Wind*, at least in English. But bird watchers come from far away to add the colorful Central American birds to their list. And they can add a lot, because there are more than fifty different species of guan. There is the Crested Guan (*Penelope purpurascens*), noted for the little crest on its head, along with its red throat and the purple around its eyes. There is the Black Guan (*Chamaepetes unicolor*), in your basic black, which is also the color of the Crested Guan's body. And then there are, among others, the Red-faced Guan, Rusty-margined Guan, Band-tailed Guan, Bearded Guan, Blue-throated Piping-Guan, White-winged Guan, Dusky-legged Guan, Wattled Guan, Sickle-winged Guan, Horned Guan, Andean Guan, Highland Guan—you get the picture.

All guans are turkey-like creatures who have been a useful link in the food chain of the human residents of Central America. They were noted in the English language as early as 1743, by George Edwards in his *Natural History of Uncommon Birds*: "The Quan or Guan, so called in the West Indies, . . . is a little bigger than a common Hen."

The Indians that named them were the Kuna of Panama and Colombia. There are about seven hundred speakers of Kuna in each country. Kuna apparently belongs to the Chibchan family of two dozen languages in Central America. In Panama, the Kuna have been granted an autonomous reserve, the San Blas Islands, where they can follow their traditional way of life and display it for tourists. The men fish, the women sew, and you can spend the night on Dolphin Island "in traditional Kuna-style huts with cozy beds and shared baths" and visit the Kuna Museum on the neighboring island of Ailigandi the next day. The main stronghold of the Kuna language, however, is on the mainland to the south in the villages of Paya and Pucuro. No other words of Kuna have migrated to English.

∼NICARAGUA

dory *from Miskito*

For hundreds of years, the smallest and plainest of boats has been called a dory. Originally it was just a log hollowed out, as it still is along the Miskito (or Mosquito) Coast of Nicaragua and Honduras. Katherine Borland of the Historical Museum of Southern Florida writes about the Miskito: "on the Atlantic Coast the dory or dugout canoe remains the major means of transportation. Thus, any adult male who grew up there knows how to build a dory. He simply goes to the forest, chooses a suitable tree, and starts chopping."

Today in the United States the name has come to mean a flat-bottomed, high-sided, sharp-prowed little sailboat. A fine modern example is the Cape Dory 10, designed in the 1960s by Carl Alberg for Cape Dory Yachts of East Taunton, Massachusetts: just ten and a half feet long, four feet wide, and weighing about 150 pounds. It was described as "an ideal tender. The Cape Dory 10 is an excellent example of traditional and functional design accomplished with modern materials. She has a rugged fiberglass hull, solid teak gunwales and seats, trimmed with bronze hardware. . . . In addition to the rudder and tiller, adjustable centerboard, she comes with a striped sail and a simple gunter rig as standard."

Miskito, to which we are indebted for this one word, is spoken by about 150,000 people in Nicaragua and 10,000 more in Honduras. It is the most widely spoken language in the Misumalpa language family. One other word from Miskito is *cohune* (1805), a palm tree whose fruits are used for oil. The Miskito people resisted both the Somoza and the Sandinista governments in Nicaragua because those regimes threatened their language and culture. The Miskito also figure in Paul Theroux's 1982 novel and the 1986 movie *The Mosquito Coast*, which featured Harrison Ford and River Phoenix.

Incidentally, although there are mosquitos along the Mosquito Coast, the name *mosquito* has nothing to do with *Miskito*. The former is Spanish for "little fly." But by the process known as "folk etymology," the name *Miskito* has sometimes adopted the spelling of the familiar word *mosquito*. It is like the occasional spelling of *wheelbarrow* as *wheelbarrel* to make it make more sense.

∾MEXICO

cenote *from Maya*

You wouldn't want your worst enemy to fall into a cenote. Or maybe you would. If so, you might be thinking of the Mayan "Cenote of Sacrifice" in Chichén Itzá, Yucatán, Mexico. According to now discredited legend, young virgins were thrown into this pool of water to placate the gods. According to still accepted legend, supported by the research of archaeologists, gold and jade objects were thrown in to placate the gods, as were chickens, turkeys, and dogs, and now and then captives of high rank. Captured enemies of lower position were not worthy of sacrifice and were used as slaves instead.

Most cenotes are not so ominous. They are natural sinkholes in limestone filled with water. Geologists tell us that sinkholes begin as underground caverns dug out of the limestone by naturally acidic ground water. When the roof of the cavern collapses, you have a cenote. Over the centuries cenotes fill with debris, even if not with sacrificial objects. Eventually a cenote can fill completely, becoming a basin in which vegetation grows.

Without any danger of being sacrificed, nowadays you can take the plunge into a cenote. There is, for example, the Grand Cenote just off the Cancún-Tuluum highway, where for a small fee you can swim in sparkling water thirty feet deep and into a cave with stalactites. "You don't need a light (the cave isn't that deep)," comments one traveler, "but I strongly recommend a snorkel and mask, because the clarity of the water, and the formations, make this an entirely different experience from ocean snorkeling."

In addition to the Maya, the Taino Indians who lived on the island where the present-day Dominican Republic is located apparently also made ritual offerings in cenotes. A 1997 archaeological expedition there found a cenote that seems to accord with Taino mythology.

Maya or Yucateco is the chief representative of the Mayan language family and the language of the ancient Mayan Indian civilization. It is spoken today by about 700,000 people in Mexico. Cenote has been an English word since 1841, when it was described in detail in an account of travel in central America. (You pronounce it with three syllables, by the way; the last *te* is a separate syllable.) It is the only Maya word in the general vocabulary of English.

∿MEXICO

chocolate *from Nahuatl*

English has had an appetite for Nahuatl words ever since 1604, when our language first tasted chocolate. In an English translation of a Spanish *History of the Indies* published that year is an account of *chocolate,* a drink made by the Aztecs of Mexico from the *cacao* bean. Both words are from the Nahuatl language spoken by the Aztecs, who considered chocolate divine, literally as well as figuratively.

Cacao was a gift from the gods; the tree on which the beans grow served as a bridge between earth and heaven. Chocolate was an everyday drink, but the Aztecs also solemnized everything from marriages to human sacrifices by having the participants drink it.

From the Aztecs the Spanish learned the art of transforming cacao beans into the chief ingredient of hot chocolate by fermenting, drying, and roasting. In 1604 the people of England could only read about chocolate; to taste it they would have to travel to Spain, if not Mexico. But in 1657 a chocolate shop opened in London, and by the end of the century chocolate houses were fashionable meeting places in town. Succeeding centuries found that chocolate was very good as a candy too, and thanks to pioneers like Milton S. Hershey, who developed the process for mass-producing the chocolate bar (not to mention Kisses), we now can indulge our chocaholic passions freely.

Even though the Aztecs were conquered by Spanish speakers nearly 500 years ago, the Nahuatl language is still spoken by nearly a million of the hundred million inhabitants of Mexico. It belongs to the Uto-Aztecan language family, which also includes Hopi, Paiute, and Shoshone. We can thank Nahuatl for about forty delicious English words, including *tomato,* also introduced to English in the 1604 translation, *chili* (1662), and *tamale* (1854), as well as *avocado* (1697) and its derivative *guacamole* (1920); the animals *coyote* (1759) and *ocelot* (1774); and the religious psychedelic drug *peyote* (1849).

⌁MEXICO

huaraches *from Tarascan*

"I looked like a maniac, of course, with my hair all wet, my shoes sopping. My shoes, damn fool that I am, were Mexican huaraches, plantlike sieves not fit for the rainy night of America and the raw road night."

So wrote Jack Kerouac in *On the Road* (1957), thereby stepping up awareness of *huaraches* in the English language. They had made their initial imprint in English earlier, in the previous century; an 1887 book about Mexico mentions "leathern aprons and sandals of the same, called *guarachi*," while an 1892 article on Spanish and Mexican words used in Texas lists *huaráchos* as "a kind of sandals worn by Indians and the lower classes generally. Used generally in the plural only."

But perhaps the greatest impression huaraches have made in English was with the help of the Nike marketing department. In 1991 and 1992, Nike introduced Air Huarache shoes for running, cross training, baseball, tennis, and aerobics. These were not typical Nike sneakers but minimalist shoes inspired by Indian sandals of sagebrush bark found in 1938 in Fort Rock Cave, Oregon, and said to be about 9,000 years old. The modern Air Huaraches used the principle of sandal straps with a sock-like insert to cushion the foot. From some people it inspired raves; on the Worldwide Sneaker Report on the World Wide Web, Air Huaraches were named "All Time Top Sneaker" by enthusiasts in Manchester and London, England; Kagoshima and Saitama, Japan; Moscow; and Barbados. Nike no longer makes Air Huaraches, but you can still buy traditional huaraches in Mexico, now sometimes made with tire tread.

Tarascan or Purépecha is spoken by about 120,000 people in Michoacán, to the west of Mexico City. It is a language with no known relatives. Huarache is the only word of Tarascan that has made its way (by means of Spanish) into English.

∿ MEXICO

Geronimo! *from Mexican Spanish*

Leaping from airplanes to land on the battlefields of World War II, paratroopers of the U.S. Army shouted the Spanish name given by Mexican soldiers to an Indian chief who had terrorized white settlers in northern Mexico and the south-western United States eighty years earlier. How did it happen that "Geronimo!" sometimes followed by an Indian war whoop became the battle cry of American paratroopers?

Apparently the immediate cause was a movie of that name that paratroopers had watched as they were beginning their training in 1940. The 1939 movie depicts Geronimo, chief of the Chiricahua Apache tribe, as a bloodthirsty villain. Portrayed by the wild-eyed actor Chief Thundercloud, the movie Geronimo is an Apache whose sole delight is slaughtering whites, preferably defenseless women and children. According to Cinebooks' *Motion Picture Guide,* "Chief Thundercloud has only one expression—murderous."

Needless to say, that movie version of Geronimo is not entirely the truth. The real Geronimo, born in 1829 in what is now Arizona, lived peaceably until Mexicans killed his wife, mother, and children in 1858. In retaliation, he led raids against both Mexican and American white settlers, then settled on a reservation. In 1876, when the U.S. government tried to move the Chiricahua to New Mexico, he took up arms again and continued his occasional raids until 1887, when he was finally captured and relocated to Fort Sill, Oklahoma. He took up farming, converted to Christianity, and became such a public figure that he was in the inaugural parade for President Theodore Roosevelt in 1905. *Geronimo's Story of His Life*, published in 1906, three years before his death, was a best seller.

Back in 1940, however, it was the ferocious warrior of the earlier film who commanded the attention of the paratroopers. It is said that Aubrey Eberhardt, a member of the first platoon testing methods of air drops in 1940, was inspired by the movie to announce that he would shout "Geronimo" as he jumped the next day. He did; his shout was heard on the ground; and the rest of the paratroopers adopted it as their call. Since then, of course, any kind of attack can be heralded in English with *Geronimo!*

In his Apache language, the warrior was known as Goyathlay or "one who yawns." It was the Mexicans who called him Geronimo, the Spanish version of the name Jerome. Numerous other words have crossed the border into English via Mexican Spanish, including Nahuatl words like *chocolate*, and more recently *chihuahua* (1858), a breed of dog named after the Mexican city, and *maquiladora* (1976), a south-of-the-border factory that uses cheap labor to make products for export to the north.

∼UNITED STATES

moccasin *from Virginia Algonquian (Powhatan)*

The arrival of three shiploads of English speakers at a place they called Jamestown on May 14, 1607, marked the

beginning of English immigration to North America and the beginning of a period of intensive immigration of American Indian words to the English language. Down the road, the first natives the English encountered were ones they called Powhatans after the name of their chief. They and the English were uneasy neighbors, but after some touchy encounters, the chief's daughter Pocahontas saved Captain John Smith's life and sent the English enough food to keep them from starving.

The Virginia Algonquians also provided important words to describe the creatures and cultures of their land, including in the first years of English presence *raccoon* (1609), *opossum* (1610), *tomahawk* (1611), and *persimmon* (1612). Among the most notable contributions was a kind of footwear unfamiliar to the English: the moccasin. In his 1612 glossary of Indian words, Captain Smith lists

"Mockasins: Shoes."

Ever since, moccasins have been admired by Americans of all ancestries. They have special potency in Henry Wadsworth Longfellow's 1855 *Song of Hiawatha*, or at least Hiawatha's moccasins do:

> He had moccasins enchanted,
> Magic moccasins of deer-skin;
> When he bound them round his ankles,
> When upon his feet he tied them,
> At each stride a mile he measured!

There are perhaps 3,000 Powhatans, or Virginia Algonquians, still living in eastern Virginia nowadays, but their Algonquian language is long since extinct.

∿UNITED STATES

sea puss *from Unquachog*

Southampton, Long Island, can claim the distinction of spawning the original sea puss. The name implies that it is a cute cousin of the seal, or perhaps a mysterious monster of the deep. Its alternative spelling *sea purse* suggests even stranger goings-on. But in fact the sea puss is not an animal or a purse at all, just an inlet connecting Mecox Bay with the ocean. Starting in the 1650s, English-speaking settlers in Southampton gave particular attention to what the local Unquachog Indians called the *sepuus* because its connection to the ocean would silt up and need to be dug open. Records of the Town of Southampton for 1653 report that "Mr Rayner & Iohn White are appointed & left to agree (if they can) with the miller concerneing the alteration of his mill to ease the town of the burthen of opening the sepoose." But the burden continued, as the record reports for 1665: "It is concluded that John Jessup shall call forth thirty men to goe to the west sepoose, and if any refuse to goe, being warned, they shall pay to ye town five shillings."

If the word were confined to Southampton, it would be hard to claim that *sea puss* is part of the general vocabulary of English. But beyond Southampton, at least in parts of the east coast of the United States, during the past century or two *sea puss* has acquired a new meaning: the undertow, a strong current near the shore moving out to sea. So in 1904 the *New York Tribune* reported, "McDonald was a good swimmer, but, getting caught in a sea puss, was shot out to the deep sea with great velocity." And from the *Baltimore Sun* in 1932: "The sea-purse swooped in and picked up a girl bather, who was suddenly seen to whirl about on the surface of the water like a cork."

The Unquachog Indians, who first named the sea puss, are long gone, and so is their language. We know, however, that it was a member of the Algonquian language family prevalent along the Atlantic coast when the first English speakers arrived. Nothing else from Unquachog has remained in present-day English.

∼UNITED STATES

manitou *from Ojibwa*

"Can you fathom the mysteries of God? Can you probe the limits of the Almighty?" Zophar the Naamathite asks Job in the New International Version of the Hebrew Bible. And the Psalmist says, in the King James version, "Great is the Lord, and greatly to be praised; and His greatness is unsearchable." Whatever the version, even the most deeply religious, perhaps especially the most deeply religious, acknowledge God to be ultimately unknowable.

And the God of the Bible has been an intimate acquaintance of English speakers ever since the first Christian missionaries converted the pagan Anglo-Saxons some 1400 years ago. If that God is beyond understanding, how much more so must be the supernatural beings that have not been part of English-speaking cultures. So this untheological book will not undertake a definitive explanation of the *manitou*. It can be said, however, that *manitou* is not the "Great Spirit," an Indian equivalent of the Christian God, as some ecumenical Christians once believed. Instead, the *manitou* in various American Indian cultures is said to be either a spiritual essence that pervades all creatures or else to be particular creatures that are divine or partly divine.

And we can definitively say this: *manitou* is an Ojibwa word. A present-day source explains of the Ojibwa, "Their religion is based on the idea that each person possesses two souls and that all is controlled by supernatural beings known as manito." The English language learned a similar word from a different Indian language, *Montoac* from Virginia Algonquian, as early as 1588. But the reason English speakers are inclined to use the Ojibwa form of the word is that a famous American poem of the nineteenth century, Henry Wadsworth Longfellow's *Hiawatha* (1855), does so, telling stories based on Ojibwa legend as accurately as contemporary research allowed. Chapter I of Longfellow's poem begins:

> On the Mountains of the Prairie,
> On the great Red Pipe-stone Quarry,
> Gitche Manito, the mighty,
> He the Master of Life, descending,
> On the red crags of the quarry
> Stood erect, and called the nations,
> Called the tribes of men together.

The setting of *Hiawatha* is the south shore of Lake Superior, where many Ojibwa still live. All told, there are about 20,000 speakers of Ojibwa in the United States and even more in Canada, about 30,000 around Lake Huron, Lake Superior, and north and west. Ojibwa comes in eastern, northern, and western varieties. It belongs to the central branch of the Algonquian-Ritwan language family. Ojibwa has given about a dozen words to English, including *pecan* (1712), *totem* (1776), and *chipmunk* (1832).

⟜ UNITED STATES

succotash *from Narragansett*

Sufferin' succotash! That now-familiar epithet was first uttered by Sylvester the cat in his Loony Tunes debut, the 1945 cartoon "Life With Feathers." It could be considered belated recognition that several centuries earlier *succotash* suffered a little in translation from the Narragansett language once spoken on Narragansett Bay in present-day Rhode Island. In 1643 Roger Williams gave "beans" as translation of Narragansett *manusqussedash* in his *Key into the Language of America,* and there is also a Narragansett word *misickquatash* meaning "ear of corn." Putting the corn and beans together in a pot, somehow we have the English word *soccotash,* first noted in a New England diary in 1751.

Perhaps succotash suffers because it isn't often considered gourmet food. Its preparation can consist of nothing more than combining a can of corn and a can of beans. But it's possible to imagine otherwise. A modern recipe by Paula Giese on her American Indian Web site calls for fresh ingredients: beans boiled with salt and rosemary, corn fried in butter then mixed with more butter, parsley, chicken consommé, and flour. The mixture is heated and stirred till it thickens, then finished by adding a cup of whipping cream and sprinkling with parsley or ground pepper. Is that better?

Narragansett, an Eastern Algonquian language, is now extinct. But it flourished during the first centuries of English-speaking settlement in New England and contributed at least a dozen words to the English language, including *tautog* (1643), *mummichog* (1787), *menhaden* (1792), and *scup* (1848), four kinds of fish; *quahog* (1753), a clam; *squash* (1634) and *samp* (cornmeal mush, 1643), as well as *papoose* (1634).

⌒ UNITED STATES

shoepac *from Unami*

Though it sounds like a designer name from a modern maker of footwear, *shoepac* is in fact an ancient American Indian invention. Apparently it began as *chipahko,* a word meaning nothing more or less than "moccasin" in the Unami Delaware language. But *moccasin* was already at home in English when speakers of English learned about the chipahko, so it gradually changed from being a synonym of moccasin to the name of a distinctive kind of Indian shoe, winterized with an extra sole. And it seems also to have been adopted as the military name for winter shoes. A 1755 letter to George Washington advises, "It would be a good thing to have Shoe-packs or Moccosons for the Scouts."

The Indian word is no kin of English *shoe,* but English speakers and writers could not resist the analogy in adapting *chipahko* to *shoepac.* It is, after all, and by coincidence, a shoe that is packed.

By the twentieth century, *shoepac* had become a standard military name for a boot designed to withstand snow and cold. It's mentioned in a memoir of the World War II Battle of the Bulge: "The wet winter months took a terrible toll on Allied troops, and Littlejohn's personnel strained to meet the ever growing demand for winter field jackets, shelter halves, wool blankets, socks, overshoes and shoepacs." Even more memorable for American soldiers and Marines were the shoepacs of the Korean War winters of 1950-52. "The Shoe-Pac consisted of a rubber foot, leather top and felt insoles," recalled one marine. "During marches the feet would perspire in the boots, and when one stopped the water would freeze and result in frostbite. It was necessary to change socks and insoles numerous times a day."

Unami is a member of the eastern branch of the Algonquian-Ritwan language family. It is spoken nowadays by about one hundred people in northern New Jersey, the Delaware Valley, and Oklahoma. *Shoepac* seems to be the only word of Unami in present-day English.

⌒ CANADA

punkie *from Munsee*

If you're attacked by a swarm of punkies, you'll probably be in the north woods rather than at a rock concert or a night club. That's because the punkies named by Munsee Indians long ago are not the in-your-face human variety but in-your-face midges, little biting bugs so small they are also called *no-see-ums*.

These punkies are less than a quarter-inch long and skinny to boot. You may not notice them because their bite doesn't register at first, but it soon can become a fierce itch and a blotch an inch across. And that's just one bite.

If you know mosquitos, you know some of the traits of *Culicoides furens* (to use their formal name). They are bloodsuckers, only the females bite, and they breed in standing water. But they don't hang around as long as mosquitos. Punkies generally swarm only for a few weeks in the spring, rather than staying for the whole summer. And they don't travel as far as mosquitos can. They are reluctant to leave the neighborhood where they grew up, so you can often escape their attack just by stepping away a few yards.

Punkies have long been known to English speakers in North America. A traveler in the colony of New York in 1769 noted, "We begin to be teazed with Muscetoes and little Gnats called here Punkies." The name ultimately derives from the word for dust or ashes in the Algonquian languages, a word that was probably the source of modern *punk*, the smoldering wick used for fireworks. *Punkie* seems to have its specific origin in *pónkwus,* a word in the Eastern Algonquian language known as Munsee. Today that language is spoken only in southern Ontario, the heart of punkie country. Munsee is a Delaware language in the eastern branch of the Algonquian-Ritwan language family. It is almost extinct; a 1991 survey located only seven or eight elderly speakers on the reservation in Ontario. Munsee is not noted as the source of any other English words.

ᨑ UNITED STATES

cohosh *from Eastern Abenaki*

What exactly is a cohosh? Good question. We know it's a potent medicinal plant that first entered our vocabulary and pharmacopeia in New England. But is it the baneberry or the black snakeroot? Or something else entirely, a blue cohosh?

Any of those answers is possible in present-day English, according to the careful account in the *Dictionary of American Regional English.* Perhaps there was some difficulty in translation when speakers of English first learned the name *cohosh* from the Abenaki Indians of New England. (We aren't sure when that was; the name appears in print in a geographical work of 1789.) Or perhaps the Abenaki used *cohosh* in a general sense that included the three plants. In any case, they all are good medicine.

For example, the root of the black cohosh, alias black snakeroot and cohosh bugbane, is, according to various authorities, an analgesic, an antirheumatic, an antispasmodic, an astringent, an expectorant, and a sedative. You can use it for pain, rheumatism, constipation, colds, coughs, and insomnia. It is said to relieve pain by constricting the blood vessels. But go easy on the dose; it's so potent that it can affect your nervous system and lower your pulse. If you get a headache, you know you've taken too much.

This variety of cohosh, known to botanists as *Cimicifuga racemosa*, is a perennial that grows on long slender stalks up to nine feet tall. Its leaves are notched like those of a maple. It has little white flowers on long upright stems, sometimes called "fairy candles." But for medicinal purposes it's the root that counts.

Eastern Abenaki, which includes a dialect known as Penobscot, is an Algonquian-Ritwan language. It may now be extinct; in 1991 that there was only one aged speaker left. But at the time of the early English-speaking settlements in northern New England, the Abenaki were important linguistic contacts. We are indebted to the Eastern Abenaki for the well-known *wigwam* (1628) and possibly *tumpline* (1796), a strap worn around the head or chest to carry the weight of a backpack.

∼UNITED STATES

hackmatack *from Western Abenaki*

Go to the wetlands of North America's northern woods, to bogs, or to the shores of lakes and streams, and you may find yourself face to face with a hackmatack. It's a kind of larch, a pine tree with an odd habit. Like other pines, it has a tall central trunk and cones and needles, but it sheds its needles in the fall and grows new ones from buds in the spring, thus being technically a deciduous tree rather than an evergreen. As a result, the hackmatack isn't good winter cover for game or hunters. But it does have its uses; it's not so hard to hack a hackmatack, as the tree is known in the north. (To the south it is more commonly called a *tamarack*. No one is sure where that name came from, though it is probably also of Algonquian origin.)

Before English speakers came to North America, Indians used the wood of the hackmatack for toboggans and arrow shafts, its roots for sewing canoes and weaving into bags, and its bark and needles as medicine. "The bark used as a decoction," wrote Mrs. Maud Grieve in *A Modern Herbal* in 1931, "is laxative, tonic, diuretic and alterative, useful in obstructions of the liver, rheumatism, jaundice and some cutaneous diseases." The tree makes good fire-wood, too.

From the Indians English speakers learned not only the name of the tree (mentioned in a history of New Hampshire in 1792) but some of its uses as well, and the settlers added new uses of their own: the roots made "knees" to support the decks of ships, the trunks became ribs of clipper ships, the soft needles filled mattresses and pillows. And the tree's root, "hard as briar," made good bowls for handmade pipes.

Western Abenaki, like Eastern Abenaki discussed under *cohosh*, belongs to the Algonquian-Ritwan family. Its speakers live in northern New England and southern Canada, but there are hardly any left; in 1991 there were only about twenty speakers of Western Abenaki, all elderly. No other words from Western Abenaki have settled into English.

⟿ UNITED STATES

squeteague *from Mohegan*

Off the Atlantic coast of the United States you will some-times find a fish called a *squeteague*, up to three feet long, dark green with purplish spotted sides, excellent for eating if you can catch it. There are only two difficulties in catch-ing a squeteague: First, it may be hard to find, because the population varies and the fish migrate up and down the coast. Second, the fish may slip away, because the flesh around its mouth is so weak that it tears rather than hold-ing the hook.

Algonquian Indians of the Atlantic coast told English speakers the name *squeteague*, which is written as *squeterg* in a Massachusetts document of 1803. The name could come from Narragansett, but it just as likely came from Mohegan *cheegut* of eastern Connecticut. Because of its weak flesh, the squeteague is also known as *weakfish* (1791), and it is also called *sea trout* or *spotted sea trout*, even though it is not a trout. To biologists it is just *Cynoscion regalis*.

Mohegan was a member of the Algonquian-Ritwan language family. There are still Mohegan Indians in Connecticut, but their language is no longer spoken. When James Fenimore Cooper wrote about "Mohicans," he was referring to a different people, properly called Mahicans, who resided in the Hudson River valley. Their descendants now have a reservation in Shawano County, Wisconsin.

∼ UNITED STATES

mugwump *from Massachusett*

From the Indians of North America, the English adventurers who came to their continent learned more than just the names of plants, animals, and tools. The Indians also taught new life styles: smoking, trading with beads (*wampumpeag*, 1627), and holding ceremonial meetings (*powwow*, 1625). They also taught about leadership. The Massachusett Indians provided the examples of *sunck*, a female chief (1676), and *mugwump*, a male. The first has sunk into oblivion; the second emerged much later as an important term in American politics.

There was no such expectation when *mugwump* was first associated with English, in Thomas Eliot's 1663 translation of the Bible into the Massachusett or Natick language, *Mamusse Wunneetupanatamwe up-Biblum God* ("The-whole holy his-Bible God"). In the genealogies of Genesis 36 and I Chronicles 1, for the English *duke* of the King James Version Eliot used *mugquomp*. Perhaps because dukes were scarce among the English-speaking inhabitants of New England, no use of *mugwump* is recorded in the English of that time.

Evidently, though, it was not forgotten. In the 1830s it appears as a somewhat humorous designation for an important person, as in *The Nation* in 1832: "the Knights of Kadosh and the Most Worshipful Mug-Wumps of the Cabletow," whatever that might mean. A book of 1835 explains that *mugwump* is "used at the present day vulgarly and masonically, as synonymous with greatness and strength." But it was in 1884 that it acquired its present political meaning. That year Republicans who refused to support the party's nominee for president, James G. Blaine, were labeled "little mugwumps" by loyalists, and since then the word has remained a term for a dissident or political independent.

Massachusett or Natick was an Eastern Algonquian language spoken in the present-day state of the same name. It is extinct, absorbed with the few remaining descandants of the tribe into the state's English-speaking culture; but it lives in our language in words like *wampum* and *squaw* (1634). Massachusett is so closely related to Narragansett that it is difficult to tell which is the source of such words as *sachem* (1622) and *powwow* (1625).

∼UNITED STATES

wapiti *from Shawnee*

The elk and its ilk are easy to confuse. What we call *elk* in North America is different from what our language calls *elk* in Europe, which is the same as the North American *moose*. Confusing? That is how *wapiti* came to be an English word, to distinguish the American elk from the quite different European one. Naturalist Benjamin S. Barton did the honors in 1806: "As the [American] Elk has not to my knowledge been described by any systematic writer on Zoology, I have assumed the liberty of giving it a specific name. I have called it Wapiti, which is the name by which it is known among the Shawnees or Shawnese Indians."

The name *wapiti* also has the advantage of being plain and descriptive, at least in its native language. In Shawnee, *wapiti* is said to mean "white rump," a distinguishing feature of the American elk. The Indian name is also a reminder that the vast herds of these animals that formerly populated North America were important renewable resources for the Indian inhabitants. Wapiti were hunted not only for their meat but for their hides, their bones, their antlers, and even their teeth. The hides made moccasins, robes, shields, and the walls of tepees. Bones and antlers made weapons and game pieces. Wapiti teeth made necklaces and decorations for clothes.

In later times, with destruction of their habitat and intensive hunting, wapiti were driven nearly to extinction by the English-speaking population of North America. But conservation laws and regulated hunting have made them abundant again. Elk (or wapiti) farming is also increasing the population.

Aside from the products already mentioned, wapiti are a source of velvet, the soft tissue of new antlers of adult males. According to a company that sells it, "Velvet antler has been used for centuries in strengthening the skeletal, circulatory and endocrine systems. Velvet antler has been shown to increase mental capacity, help PMS, impotence, and stress reduction."

Shawnee is another of the languages in the Algonquian-Ritwan family, belonging to the central branch. In Oklahoma there are still about two hundred speakers of Shawnee. *Wapiti* is the one Shawnee word that has found itself a place in English.

∼UNITED STATES

mechameck *from Menominee*

In the psychedelic sixties, everything seemed hallucinatory, including for a spell the seeds of the morning glory. Mechameck belongs to the same family as the common morning glory, has similar flowers, and is said to have certain physiological effects. But the effects of mechameck are from the root rather than from the seeds.

Mechameck is also called *bigroot, hog potato, manroot, man-in-the-ground*, and *man-of-the-earth*, and for good reason. Its perennial root is from two to eight feet—yes, that's feet, not inches—long, tapering from five inches across in the middle to two inches at the end.

In a pinch, you can get a lot of nourishment from a mechameck root. It's a close relative of the sweet potato, although it seems to be the black sheep of the family. Yellow-brown on the outside, milky on the inside, it is said to have "an acrid taste and disagreeable odor." Add to that the labor of digging it out of the ground and roasting it, and it is clear why for Indians it was only a food of last resort.

And what are the special effects of eating mechameck root? There is a clue in another of its names, *Indian purge*. That is, it is a mild laxative and diuretic. But back in 1854, John King, author of *The American Eclectic Dispensatory*, told of a more unusual property: "It is asserted that the Indians can handle rattlesnakes with impunity, after wetting their hands with the milky juice of this root."

Menominee is an Algonquian language, now nearly extinct. A survey in 1977 located only eight speakers of the

language among the 3,500 residents of the former
Menomini Reservation in northeast Wisconsin.
Mechameck first appears in English in an 1828 book of
medicinal herbs. No other words of Menominee have
made their way into English.

∽United States

wickiup *from Sac and Fox*

When roughing it was still nearly every American's way of
life, at least in the West, the Fox Indians knew how to make
the best of it with a wickiup. On a convenient spot of level
ground they would draw a circle perhaps eight feet in
diameter and dig a trench beside it. In the trench they
would put the ends of poles made from young trees or
branches. If the poles were long and flexible enough, they
would bend them into arches; otherwise they would tie
them together in the middle to make a dome five or six
feet high. Covered with small branches and grass everywhere except the doorway, this would make a snug hut. In
cold weather they would leave an opening in the roof for
smoke from a central fireplace.

There was nothing to buy, no housing to carry from
place to place. Each time they arrived at a new place, they
could build the whole thing in a few hours from locally
available materials. "They," of course, were women; the
men would be busy hunting.

In English, wickiups have been mentioned at least
since 1852, when the Portland *Oregonian* told about
Indians who "left their Wick-ey-ups at the Ogden [River]
and came and camped right by the side of us." In 1903, in
her novel *The Land of Little Rain*, Mary Hunter Austin celebrated the life of the Shoshones of the southwestern
desert: "Next to spring, the best time to visit Shoshone
Land is when the deer-star hangs low and white like a
torch over the morning hills. Go up past Winnedumah and

down Saline and up again to the rim of Mesquite Valley. Take no tent, but if you will, have an Indian build you a wickiup, willows planted in a circle, drawn over to an arch, and bound cunningly with withes, all the leaves on, and chinks to count the stars through."

Austin could be characterized as one of the earliest ecofeminists. She was also one of the first residents of the artists' colony of Carmel, California, and did her writing in a treehouse which she called her wickiup.

Though wickiups were built by many different tribes, the word apparently comes from *wiikiyaapi* meaning "lodge" or "house" in the Sac and Fox or Mesquakie language. Sac and Fox, two dialects of the same language, belong to the Algonquian language family. Nowadays the language is spoken by about seven hundred members of the tribe in Kansas, Nebraska, and Oklahoma.

∾UNITED STATES

dowitcher *from Mohawk*

Is it an elderly, dignified woman, financially well endowed? No, that's a *dowager*. Is it perhaps a stick that, held in the hands, points to water? No, that's a *dowser* or divining rod, but we're getting closer. It does have to do with the water. It's a bird, a shore bird.

As bird watchers know, you don't have to look very hard to find a dowitcher, at least if you're at the seashore in the right season. You'll be looking for a bird of medium size, with dull yellowish legs, a tail that is barred black and white, and a white *V* that extends up its back. It will have a long straight bill if it's the long-billed dowitcher and a short straight bill if it's the short-billed dowitcher.

Dowitchers breed in the north, in arctic or subarctic regions. They nest near water in meadows and bogs. Their diet is insects, seeds, and seafood. They like to prospect for small mollusks, crustaceans, and marine worms by poking their heads rapidly up and down into soft mud, a motion that reminds bird watchers of a sewing machine.

The name *dowitcher*, recorded in English as early as 1841, comes from one or more of the Iroquoian Indian languages. Which one is not certain, but Mohawk is as likely as any. It is now spoken by about 3,000 people in northern New York State and adjacent areas of Canada. No other word of Mohawk is found in the general vocabulary of English.

⌐ UNITED STATES

catalpa *from Muskogee or Creek*

The Seminole Indians of Florida gave to the English language the name of one of their most impressive trees: the catalpa. The tree is distinguished for its long narrow pods as well as its abundant white blossoms. It was noted in English as early as 1731, by Mark Catesby (1683-1749) in his book grandly titled *The Natural History of Carolina, Florida and the Bahama Islands: Containing the Figures of Birds, Beasts, Fishes, Serpents, Insects, and Plants: Particularly the Forest-Trees, Shrubs, and Other Plants, Not Hitherto Described, Or Very Incorrectly Figured by Authors. Together With Their Descriptions In English and French. To Which, Are Added Observations on the Air, Soil, and Waters: With Remarks upon Agriculture, Grain, Pulse, Roots, &c. To the Whole, Is Prefixed A New and Correct Map of the Countries Treated Of.*

"The Catalpa Tree," Catesby explains, "was unknown to the inhabited parts of Carolina, till I brought the seeds from the remoter parts of the country." And, he added, "'tis become an Ornament to many of their Gardens," as it remains today.

The language from which *catalpa* comes is Muskogee or Creek, spoken nowadays by some 10,000 Seminoles and Creeks in Florida and Oklahoma. It belongs to the

Muskogean family and is related to Choctaw. The area we now call Georgia and Alabama was the original home of the Creeks. Some of them, called Seminoles by the Spanish (from *cimarrón* meaning "wild" or "runaway"), moved into Florida and became prominent there in the eighteenth century. In the nineteenth, though they held their own against the U.S. government in what were called the Seminole Wars, most of them were forced out of their lands to Oklahoma Territory. To this day, however, some Seminoles remain on their own Floridian lands.

From Muskogee we also have the *tupelo* (1730), a swamp-dwelling tree, and *coontie* (1819) or arrowroot, formerly used as flour by the Seminoles. The names *Chattahoochee* ("marked stones") and *Miami* ("that place") are also from Muskogee.

ᔕUNITED STATES

appaloosa *from Choctaw*

This one is a fish story. True, appaloosa is best known as a favorite kind of horse—sturdy, quick, and quick-witted—developed by the Nez Percé Indians living near the Palouse River in what is now Idaho. The river, therefore, has been suspected as the source of the name. Yet the first mention of "Opelousa" horses is from an 1849 book on Texas, and there is a source of the name closer to Texas in neighboring Louisiana, the Indian tribe known as Opelousa. Neither of these tribes speaks Choctaw.

Let us rein in speculation about the horse, however, and go fishing for a moment. The earliest record of something like *appaloosa* noted in the *Dictionary of American Regional English* is for 1845, and it is for a fish in Alabama: "Right round *that* was whar I'd ketch the monstrousest, most oudaciousest Appaloosas cat, the week before, that ever come outen the Tallapoosy." This "Appaloosas cat" is a spotted catfish otherwise known as a *flathead catfish*,

Mississippi bullhead, morgan cat, pied cat, and *yellow cat,* among other names. A century after the first mention, a 1948 newspaper in Oklahoma mentioned "tackle-busting river cats, or Appaluchians."

The fish name *appaloosa* very likely comes from Choctaw *apolusa,* meaning "to be daubed" or "spotted." It is tempting to take the Choctaw word as the source for the horse name too, perhaps reinforced by the name of the Louisiana tribe, since the appaloosa horse is also spotted in the back. But Idahoans and Nez Percé might disagree, because the latter are unquestionably the source of the horse, and they were a long way from Louisiana.

Choctaw is the language spoken by Indians who lived in present-day Mississippi and Louisiana when the first Europeans arrived. It is a member of the Muskogean language family. Most Choctaw now live in Oklahoma; there are said to be about 10,000 speakers of Choctaw in a total population of 25,000. One other English word from Choctaw, transmitted to us by the French in Louisiana, is *bayou* (1763).

∾UNITED STATES

Catawba wine *from Catawba*

The tribe named the river, the river named the grape, and the grape named the wine. Or perhaps the tribe named the grape and the grape named the river. Whatever the sequence, the Indian tribe of South Carolina known as the Catawba are remembered in a grape and red wine now produced more in New York State and the Midwest than in South Carolina.

Present-day oenophiles are strangely silent on the merits of Catawba wine, but we are rescued by one of the great literary figures of the nineteenth century. In 1854, a gift from the vineyards of Nicholas Longworth of Cincinnati inspired Henry Wadsworth Longfellow to write the poem "Catawba Wine." We take this opportunity to include three of the eleven stanzas:

> . . . For richest and best
> Is the wine of the West,
> That grows by the Beautiful River [the Ohio];
> Whose sweet perfume
> Fills all the room
> With a benison on the giver. . . .
>
> Very good in its way
> Is the Verzenay,
> Or the Sillery soft and creamy;
> But Catawba wine
> Has a taste more divine,
> More dulcet, delicious, and dreamy. . . .
>
> While pure as a spring
> Is the wine I sing,
> And to praise it, one needs but name it;
> For Catawba wine
> Has need of no sign,
> No tavern-bush to proclaim it.

Catawba is still said to be the principal wine grape of Ohio.

At an earlier time, back east, the Catawba were among the first Indians to become acquainted with English-speaking settlers. They maintained friendly relations with the newcomers, taking the colonists' side in the French and Indian Wars and the Revolutionary War, and have managed to keep something of their tribal identity to the present day. Their language belongs to the Siouan family because their remote ancestors came from Siouan territory in the Black Hills of the west. Catawba is still spoken by a handful of Catawba Indians at their 630-acre reservation near Rock Hill, South Carolina. From the Catawba language we also have *yaupon* (1709), a plant whose leaves make a bitter tea that is described as "emetic and purgative."

∼UNITED STATES

tepee *from Dakota and Lakota*

Long before trailers were invented, Americans enjoyed mobile homes. Long before English was spoken in North America, Plains Indians moved from place to place throughout the year, taking their homes with them. They had lightweight, comfortable, collapsible structures that the Dakota and Lakota called *tepees* (or *teepees* or *tipis;* we agree on the English pronunciation but have not reached consensus on the spelling). The word is used in English descriptions of Indian life as early as 1743.

Tepees were tall, cone-shaped, family-sized tents made of animal skins wrapped around poles. When buffalo were abundant, tepees were made of buffalo hide. After the men hunted down the buffalo, the women prepared the hide, scraping it, soaking it for several days so the hair would be easy to remove, washing it, working in a mash made of buffalo brain, then finally sewing hides together. A dozen or more hides would be required for each tepee.

A well-built tepee would have smoke "ears" to vent fires and allow air circulation, and a dew cloth to absorb humidity and prevent drafts. It would be painted on the outside. The door faced east, away from the prevailing wind and toward the morning sun. The tepee was a sacred place as well as a residence; the floor represented the earth, the walls the sky, and the poles the pathways from earth to the world of the spirits. Behind the fireplace there would be a family altar, a simple space of bare earth on which incense was burned.

Before the Europeans came, dogs pulled the poles of the tepees when the community moved. After horses were available, they provided the motive power. Wood was scarce on the Plains, and some of the traveling was done to get wood for the poles.

Dakota and Lakota are two varieties of the language spoken by the people who call themselves collectively Oceti Sakowin. They are also known as Sioux, a term they avoid because it is a derogatory epithet originally used by their enemies the Ojibwa. The language of the Oceti Sakowin belongs to a family linguists called Siouan, which also includes Catawba. Today there are about 20,000 speakers of Dakota and 6,000 of Lakota in the Dakotas, Minnesota, and Nebraska. One other word from Dakota is *wahoo* (1857), a shrub also called *arrowwood* because it was used for arrows and *burning bush, bursting heart,* and *strawberry bush* because of its pink berries.

∼UNITED STATES

hogan *from Navajo or Dine*

Like a church for Christians or a mosque for Muslims, the hogan of the Navajo is a sacred building for religious ceremonies. Like Noah's Ark or the Ark of the Covenant, it is built to exact specifications that come from a sacred text. In the case of the Navajo, that text is the Blessing Way, a chant recited in a ceremony of that name. It gives exact specifications of the hogan built for First Man and First Woman at the beginning of our world, when they and many others emerged from the underworld. From then to the present day, to get the spiritual benefit of the hogan, Navajo have followed the directions of the Blessing Way.

A hogan is round like the sun and faces east to catch the rays of the rising sun. Two stones are buried at the entrance to support the doorway. Then the framework is built, with straight male logs and fork-tipped female logs joined together to symbolize the strong partnership between husband and wife. A hogan is said to be male if it has a pointed roof and female if it is covered with adobe to make a round roof. There is a fireplace with a chimney in the center, and designated places for sacred objects throughout the hogan.

Unlike a church, however, a hogan can also serve as a home, and until this century it was the usual Navajo dwelling. This is indicated by the word itself: *hogan* means "home" or "the home place" in Navajo. A more spacious style of hogan, making use of railroad ties laid horizontally, was introduced late in the nineteenth century. Nowadays Navajo are likely to live in conventional houses with a nearby hogan for ceremonies.

Navajo (or Dine, as its speakers prefer to call it) is a vigorously living language spoken by about 150,000 people in northern Arizona and New Mexico and southern Utah. It belongs to the Athapaskan branch of the Na-Dene language family and is closely related to Apache. *Hogan* is the one word of Navajo that is widely known in English, attested since 1871, but until recently the hogan's religious significance was little understood by *bilagáana* (non-Indians).

ᴗ UNITED STATES

Kachina *from Hopi*

The San Francisco Mountains just north of Flagstaff, Arizona, are home to spirits called Kachina by the Hopi Indians who live nearby. The Kachinas make themselves apparent in clouds, mist, and steam, but the Hopi are the ones who make them truly visible in costumes, dancing, and dolls.

Every year, according to the Hopi, just after the winter solstice, the Kachinas visit Hopi villages to renew the world. So that the Kachinas can be more clearly imagined, Hopi men wear Kachina costumes and perform dances in ceremonial chambers known as kivas. The Kachina dancers carve wooden dolls in the likeness of Kachinas that are given to girls and women so that they can have a direct connection with the Kachinas. Infants too are given Kachina dolls, not to play with but to hang on the wall so they can become familiar with Kachinas. Traditional Kachina dolls are simple wooden figures standing stiffly. Recently, in response to interest from non-Hopi collectors, some Kachina dolls have been made as action figures.

Kachinas are respected spirits, but they are not worshipped. Rather, they have a partnership with the Hopi, each giving gifts to the other. One source explains: "The Kachinas have things the Hopi want, such as rain and a guarantee of a fruitful harvest, and the Hopi have things the Kachinas want—prayer feathers, cornmeal, rituals." By one count, there are more than four hundred kinds of Kachinas, representing plants, animals, insects, warriors, runners, guards, clowns, and ogres.

There are about 5,000 speakers of Hopi, most of them living in northeast Arizona. Their language belongs to the Uto-Aztecan family. In addition to *Kachina* (1888) and *kiva* (1871), one other Hopi word that has immigrated into English is *piki* (1889), bread that is given out by Kachina dancers and is also a staple of the Hopi diet.

∾ UNITED STATES

Pima cotton *from O'Odham (Pima)*

Some of the finest cotton in the world bears the name of the Pima Indians of Arizona. But it is a twentieth-century development rather than an ancient tribal tradition. Early in this century the U.S. Department of Agriculture was developing new varieties of Extra-Long-Staple cotton at its experimental farm at Sacaton, south of Tempe in the Gila River Indian Reservation. Pima Indians cultivated the experimental crops of what was then called American-Egyptian cotton. Wanting a new name, the USDA designated the ELS cotton *Pima* in honor of the Pima workers. The first Pima cotton released by USDA was the "Yuma" variety in 1908.

Pima cotton traces its genetic ancestry to the famed cotton cultivated on the Sea Islands of South Carolina as early as the 1790s. This was interbred with varieties from Egypt to develop the Pima. Improvements in Pima cotton have continued since its introduction. "The real break-through came in 1951 when a seed was developed and introduced that produced an ELS cotton with superior fiber properties, luster and silkiness . . . as well as an unusually high yield," says the Supima Association, a trade group. "Subsequent variety releases in the 1970s, 80s and 90s included Pima S-5, S-6 and S-7, all of which boasted higher yields and better spinning characteristics."

The Pima Indians of southern Arizona speak a lan-guage that has been known as Papago-Pima, although they now prefer to call it *O'Odham* and to refer to them-selves as the Tohono O'Odham Nation. Of their total pop-ulation of about 20,000, more than half are said to be fluent in the language. It belongs to the Sonoran branch of the Uto-Aztecan language family. Aside from this use of the name *Pima*, no other words of O'Odham have been imported into English.

∿ UNITED STATES

sego lily *from Southern Paiute*

The Utah state flag has an eagle, a shield, a beehive (the famous symbol of Mormon industriousness), and a sego lily. A sego lily? Yes, and it's the state flower of Utah too, so designated by the legislature after a vote by schoolchildren in 1911. The story goes back to 1847 and the arrival of the Mormons under Brigham Young in the valley of the Great Salt Lake. Food was scarce, especially during the first winter. But the Mormons learned from the Paiute Indians of an abundant supply of food that was safely hidden from ravenous crickets and grasshoppers, the soft walnut-sized root of a lily that the Paiutes called *sego*. Scientists call it *Calochortus nuttallii*, and elsewhere in the West, outside Paiute territory, it goes by many other names, including *butterfly weed, cat's ear, fairy bell, globe tulip, Indian potato, Mariposa lily* or *tulip*, and *mountain tulip*. In Utah, however, the Paiute name remains predominant.

Above ground, the sego lily grows six to eight inches high and produces white, yellow, or pink flowers in clusters of three. But Utah honors it especially for its nutritious root. A typical story of the early years is the 1848 establishment of a fifty-acre farm in Bountiful, Utah, by the family of Daniel and Amanda Henrie. They planted four acres of corn, according to their great-granddaughter, "but the crickets took everything and the parents and brothers and sisters subsisted that first year mostly on sego lily roots, buds off the grease wood, wild greens and jack rabbits or anything they could find to eat to keep body and soul together."

The Southern Paiute language is a member of the Shoshonean branch of the Uto-Aztecan language family. There are about a thousand speakers of Southern Paiute now living in southwestern Utah and neighboring parts of Arizona and Nevada. No other Southern Paiute word has been taken into English.

∼United States

cui-ui *from Northern Paiute*

There is only one place in the world where you will find a cui-ui (pronounced kwee-wee). But it is so important to that place that the people who live there name themselves after it. Members of the Northern Paiute tribe who live at Pyramid Lake near Reno in northern Nevada call themselves the *Kuyuiodokado* or "cui-ui eating people."

Archaeologists say the first people to live along the shores of thirty-mile-long Pyramid Lake arrived more than 11,000 years ago. Paiutes say the first Woman came here after the first Man had banished their oldest son for fighting with his younger brothers and sisters. The son was sent off, with a daughter, to found the Pitt River tribe, and Man then climbed up to live in the Milky Way. That left Woman, who enjoyed her stay-at-home children but missed the banished ones so much that she wept constantly, eventually creating Pyramid Lake with her tears. Woman finally turned to stone, and you can still see her, next to her basket, on the eastern shore of the lake.

Two kinds of fish sustained the Kuyuiodokado: cui-ui and cutthroat trout. They also sustain the tourist trade at Pyramid Lake today. Earlier in the century so much of the Truckee River water that feeds Pyramid Lake was being diverted that the trout were gone and the cui-ui were on the verge of extinction. But in 1967, after a Paiute lawsuit, the federal government gave protection to the cui-ui, and with more water and a breeding program both cui-ui and trout are plentiful in the lake again.

The cui-ui is a relic of prehistoric Lake Lahontan, which once covered 8,000 square miles of northern California and Nevada. "It has a tremendous head, with a sucker mouth," explains our earliest English-language description, from a Nevada newspaper of 1877, which adds that it is "covered with ugly, shaggy fins." Though there are now millions of cui-ui, up from a mere 50,000 in the early 1980s, the fish remains on the endangered species list.

Northern Paiute, like Southern Paiute, is a member of the Numic branch of the Uto-Aztecan language family. There are still about 2,000 speakers of the language, at Pyramid Lake and elsewhere in northern Nevada and nearby California, Oregon, and Idaho. Cui-ui is the only word of Northern Paiute that has swum into English.

∿UNITED STATES

pogonip *from Shoshone*

It's a clear, cool evening in a mountain valley of western Nevada. Heat absorbed from the day's sunshine is radiating up into space, unhindered by clouds. As the temperature drops, the amount of water that the air can hold drops too. If the temperature is above freezing, the result will be a dense ground fog. If the temperature is below freezing, there will be tiny droplets of ice, a pogonip or "ice fog."

Why *pogonip?* Because this unusual weather condition was unfamiliar to the first English speakers who came upon it. They learned about it from Shoshone Indians, who had long had a name for it. It is reported as early as 1865 in a glossary of Indian words from Montana. An 1879 book published in San Francisco described it like this: "He observed what he at first supposed to be a huge bank of dark clouds descend over the valley . . . termed by the Shoshone Indians 'Pogonip.'"

Shoshone is a Uto-Aztecan language still spoken today by about 2,000 members of the tribe in Nevada, Idaho, and Wyoming. Although *pogonip* seems to be the only Shoshone word in current English, the language played an important role in an early exploration of the American West by speakers of English. It was a Shoshone, Sacajawea, wife of interpreter Toussaint Charbonneau, who turned out to be the most important guide and interpreter for Lewis and Clark's expedition of 1803–1806.

∿UNITED STATES

chuckwalla *from Cahuilla*

How much walla could a chuckwalla chuck if a chuckwalla could chuck walla? This question makes as much sense for the chuckwalla as a similar question does for the similarly named woodchuck. The name has nothing to do with chucking or wallahs (the latter a Hindi word referring to people who do particular work, like a *dictionary wallah*). Rather, *chuckwalla* is an English rendition of a Spanish rendition of a word in the Cahuilla Indian language of southern California, recorded in English since 1893.

The chuckwalla is a lizard that lives in the deserts of northern Mexico and the southwestern United States. It likes heat and doesn't start moving in the morning till the sun warms it to about 100 degrees. To cool off when the sun gets too hot, it crawls into the shade, but it can also change color to reflect more or less light and heat.

A strict vegetarian, the chuckwalla contents itself with eating fruit, flowers, buds, and leaves. Its skin hangs loosely from a plump body, and it grows to a good size, eleven to eighteen inches long. It hides from enemies by scurrying between rocks and inflating itself so that it is wedged safely in place. And since it spends most of its time quietly making itself comfortable, the chuckwalla can make a good pet.

Indians in Death Valley, California, sought it out for food. "Desert Indians all eat chuckwallas, big black and white lizards that have delicate white flesh savored like chicken," wrote Mary Hunter Austin in her novel about the Shoshone, *The Land of Little Rain* (1903).

Cahuilla is now spoken by no more than fifty people, mostly on the Cahuilla reservation in the southern California desert. It is a member of the Shoshonean language family, kin to Hopi, Comanche, Ute, and Paiute, among others. No other Cahuilla words have made their way into English.

∾ UNITED STATES

mahala *from Yokuts*

In Hebrew and Arabic, *mahala* means "tender." Although it does not appear in the Bible, the tender-sounding word has been a popular name for women in the United States. By pure coincidence, it also happens to be the word for "woman" in the Yokuts Indian language spoken in the San Joaquin Valley of California. When English speakers rushed to California for gold in the mid-nineteenth century, they heard Yokuts *mokel* and adapted it to the familiar form of *Mahala.*

In California and Nevada, at least for a while, *mahala* became the common English term for an Indian woman. It was never widely used, because English speakers already were familiar with *squaw*, a word that they had learned more than two hundred years earlier from the Massachusett Indians. The earliest evidence we have of *mahala* in English, an article in a San Francisco newspaper of 1850, in fact makes the connection: "All this is the work of the squaws—or, as they call them—'Mo-hales.'" Regrettably, the tender word did nothing to improve the status of Indian women in the eyes of English speakers.

Mary Hunter Austin's 1903 Indian novel about the Southwestern desert, *The Land of Little Rain,* notes the regional distinction in terminology: "It was Dimmick's squaw from Aurora way. If Dimmick had been anything except New Englander he would have called her a mahala." And later she writes:

> I like that name the Indians give to the mountain of Lone Pine, and find it pertinent to my subject,—Oppapago, The Weeper. It sits eastward and solitary from the lordliest ranks of the Sierras, and above a range of little, old, blunt hills, and has a bowed, grave aspect as of some woman you might have known, looking out across the grassy barrows of her dead. From twin gray lakes under its noble brow stream down incessant white and tumbling waters. "Mahala all time cry," said Winnenap, drawing furrows in his rugged, wrinkled cheeks.

In 1990 there were seventy-eight speakers of the Northern Foothill variety of Yokuts, a member of the Penutian language family. Two other varieties, Southern Foothill Yokuts and Valley Yokuts, are now extinct. The only Yokuts word that has immigrated to English is *mahala,* and it too seems virtually extinct.

⌒ UNITED STATES

abalone *from Rumsen*

The most conspicuous organ of an abalone, we are told, is its gonad. Females have a gray or green one, males a cream-colored one. In both genders, it is shaped like a crescent and extends around the side and to the rear. We are also told that abalones have hearts, but no brains. Analogies to certain sex-crazed, mindless humans are to be resisted.

What else? Abalones do have eyes, mouth, tongue. They have soft bodies, big strong feet, and big iridescent shells—just one of each per abalone. An abalone's foot has powerful suction, enabling it to stick tightly to a rock, where it can be shielded by its beautiful shell. In fact, it was the shell that was the attraction for our earliest example of the word in English: "The avelone, which is a univalve, found clinging to the sides of rocks, furnishes the finest mother-of-pearl," wrote a California author in 1850.

Abalone are mollusks, closely related to clams, scallops, and octopuses. They are found on the west coast of the United States and along the shores of other Pacific nations, as well as in South Africa. A really big abalone has a shell measuring nearly twelve inches across. The one you will eat, however, is more likely to be three or four inches. If you want to cook an abalone, be quick. You cook abalone fillets in butter in a very hot skillet for one or two seconds—that's right, seconds—on each side, then serve immediately. Longer cooking makes the abalone tough.

In their natural ocean habitat abalone are getting harder and harder to find. The United States in particular has seen its abalone harvest drop from 1,710 metric tons in 1968 to a mere 50 in 1997. However, the shortage has encouraged the beginnings of systematic abalone farming, or what we might call "abaculture"; there are now fifteen abalone farms in California. That should increase the supply.

Where did our name *abalone* come from? Apparently from a now-extinct Indian language spoken in the region of Monterey Bay, where abalone have long been harvested. The language is Rumsen, a member of the Costanoan family, all of whose languages are also extinct. Field notes from an 1884 investigation of the Rumsen language are archived at the University of California, Berkeley. Aside from that, we know very little about it.

∾United States

sequoia *from Cherokee*

When English speakers first encountered Cherokee Indians, the trees we now call *sequoias* were nowhere in sight. In fact, they were half a continent away, because the Cherokees lived in the southeastern part of what is now the United States, in North Carolina, Georgia, and Tennessee. The sequoias, meanwhile, were standing tall along the Pacific coast, as yet unnamed in English.

What connected the Indians and the trees in the nineteenth century was not the forced displacement of most of the Cherokees to present-day Texas and Oklahoma in 1838 and 1839, known as the "Trail of Tears." That brought them halfway across the continent but still far from the cool coastal climate required by the redwoods.

Rather, the English and scientific name for the trees came from the fame and accomplishments of the Cherokee Chief Sequoya. A silversmith, trader, and U.S. Army soldier who lived in Cherokee County, Georgia, in the early nineteenth century, Sequoya became famous for devising a way of writing his native language. It was not an alphabet like ours, with vowels and consonants, but a syllabary, that is, a system with separate symbols for each of the eighty syllables of Cherokee. The syllabary made written communication possible among his people, including a newspaper he published himself. It was the only writing system devised specially for an American Indian language; many others have been written down, but they all use the English (or other European) alphabet.

And so in the 1860s, when it came time to give a formal name to the world's tallest (*Sequoia sempervirens*) and one of its oldest (*Sequoia giganteum*) trees, they were named in honor of the inventive Chief Sequoya. The tall trees that grow along the coast are commonly called *redwoods*, but the older trees in the mountains have *sequoia* as their common name.

Cherokee is a member of the Iroquoian language family, along with other eastern American Indian languages such as Mohawk and Seneca. Today Cherokee has some 20,000 speakers, mostly in Oklahoma and Texas. Thanks in part to Sequoya's well-established writing system, the language continues to flourish and the number of speakers is actually growing. But no other word from Cherokee has become part of the general English vocabulary.

∾ UNITED STATES

dunk *from Pennsylvania German*

We are a nation of dunkers. What would a doughnut be without coffee, or maybe milk, to dunk it in? Who would

buy biscotti without a mocha or latte for dunking? And where would basketball be without the slam-dunk? Thanks to a small, serious band of immigrants who came to North America more than two centuries ago, we don't have to worry about those questions.

These immigrants were members of the eighteenth-century Brethren movement who fled persecution in Germany and settled in William Penn's tolerant colony of Pennsylvania. There, unmolested, they could practice their back-to-the-Bible, New Testament–centered religion. There are still Brethren churches today, one of their associations having the motto "The Bible, the whole Bible, and nothing but the Bible."

The German word *tunken* means "immerse," and the Brethren were known as *Tunker* because they took baptism seriously and insisted on complete immersion. And proper baptism required not just one but three dunkings, one for each of the persons of the Trinity. The Tunker baptized only adults because they wanted them to understand the significance of the ceremony.

In the distinctive variety of German that these Tunkers developed in Pennsylvania, the *T* became a *D*, and they became *Dunkers* of souls. There is an English-language reference to Dunkers as early as 1744. The name remained unchanged for nearly two more centuries, but in the twentieth century it dipped into everyday use. A 1919 magazine article titled "Some Notes on Dunking" includes the remark, "It should be remembered that the really fastidious dunker never burns his thumb." Today there is nothing sacred about *dunk*.

The language the Dunkers spoke became part of what we call Pennsylvania German. It is an offshoot of the German language, a mixture of dialects of Rhenish Palatinate Low German with High German and some English, so that it does not sound like anything spoken in Germany and indeed is hard for a German to understand. Today about 85,000 people in Pennsylvania, Ohio, and a number of other states speak one of the several dialects of Pennsylvania German. Like German and English, it belongs to the Germanic branch of our Indo-European language family.

Other words English has acquired from Pennsylvania German include *hex* (1830), *spritz* (1902), and *snollygoster* (1860), a name for a self-seeking politician. Pennsylvania

German is also the source of some words in Pennsylvania regional English, including *smearcase* (1829), another name for cottage cheese, and *gumband* (1959), another name for rubber band.

∿ UNITED STATES

OK *from American English*

America's greatest contribution to the English language and indeed to languages all over the world is a joke. Or at least that's how it began.

In the summer of 1838 newspaper columnists in Boston thought nothing funnier than to reduce a phrase to its initials (with an explanation in parentheses). Allen Walker Read, the premier historian of our most famous expression, found this example in the *Boston Morning Post* of June 12, 1838: "We understand that J. Eliot Brown, Esq., Secretary of the Boston Young Men's Society for Meliorating the Condition of the Indians, F.A.H. (fell at Hoboken, N.J.) on Saturday last at 4 o'clock, p.m. in a duel W.O.O.O.F.C. (with one of our first citizens.) What measures will be taken by the Society in consequence of this heart rending event, R.T.B.S. (remains to be seen)."

To add to the humor, columnists sometimes misspelled the abbreviations. One 1838 example was *O.W.*, meaning "all right," with blatant misspellings of both initial letters. That set the stage for an even more outrageous misspelling in March 1839: *O.K.*, translated as "all correct." The joke was that neither *O* nor *K* was correct.

O.K. might have died out with *O.W.*, *R.T.B.S.*, and the rest of the laughable abbreviations if "Old Kinderhook," President Martin Van Buren (born in Kinderhook, New York), hadn't running for reelection in 1840. "O.K. clubs" supporting him were established throughout the country. Old Kinderhook lost, but *O.K.* won a permanent place in American English.

Until about 1900, however, *O.K.* remained obscure. Even Mark Twain apparently never used it. But the twentieth century turned out to be an OK century, perhaps encouraged by scholarly President Woodrow Wilson's use of "okeh" on official documents. (He spelled it "okeh" because he mistakenly thought it came from the Choctaw Indian language.) It was streamlined, too, in this century, increasingly written without the periods that mark it as a mock abbreviation. We now live in an OK world where it is difficult to imagine a conversation or a computer session without frequent use of OK.

∾UNITED STATES

maven *from Yiddish*

What's the word for a know-it-all who really knows it all? We didn't have one until Yiddish gave us *maven* in the mid-twentieth century. A maven is more adept than a mere expert, more authoritative than a mere authority, sharper than a pundit, more up-to-date than a past master.

Since the word was introduced to English (with attestations going back to 1952), we have been blessed with a multitude of mavens. Leo Rosten, in his popular *The Joys of Yiddish* (1968), gave the example of a *herring maven* dreamed up by an *advertising maven.* Nowadays you can find a *sports maven*, a *political maven*, a *public relations maven*, a *principle-driven policy maven*; a *stock market maven*, a *cruise maven*, a *gift maven*; a *movie maven*, a *sci-fi maven*, even a *local historic legal maven.* There is software known as File Maven, a computer buying guide (by *Business Week*) called *Maven*, and Maven self-help videos for women. We hear of computer maven Liam Howlett, figure skating maven Christine Brennan, etiquette maven Letitia Baldrige. There is Gary Ouellet, the maven of magic, and Philip E. Schoenberg, Ph.D., Professional Speaker,

Author, and Motivator, who bills himself as Dr. Phil, the Jewish Maven. And on the Internet you will find Maven, the Virtual Know-It-All: a searchable newsletter for information and resources related to Jewish culture and Israel.

Regrettably, this word was not in the English language when Edgar Allan Poe wrote his most famous poem. He would have found it useful: "Though thy crest be shorn and shaven, thou, I said, art sure no *maven*, Ghastly grim and ancient raven wandering from the Nightly shore."

English should be so lucky to get words from Yiddish! And what a heap we've had in the twentieth century: *noshing* on *bagels, blintzes, borscht, knishes, latke,* and *lox; schmoozing, kibitzing,* or *kvetching* with *klutzes, nudniks, nebbishes, schlemiels,* or *mensches; schlepping* and *putzing,* carrying a big *shtick* with *meshuga chutzpah.* Or something like that.

Though it is written with the Hebrew alphabet, Yiddish is an Indo-European language closely related to German. The majority of Yiddish words in English share a common origin with German, but some were borrowed from Hebrew, including *maven* as well as *chutzpah, meshuga, schlemiel,* and *schmooze.* Until the Holocaust, the greatest number of Yiddish speakers were in central and eastern Europe. Today there are estimated to be about one and a half million speakers of Yiddish in the United States, another two hundred thousand in Israel, and still another two hundred thousand in Russia and other states of the former Soviet Union.

∼United States

geoduck *from Lushootseed*

It's not a gooey duck, but that's how you pronounce it: the name of a giant clam found only, or mainly, in Puget Sound in the northwestern corner of the United States. The name came into English as early as 1883, when the bulletin of the U.S. National Museum said the clam ranged from Puget Sound to San Diego. "The Geoduck is said to be of very fine flavor," explains the bulletin, "but too rich to be used constantly for food." In 1903 *Scientific American* noted its presence in Alaskan waters and said one geoduck "would afford a meal for several persons." More recently, a 1981 field guide to seashells points to its scarcity: "The Geoduck is supposedly one of the finest eating clams on the West Coast, but it is relatively scarce and difficult to dig out, so is not often sought."

How big is this sucker? The shell is about six inches in diameter, but its "foot" (actually its neck) is something else, often eighteen inches long and two inches in diameter. Geoducks average seven or eight pounds, but some have been as heavy as twenty. Burrowing into the mud under deep water, they supposedly can live for a hundred years if not harvested by humans.

Geoduck harvesting is regulated by state law in Washington, but the big clams are so valuable ($8 apiece in the Seattle wholesale market, $40 apiece delivered alive to Asia) that poaching is a serious problem.

Lushootseed, also known as Puget Sound Salish, is a Salishan language with only about fifty native speakers, but it is being revived. You can even take Lushootseed at Everett Community College in Everett, Washington. Geoduck comes from a Lushootseed word meaning something like "dig deep." Nothing aside from the big clam seems to have immigrated from Lushootseed to English.

ᴜᴜɴɪᴛᴇᴅ Sᴛᴀᴛᴇs ᴀɴᴅ Cᴀɴᴀᴅᴀ

sockeye *from Straits Salish*

If you know salmon, you know that the sockeye does not wear a sock over its eye; nor does its eye resemble a sock; nor do you fish for it by socking it in the eye. Its name, in fact, is a mistranslation of a word from a Salish language of the Pacific Northwest. One of the nineteenth-century English-speaking explorers asked a speaker of that language for the name of the distinctive red fish in that territory. "Suk-kegh," said the Indian, meaning "red fish." That had no meaning in English, so the explorer wrote it down in words that made more sense to him—"sock-eye."

Ever since, users of the English language have tried to discover the relevance of the sock and the eye. And of course there is none. It's a familiar process, called "folk etymology," in which we import a strange word and try to make sense of it by giving it a familiar look. Other notable examples of folk etymology include *woodchuck*, which has nothing to do either with wood or chucking, from Narragansett Indian *ockqutchaun; pickax*, from Old French *picois;* and *cockroach*, from Spanish *cucaracha*. As for *suk-kegh*, other early attempts to make sense of it included *saw-quai* and *suck-eye.*

If you hang around sockeye, you will soon learn the word *anadromous*. That scientific term, from the Greek, literally means "running back," and it refers to the salmon running back after a couple of years in the salt ocean to the fresh water where they were born to spawn and complete their life cycle. When they are ready to spawn, the salmon blush; that is, they change color from silver to bright red. It is said that a returning salmon can climb upstream to an elevation of 6,000 feet.

Several of the closely related Salish languages spoken in what is now Washington State, U.S.A., and British Columbia, Canada, have been proposed as the origin of *sockeye*. Halkomelem is one; Straits Salish is another. Here we will save Halkomelem for another word and allow credit to Straits Salish, which is spoken on both Vancouver Island and nearby points in Washington State. The language is nearly extinct, but there are still about thirty middle-aged and elderly speakers. No other Straits Salish words have immigrated to English.

CANADA

kokanee *from Shuswap*

If you know sockeye, you know the basics about salmon. But there is a distinctive kind of sockeye with a distinctive name: the kokanee. It distinguishes itself from other sockeye by being non-anadromous. That is, it doesn't go from fresh water to salt and back again; it spends its whole life in fresh water.

Aside from that detail, it is very much like other sockeye, with one other little difference. Where other sockeye have grown to about twenty-four inches when they are finished with their seagoing careers and return to fresh water to spawn, the mature kokanee is only about one-third that length.

The name *kokanee* apparently comes from Shuswap, a language of the Salish family spoken in south central British Columbia, Canada. It is the name they gave to a river in which kokanee salmon are found. Applied to salmon, the name appears as early as 1875, with the spelling *kik-e-ninnies* indicating an attempt to make it look a little more like an English word. Shuswap still has about five hundred speakers nowadays, but no other Shuswap words have made a splash in our language.

UNITED STATES

haddo *from Nisqually*

Although the fish that goes by this name is the most abundant of all salmon species, a haddo is hard to find. That's because it generally doesn't go by this name. More often the haddo is called a *humpback salmon* or *pink salmon* because of the hump on the back of the adult male and the pink color of its meat, the pink contrasting with the red of the more esteemed sockeye.

Like the sockeye, the haddo attains a length of about twenty-four inches when mature, and like the sockeye, most of the haddo are anadromous. (For an explanation of anadromous, see *sockeye*.)

The name *haddo* is recorded as early as 1882 in a U.S. government publication. It apparently comes from Nisqually, one of the dialects of Southern Puget Sound Salish, which is a Central Salish language. Nowadays there are about a hundred elderly speakers of Southern Puget Sound Salish. No other words of the language have been noted in English.

Haddo occasionally have also been called *lost salmon, holia*, and *dog salmon*. The term *lost salmon* was used for haddo that were occasionally found in the Sacramento River of California, far south of their usual habitat in the Northwest. *Holia* is unexplained. But the designation *dog salmon*, applied to any species deemed fit only for feeding to the dogs, indicates the disrespect in which haddo were originally held by commercial and sport fishermen. Early in the twentieth century, however, the increased demand for salmon and the dwindling supply of other salmon species changed people's minds; haddo were now "human salmon." The abundance of names reflects the abundance of the species.

~CANADA

Sasquatch *from Halkomelem*

In southwestern British Columbia, on southern Vancouver and nearby islands, live some five hundred speakers of Halkomelem, a Central Salish language in the Salish language family. And there is also said to be, somewhere in the mountains and woods known to the Halkomelem, a creature called in their language *Sasquatch*, or "hairy man."

As English-speaking enthusiasts have translated and embellished the legend for us, the Sasquatch is distinguished by more than an unusually hairy body. Modern authorities assure us that the Sasquatch is nearly human in appearance but tall as a professional basketball player, strong as a professional wrestler, nocturnal as a professional Vegas gambler, and solitary as a hermit. It eats anything that comes its way, animal or vegetable, but it doesn't go hunting. It can swim like a fish. And it can't speak, so if found it's unlikely to be interviewed on a television talk show.

Not that these authorities have actually seen a Sasquatch. But they have heard stories and reports of sightings, and they have made expeditions to the wilds of the Pacific Northwest in search of one. So far it has been as elusive as the Loch Ness Monster.

The name *Sasquatch* made its English-language appearance in an article in the Canadian magazine *Maclean's* in 1929. Since then it has spread far beyond the Halkomelem, so that today it is often used as the generic name for the "bigfoot" of North America. Around the world, other names for elusive wild men include Tibetan *yeti*, Mongolian *almas*, Chinese *yeren*, Vietnamese *ngui rung*, Sumatran *orang pendek*, and Australian *yowie* (now also a popular chocolate candy).

∿UNITED STATES

Chinook wind *from Chehalis*

Chinook Jargon, a pidgin language once widely spoken along the Pacific coast from Oregon to Alaska, made notable contributions to the English language, including one of the oddest terms we have for a person of importance, *high muckamuck* (1853), a perhaps deliberate mistranslation of a phrase that originally meant "lots of food." But one word that does not come from Chinook Jargon or the Penutian Indian language of the Chinook peoples is the name *Chinook* itself. That name came from Chehalis Indians, Salishan neighbors of the Chinook.

It is a common occurrence to have the name we use for one people come from the language of another. We follow the lead of the ancient Romans in using Germany for what the inhabitants call Deutschland. And the people who call themselves Dakota and Lakota were long known in English as Sioux, the Ojibwa Indians' name for them. Often the name a group uses for its own people is a word meaning simply "people" or "humans," while it has more colorful names for outsiders: "mountain dwellers," "tall guys," "boar hunters," "tricksters," or "people who talk funny." The latter is the meaning of the Greek word *barbarian*.

But what about the Chinook wind? It is one of many special names English has acquired for winds. The Chinook is a warm winter wind from the Southwest felt in the Northwest. The designation *Chinook* for this wind, attested in English as early as 1860, comes from the regionally prominent Chinook people and language, named, as we said, by speakers of Chehalis, which belongs to the Salishan language family. There are actually two separate Chehalis languages, Lower and Upper Chehalis; the name *Chinook* comes from Lower Chehalis. The two languages are spoken on the southwest coast and Puget Sound areas of Washington, respectively, and there are at most a couple of speakers of each left. We have no other English words from either variety of Chehalis.

⌇CANADA

potlatch *from Nootka*

If you're invited to a potlatch, don't worry about bringing a gift. Instead, you'll have to worry about bringing home all the gifts you'll get. The more overwhelmed you are by your host's generosity, the more successful the potlatch.

A potlatch is the ultimate manifestation of the principle that it is more blessed to give than to receive. If you're the host, you'll happily give away all you have, first by serving lavish food and drink, then by handing out gifts. The more generous you are, the higher you stand in the eyes of others. Furthermore, you stand a good chance of getting it all back, because the guests at a potlatch are expected to return the favor—and then some, if they want to outdo you.

Potlatches were part of the way of life of many of the Indians of the northern Pacific coast of North America. Traditional gifts included weapons, slaves, furs, and blankets. Some reports say that a particularly ostentatious host might burn the blankets that guests weren't able to take. The Canadian government banned potlatches in 1884, but they continued anyhow, becoming fully legal again in 1951.

The word *potlatch* comes to us from Nootka, a Wakashan language spoken nowadays by about six hundred people in western British Columbia and Vancouver Island. It was used in English as early as 1865, when a journal of life at Puget Sound notes: "There was going to be a great potlach at the coal-mines, where a large quantity of iktas [goods] would be given away—tin pans, guns, blankets, canoes, and money. . . . It seems that anyone who aspires to be a chief must first give a potlach to his tribe."

The Nootka word came into English by means of Chinook Jargon, the trade language of the Pacific northwest. Nootka is also the source of *chako,* the second part of the Chinook Jargon word *cheechako,* which will soon greet us when we arrive in Alaska.

⌁CANADA

pemmican *from Cree*

The high-energy fuel that transported the early inhabitants and explorers of North America was not coal, oil, or gasoline, but a concoction for human consumption known as *pemmican.* Before there were roads and canals, travelers had to use their feet for walking, their arms for paddling canoes, and their backs for carrying loads. Journeys were slow under the best of conditions, and even slower if the travelers had to hunt for their food along the way. No wonder, then, that the compact food called pemmican was produced and used in large quantities. It was the ancestor of World War II's K rations and today's military Meals, Ready to Eat.

What was it? There were just two essential ingredients: meat and fat. The meat, from buffalo, deer, or whatever other animals were available, was cut into thin strips, dried, and pounded into a paste. An equal amount of hot liquid fat or marrow was poured over it, and the mixture cooled and pressed into cakes. For flavor, cherries or berries were pounded and mixed in.

A pound of pemmican was said to be as nutritious as four pounds of fresh meat, and of course it kept much longer. Stored in rawhide bags, it would last for years. It is mentioned in English as early as 1791.

Nowadays pemmican is more likely encountered in vegetarian, low-fat versions. "Western Pemmican," a "French/Danish/English/Lenape" recipe offered by Tall Mountain and Summerwolf on a Native American Web site, calls for grinding together equal amounts of raisins, dates, and nuts, and adding honey till the mixture holds its shape.

Pemmican is a Cree word and invention, derived from the word *pime* meaning "fat." The Cree language in its various dialects is spoken by about 50,000 Cree Indians in various places in Canada. It belongs to the Central Algonquian branch of the Algonquian-Ritwan language family, closely related to Ojibwa and Montagnais. From Cree we also have *muskeg*, a mossy swamp or bog (1806), and *saskatoon* berry (1810).

⟿ CANADA

toboggan *from Micmac*

Find yourself a straight, tall birch or hackmatack. Hack it with your axe to see if it's sturdy inside. If it is, chop it down. Cut two sections, trim them with your axe, and plane them smooth to make a matching pair of boards. Then put the boards in hot water long enough to soak them through and make them limber. Bend the front edge of each board tightly around a stick to make a decorative loop. Attach crossbars to hold the two boards side by side, bend the big front loop, and tie the decorative loop to a crossbar to hold it. Let it dry for a couple of days. Then make holes in it, sew it with string, and off you go.

That's how a Cree Indian of the Mistissini tribe of central Quebec describes the making of a toboggan. You can make it long or short, depending on whether you will use it to move a whole camp or just to go out for a few days.

Northeastern Canada has lots of snow to contend with. The Europeans who first visited the eastern shores of Canada were technologically advanced over the Indians in metallurgy and manufacturing, but they were not nearly as well prepared as the Indians to get around in the winter snow. Both snowshoes and toboggans were Indian inventions that had no European equivalents. The advantage of a toboggan over a sled is that it will carry a greater load over softer snow. A sled works well on hard snow or ice, but it will get stuck off the beaten trail.

Our word *toboggan* comes from the language of the Micmac Indians in the eastern Maritime Provinces of Canada. The French learned about it first. Eventually it came into English from French, in an 1829 book called *Forest Scenes and Incidents in the Wilds of North America; Being a Diary of a Winter's Route from Halifax to the Canadas, and During Four Months' Residence in the Woods on the Borders of Lakes Huron and Simcoe:* "A tobogin is a small sleigh, drawn by men, of very simple construction, and capable of conveying from 100 to 140 pounds of clothes or other baggage."

A descendant of the toboggan is in the Winter Olympics: the bobsled, a toboggan with a steering mechanism, invented by the Swiss late in the nineteenth century.

Today there are about 6,000 speakers of Micmac in eastern Canada. Because the Jay Treaty of 1794 permits

Micmacs to move freely between Canada and the United States, substantial numbers have recently moved south. There are now said to be about 2,000 speakers of Micmac in and around Boston, Massachusetts. Micmac is a member of the eastern branch of the Algonquian-Ritwan language family. English is also indebted to Micmac for *caribou* (1665).

~CANADA

husky *from Montagnais*

The husky is an Eskimo dog, and if the words *husky* and *Eskimo* sound almost the same, it's because they are. Both are from the Montagnais name for the people who inhabit arctic regions from Greenland to Alaska.

When the ancestors of these people first arrived there, perhaps ten or fifteen thousand years ago, they found wolves adapted to vigorous survival in the cold climate. Over the years they tamed some of these wolves, harnessing them to pull sleds. These became the Eskimo dogs, or "husky dogs," as the Montagnais of southeastern Canada called them. The husky is mentioned in English in 1852 in a shipboard journal noting that a dog that "was kidnapped by the natives, and not being of a pure huski breed, would most likely be prized by them."

Actually, the husky is not a pure breed but a general type of dog descended from wolves, able to endure severe cold, and with great strength and endurance. In the twentieth century some specific breeds of husky have been developed. An "Alaskan husky" type was bred in the 1930s by mixing native huskies, wolves, and Irish setters. More recently, a miniature Alaskan husky, the Klee Kai, has been recognized as an official breed. So has the Siberian husky developed by the Chukchi people of arctic Siberia to pull sleds and herd reindeer. The Chukchi gave *kamleika* to the English language, but their dog's name came to English from the Montagnais language.

There are about 8,000 speakers of Montagnais in Quebec along the St. Lawrence River and in Labrador. It belongs to the Algonquian-Ritwan language family that was dominant along the Atlantic coast when the first English speakers came to live in North America. The word *carcajou* (1703), another name for the wolverine, also apparently comes from Montagnais.

English has two other *husky*s, the husky voice and the husky size. Both probably come from *husk,* a Germanic word that has been in English for many centuries. Neither has any relation to the name of the dog, except the accident of identical spelling.

∾CANADA

eh *from Canadian English*

There's not much difference between Canadian and American English, eh?

It's just that little uplift at the end of the sentence. Americans might instead follow a remark with *OK?* Canadians might too, because *OK* is universal. But aside from a few American regions not too far south of the border, only in Canada will you hear a quizzical, contemplative, civilized *eh* at the end of an utterance.

Canada makes a point of being multicultural, and its multiculturalism extends even to the English language. It takes some of its linguistic cues from England, some from its neighbor to the south. The Anglo-American multiculturalism is reflected even in spelling: Canadians prefer British *colour* but American *program*. Blending material from both sources, Canadians can claim that they have created a hybrid language superior to either. It's cultured like the British and brisk like the American, eh?

There are also some Canadian contributions to the English language that are used neither in Britain nor the

United States. The new *Canadian Oxford Dictionary* includes two thousand Canadianisms, including *book off* (work), *all-candidates meeting, Stanfields* (men's underwear), and *jam-buster* (doughnut). And then there's the Canadian *eh*.

It comes at the end of a sentence, any sentence, in Canadian English. And it does have a meaning. A Canadian from Kitchener, Ontario, explains that "It changes the sentence from a mere statement, to a question, or sometimes an exclamation where no answer is expected." More formally, the *Canadian Oxford Dictionary* says it is used for "ascertaining the comprehension, continued interest, agreement, etc., of the person or persons addressed."

Not a bad word, eh? Canadians didn't invent the expression or this use of it, but they are known far and wide for its cultivation. The Canadian from Kitchener remarks, "It is art. It is music. It is poetry. And goes mostly unnoticed between Canadians since it seems a natural part of the language."

Canadian English, like American, was imported from the mother country to North America starting in the 1600s. But when Americans felt a patriotic impulse to declare their linguistic independence from England, Canada remained loyal. The American influence grew in the nineteenth and twentieth centuries as industry and popular culture south of the border became increasingly prominent.

UNITED STATES (ALASKA)

mukluk *from Yupik*

To keep feet warm and toes intact during even the coldest days of an arctic winter, Native Americans long ago invented mukluks, soft-soled insulated boots that are like moccasins with risers. In the Yupik Eskimo communities of the north, mukluks were traditionally soled with seal-skin, and that is where they got their name, from the Yupik word for a seal. The earliest record of the word in English

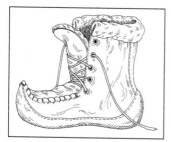

is from mountaineer Frederick Whymper's 1868 *Travel and Adventure in the Territory of Alaska:* "Their boots vary in length, and in the material used for the sides, but all have soles of 'maclock,' or sealskin, with the hair removed."

There are about 20,000 Yupik in Alaska today, more than any other Native American people, and most of them speak fluent Yupik as well as English. The Yupik language, which belongs to the Eskimo-Aleut family, has several varieties, the most widely spoken being Central Yupik. The variety known as Central Siberian Yupik, spoken by about eight hundred in Alaska and three hundred in Siberia, is the only language in the world whose original native speakers lived on two different continents.

Aside from *mukluk*, no other words from Yupik have immigrated to English, perhaps because of the complexity of the language. Yupik is known for attaching extremely long and complicated suffixes to words, so that a single word can be a whole sentence. Here is an example that means "Also, he can probably make big boats": *Angyarpaliyugngayugnarquqllu.*

If you want more about mukluks, drive to Mukluk Land in Tok, population 935, at mile 1317 on the Alaskan Highway. There, in addition to the Alaska Highway's largest mosquito, you can see the world's largest mukluk.

⁓UNITED STATES (ALASKA), CANADA, AND GREENLAND

kayak *from Inuit*

If you want to paddle a canoe on an arctic sea, learn from the Inuit: Cover the top so water won't get in. And use a two-bladed paddle so you don't have to change hands as

you paddle first on one side, then another. Snug in the middle, your legs invisible under the cover, you become one with your boat.

There is, to be sure, a down side to the kayak. If your boat turns upside down, so do you. And then there is the phenomenon known as "kayak angst." Tom Carroll, who circumkayaked Long Island in eleven days in 1993, describes it like this: "I began to feel as though my sense of balance had left me. The sky and the water were a dull silver in color. I had trouble finding the water with my paddle. I experienced the strange sensation of gliding through a silver tunnel, drifting suspended by an unseen force. A trusty low brace kept me upright and I soon realized that the ripples made by the brace in the gloss like water brought me a sense of orientation. This form of spatial disorientation or kayak angst, as it was known to the Greenlanders, would be an experience I would not soon forget."

Kayak, which appears in English as early as 1757, is not all we have learned from the Inuit Eskimo language. We have the *igloo* (1856) for a home, the *anorak* (1922) to keep us warm, and other more obscure terms such as *muktuk* (1835, whale skin as food) and *qiviut* (1958, wool of the musk ox). There is also another kind of boat, the *umiak* (1769), which holds a whole family, as opposed to the one-person kayak.

Inuit is not a single language but five closely related ones, forming a branch of the Eskimo-Aleut family. They are Northwest Alaska Inupiat Inukitut, North Alaskan Inukitut, Western Canadian Inukitut, Eastern Canadian Inukitut, and Greenlandic Inukitut. It is impossible to tell which of these is responsible for bringing the Inuit words to English. Altogether there are more than 60,000 speakers of these Inuit languages, the majority in Greenland.

~UNITED STATES (ALASKA)

hooch *from Tlingit*

An unquenchable thirst for alcoholic beverages in Alaska gave the word *hooch* to the English language. It began after the U.S. purchase of Alaska in 1867, when Congress prohibited the sale of alcoholic beverages in the territory. Unable to buy alcohol, the Tlingit Indians living in a village by the name of *Xutsnuuwú* (Hoochinoo in English) on Admiralty Island, Alaska, began making their own. It is mentioned in an 1869 report on seal and salmon fisheries: "The natives manufacture by distillation from molasses a vile, poisonous life and soul destroying decoction called 'hoochinoo.'"

During the Alaska Gold Rush of the 1890s, *hoochinoo* was shortened to *hooch* and made popular by the appetites and tales of the fortune seekers. An 1897 book, *Pioneers of the Klondyke*, says, "The manufacture of 'hooch,' which is undertaken by the saloon-keepers themselves, is weirdly horrible." Another writer describes the "hoochinoo" of the time as "made out of molasses or beans or rice or flour or anything that'll ferment. I call it squirrel whisky, because two drinks of it makes you want to climb a tree."

Ever since, *hooch* has been an uncomplimentary name for illegal or at least ill-tasting alcoholic beverages. It is used primarily in the northern and western parts of the United States, presumably by neighbors and descendants of those who returned from the Klondike. Since the 1970s, *hooch* has also been modernized to designate another illegal substance, marijuana.

Tlingit, a member of the Na-Dene language family, is still spoken. But there are only about a thousand Tlingit speakers left, mostly in the southern panhandle of Alaska, including Sitka and Juneau, the state capital. *Hooch* is the only word of Tlingit origin that has found its way into the general English vocabulary. One other Tlingit word has made it into the English vocabulary just of Alaska: *nagoonberry*, a delicious deep red berry related to the blackberry, noted in English as early as 1914.

∾ UNITED STATES (ALASKA), CANADA (YUKON)

cheechako *from Chinook jargon*

Welcome to Alaska, cheechako!

If that's the greeting you get up north, don't be insulted. In Alaska and the Canadian Yukon, *cheechako* means nothing more sinister than "newcomer" or "tenderfoot," a stage you will outgrow if you stay around. The harsh climate and terrain of Alaska do make greater demands on newcomers than the Lower 49, and perhaps that is why there is a special northern word for them.

The word was imported from Chinook Jargon into the English of that region during the Yukon gold rush that began in 1896 and is chronicled in the stories of Jack London and the poems of Robert Service. In *White Fang* (1906), London takes time at the beginning of a chapter to explain:

> A small number of white men lived in Fort Yukon. These men had been long in the country. They called themselves Sour-doughs, and took great pride in so classifying themselves. For other men, new in the land, they felt nothing but disdain. The men who came ashore from the steamers were newcomers. They were known as *chechaquos*, and they always wilted at the application of the name. They made their bread with baking-powder. This was the invidious distinction between them and the Sour-doughs, who, forsooth, made their bread from sour-dough because they had no baking-powder.

Service's third book of Yukon poems, published in

1909, is called *Ballads of a Cheechako.*

Chinook Jargon was a trade language spoken in the Pacific Northwest by perhaps as many as 100,000 Indians and the white traders and settlers who dealt with them. It was based on the language of the Chinook Indians of the lower Columbia River, but its vocabulary had many additions from English. Today there are just a few speakers of Chinook Jargon left. The Chinook language itself is extinct.

In Chinook Jargon, *cheechako* means "new come," the two parts of the word deriving from Lower Chinook and Nootka, respectively. English has gained half a dozen other words from Chinook Jargon, including *camas* (plant with edible bulb, 1805), *eulachon* (fish, 1807), *salal* (shrub, 1825), and *chum* (salmon, 1902). The motto of Washington State is the Chinook Jargon *al-ki,* meaning "by and by." But the name *Chinook,* used for a wind and a kind of salmon as well as the tribe, is not from Chinook Jargon but from the Chehalis Indian language.

⌒TERRA INCOGNITA

bamboozle *Origin Unknown*

The etymological experts are bamboozled by this one. No one knows where it came from or how long it had been around when it appeared on the London stage on November 26, 1702, and in print in the same play in 1703. This was a drama entitled *She Wou'd and She Wou'd Not* by the notable but not always esteemed Colley Cibber. In the second act, a character complains about "Sham Proofs, that they propos'd to bamboozle me with," and in the fourth, there is mention of "the old Rogue" who "knows how to bamboozle."

Like most new words, *bamboozle* encountered resistance. In a famous essay on the "continual corruption of our English tongue," Jonathan Swift, author of such notable works as *Gulliver's Travels*, complains about "certain words invented by some pretty fellows, such as *banter, bamboozle, country put*, and *kidney*." He gave an example of the "present polite way of writing": "'Tis said the French king will bamboozl us agen, which causes many speculations. The Jacks and others of that kidney, are very uppish and alert upon't, as you may see by their phizz's." (*Country put* was long ago put out of its misery; it refers to a country bumpkin. *Kidney* in this sense means temperament or disposition, and *phizz* is physiognomy or face, both rarely used nowadays. But *banter* and *bamboozle* are going strong.)

Bamboozle resembles the ten-dollar words introduced in the exuberant American frontier in the 1800s, words like *sockdolager* (1830), *hornswoggle* (1829), and *skedaddle* (1861)—all also "origin unknown." But *bamboozle* was a full century earlier, so it must have had a different source. The early 1700s were a time when words from all over the world were immigrating to English, including others discussed in this book: *catamaran* from Tamil, *shaman* from Evenki, *mongoose* from Marathi, *marimba* from Kimbundu, and *dory* from Miskito.

It's even possible that *bamboozle* was entirely made up out of thin air by an English speaker. But most new words do not come from nowhere; they are either borrowed from other languages or created by combining and reshaping current words. As more documents of the period, and more languages, are investigated, the source of *bamboozle* may one day be clear. Meanwhile, it stands in this book for all the words whose origin is yet unknown.

And they are legion. There are hundreds in the etymologies of a desk dictionary, thousands in bigger books. If "origin unknown" were a language, it would rank behind only French, Latin, Greek, and the older versions of English itself as a contributor to English. Here are a few of the other unknowns: *cuddle* (1520), *askance* (1530), *hunch* (1581), *sedan* (1635), *banter* (1676), *condom* (1706), *tantrum* (1714), *fake* (1775), *blizzard* (1829), *jazz* (1913), and *bozo* (1920). Perhaps it is appropriate that *puzzle* (1602) is one of the words whose source is a mystery.

INDEXES

WORD INDEX

Words in small capital letters are entry words. In most cases, the page number of the main entry is the first page number listed. In cases in which it is not the first number, the page of the main entry is indicated by italic type.

aardvark 93
abaca 172
ABALONE 254
abbot 115
Aborigine 188
achievement 26
ackee 76
admiral 123
ADOBE 31, *107*
agar 174
AILANTHUS 178
ailurophile 41
akee 76
AKHALTEKE 126
al-ki 277
albatross 35
alchemy 123
alcohol 123
ALGEBRA 122
algorithm 123
all-candidates meeting 272
alligator 31
almas 265
ALOHA 196
ALPACA 207
ambarella 147
amboyna 179
amen 114
ammonia 107
AMOK 18, *173*
amour 30

amusement 26
ANACONDA 146
anadromous 262
anger 18
Anglophile 41
anorak 274
aoudad 66
apartheid 93
APPALOOSA 241
appendix 40
approval 25
aquavit 20
arastra 32
archaeology 42
argali 163
ARSENIC 115
arson 26
Arthur 11
ARYAN 136
askance 278
assault 26
atemoya 172
aubade 30
Australian ballot 188
AVALANCHE 35
avocado 31, 221
AYE-AYE 98
azoth 116
azure 126

baba 53
BABEL 121

bag 18
bagel 260
baksheesh 124
balalaika 57
ballad 30
ballast 20
BALUCHITHERE 127
bamboo 174
BAMBOOZLE 277
banana 68, 71
bandalore 171
BANDICOOT 141
bandit 37
banjo 89, 90
bankrupt 37
banshee 14
banter 278
BANYAN 137, *140*
barbecue 213
bard 14
barracks 32
basalt 107
BASENJI 86
bastille 30
batik 178
bayou 242
bazaar 126
behemoth 114
BENNE 72
beret 30
berseem 108
BERSERK 17
beryl 136
BHANGRA 133
bibliophile 41
bigos 53
BIJOU 28
BIKINI 190
BILLABONG 183
billy 183
biology 42
BIZARRE 32
blintz 260
blitzkrieg 22

blizzard 278
block 24
blue norther 75
bog 14
Bohr effect 20
bok choy 158
bonanza 31
BONG 153
BONGO 84, 87
BONSAI 160
bonus 40
book off 272
BOOMERANG 182
BOONDOCKS 171
BORA 44, 75
borscht 260
boss 24
boubou 69
boutique 30
bozo 278
brainwashing 157
bravado 31
breeze 31
BRIT 8
Britain 28
Brittany 28
brocade 32
broccoli 37
brogan 14
brogue 14
BUCCANEER 208
buchu 94
bully 24
bummalo 139
bundle 24
bungalow 138, 150
BUNYIP 185
burglary 26
bushed 188
bwana 100

cabal 114
cabin 30

CACIQUE 209
caddy 174
caffe latte 37
caiman 216
calamondin 172
camas 277
cambric 25
camisole 30
camp 30
cane 30
CANNIBAL 215
canoe 216
capsize 32
CARABAO 172
carambola 139
caravan 126
carcajou 271
cargo 31
caribou 270
cashew 209
CASHMERE 132
cassava 213
cast 18
caste 34
catalog 42
CATALPA 240
CATAMARAN 145, 278
CATAWBA WINE 242
cavalier 30
cayenne 209
CENOTE 219
centum 124
chador 132
chako 267
chaparral 33
charade 30
Chattahoochee 241
chaulmoogra 150
CHEECHAKO 276
CHEESE 131
cheongsam 158
cheroot 146
cherub 114
CHIGGER 70

chihuahua 224
CHIKUNGUNYA 100
chili 221
chimpanzee 86
china 157
CHINOOK WIND 75, 265
chipmunk 227
chivalry 25
CHOCOLATE 220
chop suey 158
chow mein 158
CHUCKWALLA 251
chum 277
chutzpah 114, 260
cider 114
cigar 31
cipher 123
circus 40
clan 12
clown 22
coca 207
cockatoo 174
cockroach 31, 262
coconut 34
cocoon 30
coffee 118, 123
cogon 172
COHOSH 231
cohune 219
COLA 71
colleen 14
color 32
combe 11
comfort 26
commando 93
compatible 40
condom 278
condor 207
cookie 24
coolibah 183, 185
coontie 241
COOTER 68
cootie 174
copra 144

corgi 11
corroboree 183
cosh 9
cosmetology 42
cosmonaut 58
COSSACK 58
cotton 123
cougar 209
courtesy 25
courtly 25
cove 9
coyote 221
coypu 204
crag 11
cravat 44
crawl 18
crime 26
criminology 42
crimson 123
crowd 11
cuddle 278
CUI-UI 249
curare 216
curry 146
CZAR 56

dangle 20
DASHIKI 81
decadence 26
deck 24
defeat 26
demonology 42
dervish 118
desperado 31
DHANDH 128
DHOLE 142
dilettante 37
dim sum 158
dingo 183
dirt 18
DIVAN 117
dock 25
DODO 34
dolmen 29
dolphin 30

donnybrook 14
doom 6
DORY 218
DOWITCHER 239
DRUID 26
dumka 59
DUNK 256
dynamic 19
DYNAMITE 19
dynamo 19

ebony 107
egg 18
EH 271
eider 17
eisteddfod 11
elixir 123
embargo 31
emu 34
enormous 40
error 26
erupt 40
escargot 30
eschatology 42
Eskimo 270
eulachon 277
exit 40

faamafu 193
fajita 32
fake 278
FASHION 25
feckless 12
felony 26
fig 30
flak 22
flamingo 34
flummery 11
flunky 12
foehn 75
fossa 98
Francophile 41
fraud 26
free 6

FREEDOM 6
friend 6
frijoles 32
fuhrer 22
funk 25
futon 161

galago 71
GALAH 184
GALORE 13
gamza 45
gavial 150
gecko 174
gelada 106
genius 40
GEODUCK 260
geology 42
gerenuk 104
GERONIMO! 222
gestapo 22
GEYSER 16
geyserite 17
ghetto 37
ghibli 75
ghoul 123
gift 18
GINGER 134
gingham 174
ginseng 157
GLAMOUR 11
glasnost 58
glen 12
gley 59
GNU 91, 92
go postal 18
goa 151
gong 178
goober 90
gossan 8
GOULASH 47
gracious 25
GRAFFITI 36
Gram's stain 20
grammar 11

graphology 42
grief 26
gruesome 24
grumble 24
guacamole 221
GUAN 217
guanaco 207
guano 207
guava 213
guide 137
gulag 58
gulp 24
gum 107
gumband 258
GUMBO 88
GUNG HO 156
GURU 137

haček 51
HACKMATACK 232
HADDO 263
haiku 161
hallelujah 114
hallucination 40
halvah 47
hamburger 22
hammock 213
hangul 159
HARMATTAN 75
hashish 123
heath 45
HEATHEN 45
hetman 59
hex 257
hit 18
HOGAN 245
honcho 161
honor 25
HOOCH 275
hooligan 14
HORA 46
HORDE 51
hornswoggle 278
howdah 132
HUARACHES 221
hubbub 14

hula 198
hunch 278
hundred 124
hunk 22
hunky 23
HUNKY-DORY 22
HURRICANE 211
HUSKY 270
hustle 24

iceberg 20
idea 40
igloo 274
iguana 210
impala 94
INDABA 93
indri 98
insane 40
intelligentsia 58
ipecac 209
iroko 82
Islam 123
ivory 107

jabiru 206
jacana 206
jackfruit 144
Jacobson's organ 20
JAGUAR 205
jai alai 33
jambuster 272
jasmine 123, 126
JAVA 177
jazz 278
jerk 207
jerky 207
jockey 12
John Canoe 77
joy 26
juggernaut 138
JUJU 79
JUKE 69, 211
JUMBO 67
jungle 138
junk 178

junta 35
JUSTICE 39
JUTE 137, *149*

KACHINA 246
kaddish 115
kahawai 189
kai 189
kakaki 80
kamikaze 161
KAMLEIKA 165, 270
KANGAROO 180
kantele 55
karaoke 161
kauri 189
kava 192
KAYAK 273
kelly green 14
ketchup 174
key 213
khaki 132
khamsin 75
kiang 151
kibbutz 114
kibitz 260
kielbasa 53
kikepa 193
kimchi 159
KINDERGARTEN 21
kiosk 118, 124
kitsch 22
kiva 247
KIWI 189
klutz 260
knish 260
koala 183
KOKANEE 263
kolache 51
komondor 48
kookaburra 184
kouprey 154
kowhai 189
kowtow 157
kudzu 161

KUGELI 53
kumara 189
kumquat 158
kurrajong 183
KURU 179
kvetch 260
KWANZAA 82, *99*
KWASHIORKOR 73

LABRISH 214
LAGNIAPPE 206
LAH 174
lama 151
landscape 24
latke 260
latte 37
lauan 172
LAVALAVA 192
leader 137
lechwe 95
LEGO 20
lei 198
leisure 26
LEKVAR 48
lemur 98
leprechaun 14
levanter 75
Lhasa apso 151
libeccio 75
libel 26
liberty 7
LINGO 29
llama 207
loch 12
logy 42
loose 18
loot 138
low 18
lox 260
luau 198

Mafia 39
magazine 123
MAHALA 252

mahi-mahi 196
mallee 187
mamba 94
MAMMON 114
mammoth 57
manager 37
MANGO 143
mangrove 213
MANITOU 226
manna 114
maquiladora 224
MARIMBA 89
MAVEN 259
mazurka 53
MBILA 97
MBIRA 95
MECHAMECK 237
meditate 40
menhaden 228
menhir 29
mensch 260
MERENGUE 213
Merlin 11
meshuga 260
messiah 114
metheglin 11
Miami 241
MILO 94
miniature 37
Mir 58
mirador 32
misdemeanor 26
mistral 75
MOCCASIN 224
MOGUL 162
MOJO 83
molasses 34
MONGOOSE 138
MONIKER 14
monsoon 75, 123
moped 19
mosquito 31, 219
muffin 22
MUFFULETTA 38
MUGWUMP 234

MUKLUK 272
muktuk 274
mulligatawny 146
mumbo jumbo 67
mummichog 228
mummy 126
MUNTJAC 176
museum 40
muskeg 268
muumuu 198

nabob 132
nadir 123
nagana 94
nagoonberry 276
narwhal 17
nawab 132
nebbish 260
Negus 106
neurology 42
ngui rung 265
nickel 19
noble 25
nomoli 73
nosh 260
nudnik 260
NUGGET 187
NUNCHAKU 161
nutmeg 30
nutria 204

O'NYONG-NYONG 102
OASIS 106
OBEAH 77
ocelot 221
odd 18
oenophile 41
OK 258, 271
OKRA 80, 88
ombudsman 19
omertà 39
oology 42
opah 81
opera 37

opossum 224
orang pendek 265
orangutan 174
orienteering 19
OUABAIN 103
ouch 22

padauk 152, 179
paddy 174
pagoda 34
pajamas 138
PAL 9
palanquin 136, 178
palaver 34
pampa 207
PAMPER 23
pampero 75
panda 148
panga 100
papoose 228
paprika 48
PARADISE 124, *125*
pareu 193, 195
pariah 146
PARKA 164
pasta 37
pastrami 47
patchouli 146
patio 31
pecan 227
peccary 216
pedophile 41
PEMMICAN 267
PENGUIN 10
perfume 30
perjury 26
persimmon 224
petunia 209
peyote 221
Pharisee 115
Philadelphia 41
philanthropy 41
philharmonic 41
philodendron 41

philology 42
philopatrodomania 41
PHILOSOPHY 41
phony 14
piano 37
pickax 262
pika 164
piki 247
PIMA COTTON 247
piranha 209
pirogue 216
pirohi 49
pistol 51
pitta 142
PLACER 31
plaid 12
plaza 31
pleasure 26
plump 24
POGONIP 251
pogrom 58
polka 53
POLO 129
polonaise 53
PONCHO 204
porbeagle 8
port 34
portfolio 37
postal 18
potato 213
Potemkin village 57
POTLATCH 266
potto 71
powwow 234, 235
praise 26
propaganda 40
psychology 42
puck 14
puli 48
punk 230
PUNKIE 230
purdah 132
putz 260
puzzle 278
python 147

qiviut 274
quahog 228
quarter 25
quinine 207

raccoon 224
rampage 12
ranch 31
rant 24
rattan 174
REASON 25
rendzina 53
RIP 24
ROBOT 50
royal 25
rumple 24

sachem 235
salad 30
salal 277
samovar 57
samp 228
sampan 158
SAMPOT 154
samurai 161
Santa Ana 75
sarong 174, 193
sash 123
saskatoon 268
SASQUATCH 264
SATEM 123
SAUNA 54
savanna 213
savvy 34
sayonara 161
schadenfreude 22
schlemiel 260
schlep 260
schmooze 114, 260
scholar 42
school 42
schwa 114, 116
scoff 20
scour 24

scuffle 19
scup 228
SEA PUSS 225
sedan 278
seersucker 126
SEGO LILY 248
Semtex 51
SEQUOIA 255
serendipity 126
SEROW 148
sexology 42
SHAMAN 163
shampoo 138
shamrock 14
shar-pei 158
SHASHLIK 59
shea 70
shebeen 14
sherbet 118
sherry 31
SHIBBOLETH 113
SHISH KEBAB 60, *118*
shiv 9
SHOEPAC 229
shtick 260
Siamese 153
SIESTA 30
sifaka 98
silo 31
simoom 75
simoon 75
sirocco 75
skedaddle 278
skill 18
skin 18
skirt 18
skoal 20
skosh 161
SKUA 15
skulk 20
sky 18
slander 26
slim 24
slip 24
slivovitz 44

slob 14
slogan 12
slurp 24
smearcase 258
smithereens 14
smorgasbord 19
smuggle 24
snack 24
snollygoster 257
snoop 24
sockdolager 278
SOCKEYE 261
sonnet 30
sophisticated 41
sophomore 41
spinach 126
spoor 93
sport 26
springbok 93
spritz 257
spry 19
spunk 12
sputnik 58
squash 228
squaw 235, 253
SQUETEAGUE 233
stagger 18
stampede 31
Stanfields 272
studio 37
subgum 158
SUCCOTASH 228
suds 24
sulu 193
sumo 161
sunck 234
SUNI 101
sushi 161
syrup 123

TABOO 191
TAE KWON DO 158
TAHR 147
take 18

tamale 221
tamarau 172
tanager 209
TANGO 31, *82*
tanrec 98
tantrum 278
tapa 196
tapioca 209
tapir 209
tariff 37
TATTOO 194
tautog 228
tea 157
teak 144
TEFF 104
tefillin 115
television 42
TEMPEH 175
tenrec 98
TEPEE 244
terminology 42
terrace 30
testament 40
TET 155
thamin 152
their 18
theology 42
they 18
thrift 18
thug 138
TIKI 195
tillandsia 55
TIMBUKTU 66
tobacco 213
TOBOGGAN 268
tomahawk 224
tomato 221
tong 158
tope 134
topi 100
torture 26
totem 227
toucan 209
treason 26

TREK 92
troll 20
troubadour 30
trousers 12
truffle 30
tsar 57
TSETSE 90, 94
tsine 152
tub 24
tucktoo 152
tulip 118
tumpline 232
tuna 31
TUNDRA 55
tupelo 241
turban 118
tycoon 161
typhoon 158

U 152
ufology 42
ugly 18
uhlan 53
ukase 57
ukulele 198
ultimate 40
umbrella 37
umiak 274
UNIVERSE 39

vacuum 40
VAMPIRE 42
vanilla 31
veldt 93
velour 30
veranda 138
vice 26
vicuña 207
VINDALOO 139
viola 30
vizsla 48
VOODOO 76
vug 8

waddy 183
wahoo 245
walkabout 188
wallaby 183
wallah 252
wallaroo 183
walrus 20
wampum 235
WAPITI 235
waterzooi 25
weak 18
whiskey 14
WICKIUP 238
wigwam 232
wildebeest 92
will 40
window 18
wok 158
wombat 183
won ton 158
woodchuck 262
wow 12
wrasse 8

YABBER 186
yak 151
yam 68, 84
yang 157
yarmulke 118
yaupon 243
YEN 157
yeren 265
YETI 150, 265
yin 157
ylang-ylang 172
yo-yo 171
yogurt 118
yowie 265

zeal 42
ZELKOVA 120
zenith 123
ziggurat 122
ZOMBIE 85
zori 161
ZOUAVE 65
ZOUK 210

LANGUAGE INDEX

In most cases, the page number of the main entry is the first to follow the language name. In cases in which it is not the first number, the page of the main entry is indicated by italic type.

Afrikaans 92
Akkadian 121
Ambonese 178
American English 258
Amharic 104
Arabic 75, *122*, 252
Aramaic 114
Araucano 204
Arawak 209
Armenian 118
Australian English 187
Avestan 123
Aymara 207

Balti 129
Baluchi 127
Bambara 69, 211
Basque 32
Bengali 149
Berber 66
Bisayan 172
Breton 28
Bulgarian 44
Burmese 152

Cahuilla 251
Canadian English 271
Cantonese Chinese 157
Carib 215
Catalan 31

Catawba 242
Cebuano 172
Chaga 101
Chehalis 265
Cherokee 255
Chinese 156, 265
Chinook Jargon 276
Choctaw 241
Chukchi 165, 270
Coptic 107
Cornish 8
Cree 267
Creek 240
Creole French 210
Crimean Turkish 59
Czech 50, 53

Dakota 244
Danish 20
Dharuk 182
Dine 245
Dutch 23

Eastern Abenaki 231
Efik 77, 83
Egyptian 106
English 6, 75, 137, 271
Evenki 163
Ewe 76

Faroese 15
Fijian 193
Finnish 54
Flemish 24
Fore 179
Fox 238
French 25, 53, 75, 116, 137, 262
French, Lesser Antillean
    Creole 210
Frisian 22
Fula 83

Ga 73
Galibi 71
Ganda 102
Gaulish 26
Georgian 120
German 21, 75, 116
German, Pennsylvania 256
Gothic 45
Greek 19, *41,* 116, 147, 212
Guaraní 205
Gujarati 140
Guugu Yimidhirr 180

Haitian Creole French 213
Halkomelem 264
Hausa 79
Hawaiian 193, *196*
Hebrew 113, 116, 252
Hindi 137, 150, 252
Hopi 246
Hottentot 92
Hungarian 47

Ibibio 78, *82*
Ibo 78, *80*
Icelandic 16
Indonesian 175, 193
Inuit 273
Irish 13
Italian 36, 75

Jamaican Creole English 214
Japanese 160
Javanese 177

Kabyle 65
Kalihna 71
Kannada 142
Kashmiri 132
Kélé 84
Khmer 154
Kikongo 86
Kimbundu 86, *89*
Kongo 85
Konkani 139
Korean 158
Kuna 217

Lakota 244
Lappish 55
Latin 7, *39,* 116
Lepcha 148
Lesser Antillean Creole
    French 210
Lingala 86
Lithuanian 53
Luganda 103
Lushootseed 260

Makonde 100
Malagasy 98
Malay 173
Malayalam 143
Malaysian English 174
Malinke 68, 72
Mandingo 67
Maori 189
Mapudungun 204
Marathi 138
Marquesan 195
Marshallese 190
Massachusett 234
Maya 219

Mende 72
Menominee 237
Mexican Spanish 222
Micmac 268
Miskito 218
Mohawk 239
Mohegan 233
Mongolian 162, 265
Montagnais 270
Munsee 230
Muskogee or Creek 240

Nahuatl 220
Nama 92
Narragansett 228, 262
Natick 235
Navaho 245
Nenets 164
Nepali 147
Nisqualli 263
Nootka 266
Northern Paiute 249

O'Odham 247
Ojibwa 226
Okinawan 161
Old Norse 17

Pali 134
Pennsylvania German 256
Persian 116, *125*
Pima 247
Polish 49, *51*
Portuguese 34, 75
Powhatan 224
Provençal 29
Puget Sound Salish 261
Punjabi 133

Quechua 206

Romani 9
Romanian 46

Romansch 35
Rumsen 254
Russian 49, *56*

Sac and Fox 238
Salish 261
Sami 55
Samoan 192
Sanskrit 136
Scots 11
Serbo-Croatian 42
Shawnee 235
Shelta 14
Shona 95
Shoshone 251
Shuswap 263
Siamese 153
Sicilian 38
Sindhi 128
Singaporean and Malaysian
    English 174
Sinhala 146
Slovak 48
Somali 103
Sotho 94
Southern Paiute 248
Spanish 30, 83, 85, 204, 219, 262
Straits Salish 261
Sumatran 265
Sundanese 176
Swahili 99
Swedish 19
Syriac 115

Tagalog 171
Tahitian 193, *194*
Taino 211
Tamasheq 66
Tamil 145
Tarascan 221
Telugu 141
Temne 71
Thai 153

Tibetan 150, 265
Timbuktu Tamasheq 66
Tlingit 275
Tongan 191
Tshiluba 88
Tswana 90
Tupí 208
Turkish 117
Turkmen 126
Twi 75, 78

Ukrainian 58
Unami 229
Unknown 277
Unquachog 225
Urdu 131

Venda 97
Vietnamese 155, 265

Virginia Algonquian 224
Visayan 172

Welsh 10
Wemba 185
Western Abenaki 232
Wiradhuri 183
Wolof 70
Wuywurung 186

Xhosa 91

Yiddish 259
Yokuts 252
Yoruba 81
Yupik 272
Yuwaalaraay 184

Zulu 93

C O U N T R Y   I N D E X

Algeria 65
Angola 85, 89
Armenia 118
Australia 180, 182, 183, 184, 185, 186, 187
Bangladesh 149
Belgium 24
Bhutan 148
Bolivia 207
Bosnia-Herzegovina 42
Botswana 90
Brazil 208
Bulgaria 44, 45
Cambodia 154
Cameroon 83
Canada 230, 261, 263, 264, 266, 267, 268, 270, 271, 273
Canada (Yukon) 276
Chile 204
China 156, 157
Congo 85
Congo, Democratic Republic of the 85, 86, 88
Croatia 42
Cuba 211, 215
Czech Republic 50
Democratic Republic of the Congo 85, 86, 88
Denmark 20
Egypt 106, 107
England 6, 8, 9
Ethiopia 104
Faroe Islands 15
Finland 54
France 25, 26, 28, 29
Gabon 84
Gambia 67

Georgian Republic 120
Germany 21
Ghana 73, 75, 76
Greece 41
Greenland 273
Guadeloupe 210
Guyana 209
Haiti 211, 213
Hungary 47
Iceland 16
India 131, 132, 133, 134, 136, 137, 138, 139, 140, 141, 142, 143, 145, 148
Indonesia 175, 176, 177, 178
Iran 123, 125, 127
Iraq 121, 122
Ireland 13, 14
Israel 113
Italy 36, 39
Italy (Sicily) 38
Jamaica 214
Japan 160, 161
Korea 158
Lesotho 94
Liberia 72
Lithuania 53
Madagascar 98
Malaysia 173, 174
Mali 66, 67, 68, 69
Marquesas Islands 195
Marshall Islands 190
Mexico 219, 220, 221, 222
Mongolia 162
Myanmar 152
Nepal 147
Netherlands 22, 23
New Zealand 189

Nicaragua 218
Nigeria 77, 79, 80, 81, 82
Norway 17
Okinawa 161
Pakistan 127, 128, 129, 131, 133
Panama 217
Papua New Guinea 179
Paraguay 205
Peru 206
Philippines 171, 172
Poland 51
Portugal 34
Puerto Rico 211
Romania 46
Russia 55, 56, 163, 164, 165
Samoa 192
Scotland 11
Senegal 70
Sierra Leone 71, 72
Singapore 174
Slovakia 48
Somalia 103
South Africa 90, 91, 92, 93, 94, 97
Spain 30, 31, 32
Sri Lanka 146

Sweden 19
Switzerland 35
Syria 114
Tahiti 194
Tanzania 99, 100, 101
Thailand 153
Tibet 150
Tonga 191
Turkey 115, 117
Turkmenistan 126
Uganda 102
Ukraine 58, 59
United States 224, 225, 226, 228, 229, 230, 231, 232, 233, 234, 235, 237, 238, 239, 240, 241, 242, 244, 245, 246, 247, 248, 249, 251, 252, 254, 255, 256, 258, 259, 260, 261, 263, 265
United States (Alaska) 272, 273, 275, 276
United States (Hawaii) 196
Unknown 277
Vietnam 155
Wales 10
Yugoslavia 42
Zimbabwe 95, 97